HUNT THE BISMARCK

HUNT THE BISMARCK

The pursuit of Germany's most famous battleship

ANGUS KONSTAM

OSPREY PUBLISHING
Bloomsbury Publishing Plc
PO Box 883, Oxford, OX1 9PL, UK
1385 Broadway, 5th Floor, New York, NY 10018, USA
E-mail: info@ospreypublishing.com
www.ospreypublishing.com

OSPREY is a trademark of Osprey Publishing Ltd

First published in Great Britain in 2019

ISBN: HB 978 1 4728 3386 0; PB 978 1 4728 3387 7; eBook 978 1 4728 3385 3; ePDF 978 1 4728 3384 6; XML 978 1 4728 3383 9

19 20 21 22 23   10 9 8 7 6 5 4 3 2 1

Maps by Nick Buxey
Index by Alan Rutter

Typeset by Deanta Global Publishing Services, Chennai, India
Printed and bound in Great Britain by CPI (Group) UK Ltd, Croydon CR0 4YY

Front cover: HMS *Hood* as viewed from HMS *Repulse* whilst on patrol in the North Sea on 1 September 1939. (Photo by Fox Photos/Hulton Archive/Getty Images)
Back cover: HMS *Rodney* cruising off Scapa Flow with the Home Fleet. (Photo by Keystone/Hulton Archive/Getty Images)

Editor's note
For ease of comparison please refer to the following conversion table:
1 mile = 1.6km
1 yd = 0.9m
1 ft = 0.3m
1 in = 2.54cm/25.4mm
1 lb = 0.45kg

Osprey Publishing supports the Woodland Trust, the UK's leading woodland conservation charity.

To find out more about our authors and books visit www.ospreypublishing.com. Here you will find extracts, author interviews, details of forthcoming events and the option to sign up for our newsletter.

Contents

CONTENTS

Prologue

The clock on the bridge of the *Bismarck* read 05.53.[1] At that moment, virtually everyone on the bridge was watching the two dark shapes on the southern horizon. Were they just British cruisers, or were they battleships? Then, the watchers saw a ripple of orange light erupt from the front of the lead ship. To some, it looked like a flash of lightning. They were firing. At a range of 25,000 yards (12.5 miles), a 15in. shell has a flight time of around 50 seconds. The men on the bridge could do nothing but wait. Seconds later, the same flashes were seen from the second British ship. Then, with a roar like an express train, the first shells arrived.

In fact, *Hood* was firing on *Bismarck*'s consort, the cruiser *Prinz Eugen*, which was steaming ahead of the huge German battleship. That roar came from the shells fired by the second enemy ship, and when they landed a few hundred yards past *Bismarck* they threw up six huge water spouts. Those weren't cruisers out there. Those shells had come from a battleship!

On the telephone, Korvettenkapitän (Lieutenant Commander) Schneider asked permission to open fire. His eight 15in. guns had been tracking the lead enemy ship, and he was ready. Someone shouted out 'The *Hood* – it's the *Hood*!' So, the target was the battlecruiser *Hood* – that legendary icon of British seapower. Then, Kapitän Lindemann picked up the bridge telephone. 'Permission to open fire.' Seconds later, Schneider's great guns erupted in similar flashes of orange flame. The duel had begun.

By then, the second British ship had been identified as one of the new King George V class battleships.[2] She carried ten 14in. guns. *Hood* carried eight 15in. ones, as did *Bismarck*, while the *Prinz Eugen* only had eight 8in. guns. So, the Germans were outgunned, but far from outclassed. On both sides, the gunnery teams watched for the splashes as their shells landed, and corrected their aim. The range was still dropping, even though at 05.54 the German ships turned slightly to starboard. They had the edge now – all their guns could fire, while only the front turrets on the British ships could bear on the enemy. *Prinz Eugen*'s smaller guns had a greater rate of fire, so her shells were soon falling around the *Hood*, and she scored the first hit of the battle, and started a small fire. By now, though, the shells from the bigger guns were also straddling their targets.

Admiral Lütjens ordered the *Prinz Eugen* to switch her fire to the British battleship and to drop astern of *Bismarck*, so the German battleship had her own duel with the enemy battlecruiser. By her third salvo, *Bismarck*'s shells were straddling *Hood*, their splashes falling all around her. They had found the range. So, at 05.59 Schneider fired three more rounds in quick succession, 30 seconds apart. By now the range was down to 18,000 yards (9 miles), and the flight time was just 30 seconds. The first of these straddled the *Hood* again, without scoring any hits. Then, at 06.00, with the *Bismarck*'s fifth salvo, one of the German shells struck home.

Nobody really knows for certain what happened. Some observers on the German ships saw a pillar of flame rise up beside the *Hood*'s mainmast. That may have been an explosion caused by the fire started by *Prinz Eugen*'s shells, or it may have been from another shell from *Bismarck*'s fight salvo. A fraction of a second later, a German 15in. shell smashed through the afterdeck of the *Hood*, somewhere near 'X' turret. When it exploded deep inside the battlecruiser, it ignited the charges in one of the ship's after magazines. On *Hood*'s bridge, they felt a jolt, and they knew they'd been hit.[3] Then the helmsman reported the wheel wasn't responding. In fact, when the magazine exploded, the blast had ripped the stern off the ship.

On the *Bismarck*, Kapitänleutnant (Lieutenant) von Müllenheim-Rechberg was watching the pursuing British cruisers shadowing the German ships when he heard a voice on the intercom say, 'She's blowing up.' He quickly peered through the port-side gunnery director. There was no sign of the *Hood*. Where she should have been there was only a colossal pillar of black smoke. Then, at its foot, he made out the bow of the battlecruiser, sticking up out of the sea at an angle. It was true. *Hood* had been torn in two. As he watched, he saw another orange flash. It was the *Hood*'s forward guns, firing one final salvo, her gun crews refusing to acknowledge that their ship was sinking beneath them.

On *Bismarck*'s bridge, the ship's navigator watched as the *Hood* split in two, and a fireball enveloped her. Then came the shockwave. Even 9 miles away from the blast, he felt every nerve being yanked out of his body. In those moments, or in the minutes that followed, the mangled battlecruiser became a great steel coffin for 1,415 of her crew. There were only three survivors.

Time, Speed, Distance and Bearing

On 18 May 1941, when the *Bismarck* sailed from Gotenhafen (now Gdynia in Poland), she was operating under Central European Time (CET), which was one hour ahead of Greenwich Mean Time (GMT). However, due to the season, this had been changed to Central European Daylight Savings Time (CEDST), which was two hours ahead of GMT (making it GMT+2). At the time, Great Britain was also operating in the same time zone, which they called British Double Summer Time (BDST). So, both British and German clocks were aligned, at GMT+2.

What complicates this is time zones. The further west a ship sails, the later sunset becomes. The North Atlantic spans five time zones, and so warships crossing from one zone to another would normally alter their ship's clocks to conform to the new time zone. To simplify things, on 23 May, as his ships were approaching the Denmark Strait, Admiral Lütjens ordered that at 13.00 his force would switch to Central European Time, at GMT+1. That put them an hour in front of both their own naval headquarters in Berlin and the British Admiralty in London.

For the most part, British warships operating in the eastern region of the North Atlantic were also either one or two hours ahead of London, depending on the time zone in which they were operating. To simplify this, within the Home Fleet, signals were usually dated and timed in accordance with BDST. However, times in ships' logs conformed to the time zone. To simplify all this, unless otherwise noted, the times in this book are given in CET (or GMT+1). So, for instance, *Bismarck* left her berth at Gotenhafen at 11.30 (CEDST). She remained in this time zone until the time of Lütjens' switch to CET five days later, and so the narrative waits until 13.00 that day to switch to the new time zone, allowing the cumbersome 'CEDST' label to be dropped.

Other conventions are more straightforward. A warship's speed through the water is given in knots, which represent its speed in miles per hour.[1] Since 1929, the mile was officially defined as 2,025 yards (1,852m). So, a ship moving at 30 knots will cover 30 miles in the space of an hour, or half a mile per minute. Incidentally, until 1970, the British still clung to an Admiralty mile, which was a yard longer. Historically, a mile equated to a minute of latitude, or one-sixtieth of a degree of latitude. A mile is divided into ten sub-units, called cables.

To confuse matters, for the sake of naval gunnery, a mile was defined as 2,000 yards (1,829m). These were sea miles, and so when the *Hood* engaged the *Bismarck* at a range of 25,000 yards (22,860m), that equates to 12.5 sea miles. The Germans, of course, calculated range in metres rather than yards. A sea mile is 2,000 yards (1,829m), and so is slightly shorter than a nautical mile, and a land mile is 1,760 yards (1,609m). So, the convention we'll adopt here is to give speed in knots, and therefore the distance travelled in nautical miles, while for gunnery, ranges will be given in yards or sea miles, rather than their equivalent in metres.

Finally, a word on courses and bearings. These are determined by the compass, divided into 360 degrees. The four cardinal points are North (0°, or 360°), East (90°), South (180°) and West (270°). On a warship of this period, port lay to the left-hand side, and starboard to the right. These were linked to the colours used in navigation lights, with red representing port and green denoting starboard. To a shipboard observer looking forward, objects at roughly 90 degrees to the direction the ship was facing were deemed to be on the beam – either to port or starboard. An object forward of this was deemed 'on the bow', and behind it as 'on the quarter'. So, an enemy ship spotted ahead of the ship and to the left was deemed as being 'off the port bow'.

Preface

Almost 80 years ago, a mighty German battleship set out on its first operation. She never returned. Enshrouded in the cold waters, the battered and corroding remains of this great warship now lie in the Stygian darkness some 15,700ft below the surface of the Atlantic Ocean.[1] This battleship, the *Bismarck*, is gone, but not forgotten. At the time of her sinking, the attention of the world was focused on her and the dramatic events surrounding her sortie into the Atlantic.

While the glare of this attention has dimmed over the intervening years, the *Bismarck* and her last nine days retain an enduring fascination. This is hardly surprising. The story of her final voyage is one that involves triumph over adversity, a nail-biting hunt for an elusive foe, the clash of steel titans, and gut-wrenching human tragedy. Entwined in this are the constant threads of luck and chance, more than a few unanswered mysteries, and the fate of thousands of sailors caught up in great events. Above all, though, this remains one of the classic tales of the sea.

The battleship *Bismarck* first fired her big guns in anger soon after dawn on 24 May 1941. Although she might have been the largest and most modern battleship in the world, she wasn't the biggest warship, nor the most prestigious.

That position was held by the British battlecruiser *Hood*, as elegant as she was impressive. For two decades, she had been the embodiment of British seapower, and a source of great national pride. Now, that morning in the freezing waters to the west of Iceland, she would fight a duel to the death with her German nemesis.

This 20-minute fight – the Battle of the Denmark Strait – ended in the complete destruction of the *Hood* and the crippling of another British warship, the brand-new battleship *Prince of Wales*. This clash between the *Bismarck* and the *Hood* is probably the most famous naval battle of the modern age. Ironically, though, it ultimately helped seal the fate of the *Bismarck* and her crew. The damage she sustained, light though it was, forced the German commander, Admiral Lütjens, to rethink his plans. Ultimately, that involved the return to a friendly base for repairs. In the meantime, the British Home Fleet had put to sea and was eager for revenge.

What followed was a chase that was every bit as dramatic as the battle in the Denmark Strait. It saw the *Bismarck* and the accompanying cruiser *Prinz Eugen* shake off a carrier strike, then evade the British, allowing both ships to disappear into the vastness of the Atlantic Ocean. The two German warships parted company, and as the cruiser hunted for convoys, the *Bismarck* set a course towards the German-occupied French port of Brest, where she could be repaired. Then she would try her luck again. For a nerve-wracking 31 and a half hours, *Bismarck* remained at large, and undetected. Then she was spotted by the crew of a flying boat, roughly 150 miles south-west of the Irish coast. The chase was on.

The problem, however, was that most of the pursuers were in the wrong place. Admiral Tovey's Home Fleet was far to the west, while Force H to the east – between *Bismarck* and the French coast – was too weak to stop her. So, it looked like *Bismarck* was going to evade her pursuers. Eventually, it all came down to one final strike from the British aircraft carrier *Ark Royal*, carried out by a dozen antiquated biplanes. Amazingly, and against all the odds, one of their torpedoes struck *Bismarck*'s rudder. This was her Achilles heel. It jammed to port, and although *Bismarck* limped on, steering an erratic course, it meant that the British Home Fleet could now overhaul her.

The final act of the great drama took place the following morning, when Tovey's battleships *King George V* and *Rodney* caught up with *Bismarck* and their guns quickly pounded her into floating scrap. Even this was a last-ditch effort, as the British ships had barely enough fuel remaining to make it back to port. Her guns silenced and her decks ablaze, the once-proud German battleship was left wallowing in the swell. As her own crew detonated scuttling charges, the British closed in to finish her off with torpedoes. So, *Bismarck* finally rolled over and sank. Of her 2,200-strong crew, there were only 114 survivors.

In this brief nine-day campaign, two great warships were sunk – the pride of their respective navies – and more than 3,500 sailors lost their lives. That alone would have been enough to make this struggle one of the most important ones of World War II. However, the *Bismarck*'s last voyage was so much more than that. First, there were the mysteries surrounding the operation, some of which remain unanswered. While some of these stem from the decisions made by Admiral Lütjens and Admiral Tovey, perhaps the biggest one surrounds the sinking of the *Bismarck* herself. Was she sunk, or did she scuttle herself? Add to that the sheer drama of her pursuit, the all-or-nothing carrier strikes at the eleventh hour and the odds-defying torpedo hit and you have the makings of a naval classic.

Of course, this story has been told many times before. Versions range from the official British history published in 1954[2] and C. S. Forester's dramatised version, which came out five years later. An excellent film came out in 1960, based on Forester's book, and since then there's been a steady stream of books on the German battleship and/or her Atlantic sortie. Some of these are somewhat dated, while others are filled with technical analysis and statistics. Another was written by a German survivor, a young officer, while others focus on certain aspects of the bigger story, such as the battle in the Denmark Strait. So, why publish another version of the same tale?

One reason is that despite the numerous books on the *Bismarck*'s last voyage, most aren't particularly accessible to readers who lack a solid grounding in modern naval tactics and technology. Accounts often get bogged down in unnecessary detail, while leaving out the very important human aspect of the story. Others go the other way, obscuring the historical narrative with clichés and needless speculation, or resorting to repeating old historical dogmas, wrapped up in a slightly newer package. Few of these match the elegant prose of Ludovic Kennedy's *Pursuit* (1974), written by someone who actually witnessed the *Bismarck*'s final battle.[3] That, though, will soon be half a century old. Historical tastes have changed since then. So, despite all that's been written, there's room for at least one more book – another readable narrative of the *Bismarck*'s final nine days, written by a naval historian who can cut through the technicality to retell this classic naval tale to a modern audience.

Angus Konstam
Orkney 2019

Chapter 1

The *Bismarck*

THE CEREMONY

For late August it was an unusually cold and blustery day.[1] An unseasonable weather front had crept in, and a chilly east wind now blew across the Hamburg waterfront. It was almost as if autumn were trying to come early. On the quarterdeck of the new battleship, the bandsmen mouthed their breath into their brass instruments to keep them warm, while the sailors arrayed beside them had their caps jammed firmly on to their heads to prevent them from being blown overboard. The date was 24 August 1940, and the new ship these men were standing on was officially known as Battleship 'F'. In a few minutes, after a brief ceremony, it would be inducted into the German navy – the Kriegsmarine – and its new name would officially be prefixed with 'KMS', which meant that it was now a Kriegsmarine ship. At the same moment, Battleship 'F' would become Nazi Germany's newest warship and first modern battleship. That name, used by the designers and builders, would be replaced with her proper name. At that moment she would become the *Bismarck*.

A small raised platform had been erected at the after end of the quarterdeck, and the crew of this mighty new ship – all 2,000 of them – were ranged in fairly neat rows, occupying most of the available deck space on both sides of the ship, from bow to stern. The upper deck of a modern battleship was no army parade ground, though. Instead, it was broken by numerous deck fittings, hatches, capstans and stern anchor cables. Most of all, it was dominated by four immense gun turrets, which loomed over the waiting sailors and gave a menacing air to the proceedings. Still, petty officers tweaked their men into line and officers nervously fingered their ceremonial swords and checked that everything was as it should be – from the neatly coiled ropes and polished fittings to the neatness of the men's uniforms. Then a nervous excitement swept through the array, and the ship's executive officer called the assembled ship's company to attention, and to face to starboard.

At that moment, a sleek white motorboat appeared and drew smoothly alongside the starboard gangway. The first man to step aboard from her was the ship's new commanding officer: Kapitän Ernst Lindemann – a tall, thin man with a ramrod-straight back and a lean face. That cold morning, he wore a long naval overcoat, as did his officers, and a pair of leather gloves. His slightly prominent ears were obscured by his black braided cap, and as usual his black shoes were polished to perfection. So, too, of course were those of his men – the whole crew was looking its best. When he appeared at the top of the gangway, the waiting armed honour guard snapped to attention, and the cluster of officers gathered there all saluted. As the ship's bugler played, Lindemann returned the salute.

After that, the first man to step forwards with words of welcome was his executive officer, or first lieutenant in British parlance, Fregattenkapitän (Commander) Hans Oels. He was known as a strict disciplinarian, and a stickler for rules and regulations. Still, as the captain's deputy, that was his job – and that morning he wanted to make sure everything went according to plan. The ship's company was divided into 12 groups, or 'Divisions', each with an officer in charge of them. Minutes before, each of these officers had reported to Oels at the gangway, telling him that their men were all present and ready for inspection. Therefore, when his captain arrived, Oels was confident that everything was in order. The welcome complete, Lindemann turned forward and began his inspection of the crew.

Each of the *Bismarck*'s ten divisions was divided by job, with four seamen's divisions, three technical ones, two for flak gunners, and three more for various other roles. Kapitän Lindemann acknowledged the salute of each of these divisional officers and inspected the men, stopping occasionally to have a quiet word with them. Some of these sailors were men who had served under him before, in the cruiser *Admiral Scheer*, or in various shore bases. He worked his way forwards along the port side of the ship, then inspected his way down the starboard side. In the waist, near the starboard gangplank, was an armed honour guard, who snapped to attention as their captain approached. Keeping pace behind Fregattenkapitän Oels was Kapitänleutnant (Lieutenant) Burkhard von Müllenheim-Rechberg, the new battleship's fourth gunnery officer. His job was to note down any comments or criticisms made by his two superiors.

All the while the band played martial airs. Finally, Kapitän Lindemann reached the quarterdeck, and after inspecting the last divisions of seamen standing to attention there he mounted the small platform. On Oels' order, the ship's company turned and faced aft. In front of Lindemann, gathered beneath the muzzles of 'Dora' turret, were representatives of the Blohm+Voss shipyard, who technically still owned the great ship. Those civilians and the sailors standing on the quarterdeck strained to catch their captain's words. For those further forwards, a microphone linked to loudspeakers carried his words. As he started to speak, two signal petty officers moved behind him carrying a neatly folded bundle – the battleship's new ensign. With practised hands, they clipped it to the waiting halyards and waited for their next order. Meanwhile, their captain's words echoed around the otherwise silent ship.

'Soldiers of the *Bismarck*,' began Lindemann. In the Kriegsmarine, sailors were officially called 'soldiers'. He continued, 'Commissioning day for our splendid ship has come at last.' The captain then went on to thank the men of the Blohm+Voss shipyard for producing such an incredible ship, and doing it ahead of schedule. He called on her crew to weld her into a truly effective instrument of war. Next, he spoke briefly of the war and his expectation that *Bismarck* would play her part, and he then quoted the ship's namesake – Germany's 'Iron Chancellor' Otto von Bismarck, who once said: 'Policy is not made with speeches, shooting festivals or songs. It is made only by blood and iron.' Lindemann was sure this mighty new battleship would honour those words.

His speech done, he turned aft, and with the entire crew standing to attention and officers saluting, Lindemann gave the order: 'Hoist flag and pennant!' With that, the two signalmen tugged on the halyard, until the red, black and white ensign of the Kriegsmarine was flapping in the fresh breeze. Simultaneously, the ship's commissioning pennant broke out on the battleship's mainmast. The band began playing the familiar strains of Haydn's '*Deutschlandlied*', the national anthem. With the unfurling of that flag and pennant, the battleship *Bismarck* officially became the latest addition to the German navy. Few who witnessed the simple naval ceremony would have imagined that in just nine months' time the neat decks of that great battleship would be a tangled mess of ripped steel, and her battered remains would be lying 15,700ft below the surface of the Atlantic, or that Lindemann, Oels and all but a handful of the seamen who stood to attention that cold August day would be dead.

BATTLESHIP 'F'

The *Bismarck* didn't just emerge fully formed from the drawing board and the shipyard.[2] She was the end result of an evolutionary chain that stretched back to the dreadnoughts of Kaiser Wilhelm's Imperial Germany Navy. At the Battle of Jutland in May 1916, the German High Seas Fleet was not only outnumbered by the British, but they were outgunned as well. That said, the German 12in. gun carried by its more modern dreadnoughts was better than its British equivalent, and almost as effective as the 13.5in. guns mounted in the British 'super dreadnoughts'. However, Jutland proved the superior hitting power of the latest 15in. guns used in the latest British 'fast battleships'. The Germans had their own 15in. guns though, and just six weeks after the battle the first of Germany's Bayern class dreadnoughts were commissioned into service. Now, at last, the High Seas Fleet had dreadnoughts with the firepower to counter these new British leviathans.

By war's end in 1918, only two of these new dreadnoughts had been completed. Although never tested in a real battle, they proved their worth bombarding shore targets in the Baltic. With a range of almost 18 nautical miles, and with excellent range-finding and fire control equipment, these were probably the most potent naval guns of their day. Germany's defeat, however, and the savage naval restrictions imposed on the country by the Treaty of Versailles (1919), meant that there was no place for such ships in the Reichsmarine. With the old wartime dreadnoughts either scuttled or disposed of, this new German navy was restricted to a small coastal defence fleet. Its strength was limited to just six pre-dreadnought battleships, while no new armoured ships could be built to replace them if they displaced more than 10,000 tons. Essentially, the Versailles treaty meant the end of the German navy as a potent force.

The Washington Naval Treaty of 1922, signed by the wartime Allies, was designed to prevent a post-war arms race.[3] It limited the size of new battleships to 35,000 tons, and allowed everyone to scale back their wartime fleets. Naturally, Weimar Germany was excluded from the treaty, and they still were when it was revised eight years later. However, when a fresh naval conference was held in Geneva in 1932, German delegates were invited to attend, despite strong French objections. This was a tacit recognition that Germany had started rebuilding its ageing fleet, even though it was still constrained by the iron-bound restrictions of the Versailles treaty. The Reichsmarine had started the ball rolling by building three new armoured ships. The first *Panzerschiff*, the *Deutschland,* was launched in May 1931. This effectively represented the start of Germany's naval recovery.

In warship terms, these were neither fish nor fowl. The British dubbed them 'pocket battleships', because they carried six 11in. guns apiece, mounted in a pair of triple turrets.[4] However, their armour was that of a contemporary heavy cruiser, and their diesel engines, though reliable and giving the ships a healthy range of operations, were generally slower than the steam turbines fitted in most contemporary cruisers. So, although they had the firepower to do some real damage in a fight, they didn't have the speed to run away from danger. In the Battle of the River Plate, fought in late 1939, the *Panzerschiff Admiral Graf Spee* was forced to retire from a fight with three lighter British cruisers. So, while they had their strategic uses – and the German navy had a definite role for them – they were little more than well-armed commerce raiders.

Next, German naval architects began drawing up secret plans for two much larger battlecruisers, each armed with nine 11in. guns. These were drawn up in secret, because at 19,000 tons apiece they were almost twice the displacement limit stipulated by the Versailles treaty. In fact, these warships, which became the *Scharnhorst* and the *Gneisenau*, would eventually displace more than 35,000 tons.[5] Of course, drawing up plans was one thing. Building them in contravention of the treaty was another matter entirely. What that required was a strong political will to defy the treaty, both inside Germany and on the diplomatic stage. That, of course, was just about to happen.

In the national elections of 1928, the extreme right-wing Nationalsozialistische Deutsche Arbeiterpartei (NSDAP), or 'Nazi Party', polled less than 3 per cent.[6] However, the party's paramilitary wing – the 'brownshirts' – helped raise the Nazi profile through intimidation and violence. As a result, by 1932 the Nazis had become the largest party in the German Reichstag. In January 1933, President Hindenburg appointed the NSDAP leader Adolf Hitler as the new German chancellor, hoping that this would defuse the fraught political situation.

Instead, it gave Hitler the opportunity to seize control of the state. Political opponents were silenced, and civil liberties suspended. Soon, rival political parties were disbanded and Germany became a one-party state, ruled over by Hitler, who increasingly assumed full dictatorial powers. So began Hitler's Third Reich – the darkest period in German history.

In March 1935, Hitler abrogated the Treaty of Versailles. He also withdrew Germany from the League of Nations and the Geneva Naval Conference – an act that left the Reichsmarine free to build its new battlecruisers and any other warships it fancied. Still, Hitler recognised that the dominant naval power in Europe was still Great Britain, and he needed their support for this naval expansion, or else risk a fresh blockade of the kind that brought Imperial Germany to its knees in 1918. So, he opened a diplomatic dialogue with the British, which in June 1935 resulted in the Anglo-German Naval Agreement.[7] This effectively ripped up the limitations of Versailles and replaced them with a new lot of guidelines, which set the relative size of the British and German fleets. Just as importantly, Germany was now free to build battleships of up to 35,000 tons.

This was just as well, as the previous month, work had begun on building two new battlecruisers – *Scharnhorst* and *Gneisenau*. They would push the new displacement ceiling to its limit. The term 'battlecruiser' was something of a misnomer, however. As any naval architect knows, designing a warship involves a balancing act between speed, protection and firepower. If you favour one element of this trinity it usually means sacrificing another part of it. The battlecruisers that saw service during World War I were capital ships, for which protection was sacrificed in exchange for speed. The danger of this was exposed at Jutland when four British battlecruisers blew up, while one German battlecruiser was so badly battered it had to be scuttled. In 1941, the Royal Navy still had three battlecruisers in service – *Hood, Repulse* and *Renown*. All would play a part in the drama to come. By contrast, the two new German warships were well armoured – their sacrifice had been in firepower rather than protection, as they only carried 11in. guns.[8] Still, they represented a major step forwards for the German navy.

At the same time, the Reicshmarine changed its name. From 1935 onwards, it would be known as the Kriegsmarine, or 'battle fleet'. Work also began on a pair of new heavy cruisers, a powerful force of destroyers and, even more importantly, a new and formidable U-boat fleet.[9] This, though, wasn't enough. In 1935, plans were already under way for the design of a pair of battleships – warships that would be more powerful than anything else in European waters. So, after casting off the restrictions of Versailles, and ensuring the tacit approval of Britain for their naval expansion, Nazi Germany was free to flex its growing industrial and technological muscle and build a modern new battleship that reflected its growing sense of national pride and military might. They even had the means to do this, thanks to the *Schiffbauersatzplan* (Replacement Ship Construction Programme), a rolling programme funded by the Reichstag to replace Germany's ageing pre-dreadnoughts. This scheme had been used to fund the building of the Deutschland class, as well as the *Scharnhorst* and the *Gneisenau*. Now it would be used again, for the building of a true battleship.

In fact, plans for this modern battleship had first been drawn up as early as 1934, and by the following year they were well advanced. Once again, this work was shrouded in secrecy. Officially, the project was code named *Schlachtschiff* 'F' *Ersatz*

Hannover (Battleship 'F', *Hannover* Replacement), as it was meant to involve a replacement of the old pre-dreadnought battleship *Hannover*, which had been decommissioned in 1931.[10] This, though, would be no mere replacement. If the *Hannover* had been a Ford Model T, this new ship would be a luxury Mercedes-Benz, Duesenberg or Jaguar – three times as large and immeasurably more powerful. The design would change a lot on the drawing board, and even during construction, but what finally appeared on the slipway was arguably the finest capital ship of her day – the battleship *Bismarck*.

The man in charge of her design was Dr Hermann Burkhardt (1881–1969), the chief of the Department of Ship Construction, who was based in Kiel. His initial brief from the navy was to produce plans for a battleship of no more than 35,000 tons. That ceiling was a diplomatic one since it conformed to the restrictions of the Washington Naval Treaty, and later the Anglo-German Naval agreement. The brief wasn't just for one ship, either: he was told he would be building two ships – Battleships 'F' and 'G' – the latter becoming *Bismarck*'s sister ship the *Tirpitz*. In late 1934, he presented his plans for a ship mounting 13in. guns, like the battleships of the French Dunkirque class, to Admiral Raeder, commander-in-chief of the Reichsmarine. However, Raeder told Burkhardt to revise his designs so that Battleship 'F' carried 13.8in. pieces instead. Raeder's other stipulation was that the new ship should be able to pass through the Kaiser Wilhelm Canal, allowing easy transit between the North Sea and the Baltic. So, Burkhardt and his team went back to the drawing board.

By early 1935, the German naval command felt they could break through the 35,000-ton ceiling, which gave the designers a little more flexibility in balancing that trinity of speed, protection and firepower.[11] That summer, Raeder changed the plans again, now demanding that she carry 15in. guns, in four twin turrets. He felt that any delay in completing the design was worth it in terms of the extra firepower the ship would have. Other design problems, such as the type of propulsion system used and the scale of the ship's armour, were also overcome that summer. While changes were still being made, the final design of Battleship 'F' was finally taking shape. So much so, in fact, that by the autumn Raeder felt confident enough to officially order Battleship 'G' – the *Tirpitz*. In November, the final set of plans for Battleship 'F' was approved and the construction was duly awarded to the Blohm+Voss shipyard in Hamburg. Work was scheduled to begin the following summer, for delivery in the autumn of 1939.

That, though, was only the start. Other plans and contracts were drawn up for everything from the guns and steam turbines to the ammunition hoists, galley equipment and plumbing systems. Building a modern warship was a complex business, involving not only the designers, the navy and the shipyard, but also myriad other contractors, both large and small. Meanwhile, Burkhardt and his team in Kiel continued to make a host of other modifications, largely caused by Raeder's insistence on 15in. guns and a speed of 30 knots.[12] That meant a slight reduction in armour thickness to compensate, and last-minute changes to the propulsion system. By then, however, international events had rendered the old 35,000-ton limit irrelevant. Japan, the USA and Italy were all known to be planning to build battleships that broke the treaty ceiling, so effectively the gloves were now off. This removed any lingering diplomatic doubts about the construction of Battleship 'F'. So, after a brief ceremony, the keel of Battleship 'F' was finally laid on 1 July 1936.

BUILDING THE *BISMARCK*

For just over two-and-a-half years, the battleship grew one weld at a time.[13] Slipway 9 of the Blohm+Voss yard was a place where shipbuilding magic happened. The yard lay on the south bank of the Elbe, across the river from the bustling heart of Hamburg. It had built some of the Kaiser's great warships, but now it was the scene of something even more spectacular – the construction of Germany's first truly modern battleship.

Building a battleship was a long and complex process. First came the great keel, and then the frames and bulkheads that gave the web of steel the skeletal appearance of a ship. If the keel was the spine of the ship, the frames at right angles to it were its ribs. Banding these together was a series of longitudinal frames and transverse bulkheads. These would eventually divide the battleship into 22 watertight compartments, which, together with her double bottom, were there to make sure she stayed afloat, even if her hull were to be pierced by enemy shells. Work continued steadily, and bit by bit the great ship took shape.

By the coming of spring in 1937, most of the framework of her hull had been completed.[14] That meant that the builders could start attaching her outer skin of hardened steel plates. The armour of Battleship 'F' was concentrated in a citadel in the centre of the ship, protecting the magazines and engines. Forward and aft of this, the battleship would be less well protected. The central armoured citadel, however, was considered proof against hits from most calibres of naval guns. It was topped by an armoured deck, which was actually below the ship's upper deck. This great armoured box was pierced by circular shafts, designed to house the ship's four great gun turrets and her six secondary ones. By the end of the year, this armoured citadel had been completed, and most of the upper deck built and plated in. Then came the adding of the great tubular steel barbettes that would house the gun turrets, and the plating in of the bow and stern.

The work continued steadily throughout 1938, while close by the first of the Kriegsmarine's new heavy cruisers was being fitted out. Named the *Admiral Hipper*, she for all practical purposes looked like a slightly smaller version of the new battleship, or rather she would when *Bismarck* was completed.[15] Over in the Germaniawerft shipyard in Kiel, meanwhile, the *Hipper's* sister ship the *Prinz Eugen* was still on the stocks – she would be launched that August. Back on Slipway 9, the *Bismarck* was looking increasingly impressive.[16] A steady succession of trains brought high-tensile steel plate directly to the shipyard, and one by one, plates were hoisted into position and welded into place. Once the hull was complete, work began on her superstructure. Her construction was planned with meticulous attention to detail, and so by the end of the year it was clear the new battleship would be launched on schedule, in early 1939.

So it was that on St Valentine's Day 1939, a select crowd of guests took their seats on the platforms surrounding Slipway 9.[17] The shipyard workers stood in the background. In all, 60,000 people watched the ceremony that followed. At noon, the German Führer Adolf Hitler left Hamburg's prestigious Hotel Atlantic and boarded a yacht, which took him across the river to the shipyard. The rest of the Nazi inner circle – Göring, Himmler, Goebbels, Hess, von Ribbentrop, Keitel and Bormann – were already in their seats. Once he'd arrived, Hitler mounted the rostrum, and at 13.00 the launching ceremony began. Hitler gave a brief speech, announcing for the first time that Battleship 'F' would be named after Germany's great statesman Otto von Bismarck. Then, he was joined by Dorothee von Löwenfeld-Bismarck, the granddaughter of the 'Iron Chancellor'. She named the ship after her famous grandfather, and a bottle of sparkling wine was duly smashed against her bows. The band then played the '*Deutschlandlied*' as the newly named battleship slid into the River Elbe.

The ceremony over, tugs towed the *Bismarck* to the nearby Equipping Pier, where her fitting-out would take place. This involved another year or more of work; at the moment, *Bismarck* was merely an empty steel shell. This was the period when she would be turned into a functioning warship. *Bismarck* was still alongside the Equipping Pier when the war broke out seven months later. The work continued, although now flak batteries ringed the shipyard and searchlights probed the night sky over Hamburg.

The winter of 1939–40 was a harsh one, and ice covered the basin. Nevertheless, by January, the last of the battleship's four great gun turrets was in place and the final phase of fitting-out began. In April 1940, the first of her crew arrived, although initially they were housed in barrack ships berthed nearby.

Their ship was still a mess, with electricians, engineers, fitters, carpenters, metalworkers and even plumbers working hard to complete it. Wiring lay everywhere and vital equipment was being installed. Still, these sailors had to learn their way around their new ship and, even more importantly, they had to familiarise themselves with her machinery and weaponry. Everything gradually took shape, though, and by the summer *Bismarck* was moved into a dry dock to have her propellers fitted and her underside painted. By then, all that was left were a few finishing touches and last-minute snagging. Once that was done, and her captain and a team of naval inspectors officially approved the work, the shipyard would be ready to hand the completed ship over to the navy. That was what happened on commissioning day, when *Bismarck* officially became part of the Kriegsmarine.

THE LIEUTENANT'S NEW SHIP

That June, the battleship's fourth gunnery officer joined his new ship.[18] Kapitänleutnant Burkard von Müllenheim-Rechberg came from Alsatian nobility, and at 29 he was already an experienced officer; before the war, he'd even served as a junior naval attaché in London. He'd been on other warships during his career, but nothing compared to the *Bismarck*. His account of her reflected the young man's sense of pride in his imposing new ship. He began with her bare statistics: '*Bismarck* had a net displacement of 45,928 metric tons, and a full-load displacement of 49,924.2 metric tons. Her overall length was 251m, her beam 36m, and her designed draft was 9.33m, or at maximum displacement, 10.17m.'[19] As a gunnery officer, he was particularly impressed by the wide beam, which made for a stable gun platform. In fact, she could barely scrape through the Kaiser Wilhelm Canal – Dr Burkhardt had pushed that aspect of her design to the limit.

Müllenheim-Rechberg emphasised the underwater protection afforded by her double bottom, her torpedo bulkheads – which acted like a sacrificial layer outside the main hull – and her 22 watertight compartments. Any warship was vulnerable to torpedo attacks by aircraft, submarines or destroyers, and it was almost impossible to make the ship impervious to their blast. So, the idea was to create an outer hull that would absorb the detonation, and thus avoid serious damage to the inner layer of the hull. The wide beam of the *Bismarck* made this system particularly effective.

The lieutenant was just as impressed by the ship's armour. Again, while *Bismarck* carried 18,000 tons of armour, made from plates of specially hardened Wotan steel, it was almost impossible to protect everything. So, as the lieutenant put it, it was concentrated where it was needed the most: 'The ship's outer shell was covered by an armoured belt, whose thickness varied up to 320 millimetres, and which protected such important installations as the turbines, boilers, and magazines. Higher up, the armour was between 120 and 145mm thick and it formed a sort of citadel to protect the decks above the armoured deck.' He added that this armoured deck was up to 4.3in. thick, although the main deck above it was only protected by 2.4in. of armoured plate – enough to protect against shell splinters and not much else. This was enough, though: the vital parts of the ship were superbly protected. As in most warships of the time, some areas of the ship lacked full armoured protection, in part to keep her weight down and maintain that all-important balance between protection, firepower and speed. After her sinking, Allied naval analysts reckoned *Bismarck* had achieved a near perfect balance between these three factors, and was actually better designed than the latest British or American battleship. Any way you look at it, *Bismarck* was well protected.

Müllenheim-Rechberg went on to describe *Bismarck*'s propulsion system – her three propellers, powered by steam turbines and 12 high-pressure boilers: 'The plant was designed to provide a top speed of 29 knots at a total horsepower for the three [propeller] shafts of 138,000, but at the normal maximum of 150,000, the speed was 30.12 knots.'[20] He couldn't help adding: 'The *Bismarck* was one of the fastest battleships built at this time.' He then touched on her cruising abilities: 'Her maximum fuel capacity was 8,700 tons, which gave her an operating range of 8,900 miles, at a speed of 17 knots, and 9,280 miles at 16 knots.' That was a remarkable range for a turbine ship of that day, and it shows, from the outset, that the *Bismarck* was intended for high-sea operations. He described her two electrically powered rudders, and her battery of powerful electrical generators, but his main fascination still lay with the ship's weaponry.

'The battleship's main armament consisted of four double 15in. turrets, two of which, Anton and Bruno, were mounted forward, and two, Caesar and Dora, aft. Their maximum range was 36,200m.'[21] These guns were hugely impressive, with barrels almost 66ft long. It wasn't just the guns that impressed the lieutenant, either – it was the whole complex array of magazines, hoists, rangefinders, analogue computers and fire control equipment that kept them supplied with their huge shells, and made sure they hit their target. Each turret weighed a little over 1,000 tons, but they were so well balanced on rollers that they could turn quickly and easily to face their target. The shells, which weighed almost 800kg (0.75 ton), were brought up to the turrets on mechanical hoists, and hydraulic rammers fed them into the gun breeches.

Analogue computers used things like speed bearing, wind direction and humidity to work out where the barrels should be aimed, and once a firing solution had been found, the guns were trained and fired.[22] To a gunner like Müllenheim-Rechberg, there was nothing to match the *Bismarck*'s firepower. The lieutenant admired almost as much the battleship's other weaponry – her 12 6in. guns in six twin turrets, and her formidable array of light, medium and heavy anti-aircraft (or flak) guns. These were backed up by an impressive fire control system that allowed the ship to lay down a devastating barrage of flak – the bigger guns creating a wall designed to stop enemy planes, while the smaller ones actually targeted individual aircraft. A radar system gave the ship a degree of warning of enemy surface or air threats, while hydrophones did the same for enemy submarines. Müllenheim-Rechberg found it all very impressive. With some justification he described the *Bismarck* as 'a floating gun platform'.

With the crew of 103 officers and 1,962 men assembled, the *Bismarck* also contained everything required to keep them fed, clothed and healthy.[23] She was fitted with state-of-the-art galleys, while cold stores and freezers were crammed with food. This was served in large dining areas or in the wardroom. The ship had her own bakery and even a bar serving beer. Stores were filled with clothing, while a laundry kept uniforms clean. *Bismarck* also boasted a tailor's shop and a cobbler. The health of the crew was maintained by a medical team, headed by skilled doctors using a full operating theatre, a dental surgery and a pharmacy. Hygiene was maintained by showers and washing facilities, while mess decks were kept scrubbed and clean. In effect, *Bismarck* was a small floating town, albeit one with an all-male population.

So, with her crew on board, *Bismarck* was now ready to begin her sea trials.[24] This was the process whereby her performance would be tested, and her engines put through their paces. The Kriegsmarine policy was that no commissioned warship could be considered operational until these trials had been completed, and that any snags that emerged were dealt with – something that involved her returning to Hamburg. Only once this had been completed could the training of her crew begin and then, finally, after these trials and training periods had been completed, the Kriegsmarine would be willing to declare the new ship fully operational. Thus it was that on 14 September 1940 the great battleship was edged away from the quayside, and with the help of tugs made her way into the River Elbe. From there, she faced a 40-mile journey to Brünsbuttel, and the western end of the Kaiser Wilhelm Canal.

That night she anchored off Brünsbuttel, and fired her guns in anger for the first time, as her flak batteries engaged a formation of British bombers on their way to Kiel.[25] The next day, she entered the canal, Kapitän Lindemann nervously watching the battleship pass through it with just centimetres to spare on either side. As Müllenheim-Rechberg put it: 'The slightest error … could have had disastrous consequences'. However, all went well, and by the evening of the 17th *Bismarck* was safely berthed alongside the Scheerhaven – the naval wharf in Kiel. Eleven days later, on 28 September, she left Kiel and headed out into the Baltic. That was when her eight weeks of sea trials started in earnest.

These began with the testing of her engines, and her speed trials. It was found she could easily make 30 knots. Lindemann put her through a range of evolutions, including high-speed turns and rapid changes of speed. The ship responded perfectly. On 12 November, Raeder came aboard to inspect her as she lay off Gotenhafen and additions were made to her weaponry, including the adding of two new twin 4.1in. flak mounts. Eventually, the trials were deemed a success, and in early December the *Bismarck* returned to Kiel. By 9 December she was back alongside the Equipping Pier in the Blohm+Voss shipyard, ready for any problems to be dealt with. In fact, there were very few.

So, Kapitän Lindemann officially thanked the crew for their efforts, and told them that after some well-deserved

Christmas leave they would return to the Baltic, for their working up, or crew training.²⁶ Then, once *Bismarck* and her crew had been welded into a fighting machine, they would become fully operational and embark on their first operation. On 16 December, Müllenheim-Rechberg left Hamburg for two weeks of skiing in Bavaria.²⁷ Others went home to their families or enjoyed the delights of Hamburg. Meanwhile, the shipyard workers trooped back on board to make sure the battleship would be ready for her crew when they returned. This completed, *Bismarck* was now a fully functioning warship, and the pride of the German navy. Soon, in a very few months, she and her crew would be able to play their part in the war.

Chapter 2

Germany's Atlantic Strategy

RAEDER'S VISION

Bismarck, like the other Kriegsmarine ships that came before her, had a clearly defined job to do. The Kriegsmarine's construction programme, from its capital ships like *Bismarck* to its U-boat fleet, was in the business of 'sea denial'. This was a term first coined by Alfred Thayer Mahan, the hugely influential American naval strategist whose writing in the 19th century was read by Kaiser Wilhelm II and whose words lay behind his enthusiasm for a powerful German navy.[1] However, the German Kaiser realised that he would never be able to build a fleet large enough to rival that of the British Royal Navy.[2] Instead, his battle fleet had a more limited aim – the pinning-down of British naval resources. That, ultimately, would allow his U-boat fleet to set about the job of cutting Britain's vital maritime supply lines. The survival of Great Britain relied on a steady supply of foodstuffs and raw materials, all of which were imported by ships. By sinking these ships, and so severing these supply lines, Germany could bring Britain to its knees.

During World War I, this plan came close to succeeding.[3] Only by diverting considerable resources to the protection of her sea lanes could Britain avoid catastrophe. So, Britain organised convoys to protect her merchant ships, and developed new anti-submarine technology. This, and the entry of the USA into the war, helped tip the balance, and the Kaiser's stratagem was foiled.

The Royal Navy, meanwhile, played a different game. Its role was 'sea control' – in effect maintaining full control of the seas by using the fleet to protect the sea lanes and deny the enemy access to them. It was a far more ambitious policy, but then the Royal Navy was large enough to make it work. Sea denial, by contrast, was less ambitious, and for Germany it recognised the limitations of its much smaller navy. If you couldn't seize control of the seas, then at least you could choke Britain's maritime lifeline enough to deny control of the high seas to the enemy.

In fact, in the days of Weimar Germany, Britain was never seen as a potential enemy. Instead, in 1928, when Admiral Erich Raeder became the head of the Reichsmarine, France was considered Germany's most likely adversary.[4] While the French fleet was powerful, it had to divide its forces between the Atlantic and the Mediterranean. So, if the German navy were built up then it might conceivably be able to strangle France's maritime links to her Atlantic and Channel ports, and with her overseas colonies. It was a very limited objective but one Raeder felt he could achieve, which was why he approved the building of the Deutschland class of 'pocket battleships'.[5] While they lacked the firepower to take on French capital ships, they were perfectly suited to the role of commerce raiding, and therefore of 'sea denial'. So, too, were the small fleet of U-boats that Raeder was secretly building.

When Hitler came to power in 1935 this whole strategic plan was turned on its head. The abrogation of the Treaty of Versailles and the Anglo-German Naval Agreement meant that Raeder could now build pretty much what he wanted.[6] So, the Kriesmarine began a construction programme that saw the expansion of the fleet, in line with Hitler's more aggressive foreign policy, which added Poland and the Soviet Union to the list of potential enemies. However, both of these countries had even smaller navies than France. So, with a slightly larger Kriegsmarine, this raised the possibility of achieving control of the seas against them. In short, although any military campaign against any of these three countries would predominantly be decided on land, a larger fleet would give Raeder's navy the chance to play a greater part in the conflict.

It was only in 1938 that Hitler began to consider a possible war with Great Britain.[7] At this point it was clear that the Kriegsmarine wasn't up to the task of challenging the Royal Navy. Even in 1939, it would have less than one-tenth of the strength of the British fleet. This meant that Germany needed to re-evaluate its plans for the Kriegsmarine, and also had to expand it. So, towards the end of 1938 Raeder came up with a long-term programme of naval expansion – one that far exceeded the limits imposed by the Anglo-German Naval Agreement of just three years before. This programme, known as 'Plan Z', was approved by Hitler in January 1939.[8] It involved the commitment of more than 33 million marks over the next seven years, and the building of a decent-sized battle fleet that included battleships, aircraft carriers, cruisers and a huge force of U-boats. Underpinning it was Hitler's assurance to Raeder – now a Grossadmiral – that any war with Britain wouldn't take place before January 1946 – seven years from then. In fact, the peace lasted barely seven months.

The coming of war with Britain and France in September 1939 meant that Plan Z was now dead in the water. The first casualties were the capital ships – a new group of 'H' class battleships that would have been even larger than *Bismarck* – and an aircraft carrier.[9] By September, work had begun on two of the battleships, while the carrier *Graf Zeppelin* was already being fitted out in Kiel. Raeder understood his fleet would only get limited resources now; economic efforts would be concentrated on the army and air force. He therefore had to prioritise, which meant focusing on U-boats and smaller warships, which could be built quickly, rather than large capital ships. So, the two 'H' class battleships that had just been laid down in Hamburg and Bremen were scrapped before their keels were even finished. The *Graf Zeppelin* suffered a lingering death. She had already been launched and was being fitted out. However, the Luftwaffe, who would have supplied the planes and pilots, were lukewarm about the project, and in May 1940 work on her was halted.

Essentially, then, Raeder and his *Oberkommando der Marine* (OKM, or German Naval High Command) had to wage a war for which they were unprepared, and do so with the limited resources they had at hand. Certainly, new ships were being completed, including *Bismarck*, *Tirpitz*, a third Admiral Hipper class heavy cruiser and a host of new destroyers and U-boats.[10] The OKM was divided into several departments,[11] the most important of which was the *Seekriegsleitung* (SKL, or Naval Warfare Command). This was responsible for strategic planning, the allocation of naval ships and resources, and the oversight of specific operations. Officially, Raeder was in charge of it, but it was his chief-of-staff Admiral Otto Schniewind who effectively ran the department. This meant that in the autumn of 1939, both Raeder and Schniewind had to come up with a whole new strategic plan, based on a war their Führer had assured them wouldn't happen.

In 1939, the Royal Navy had 12 battleships, three battlecruisers and six aircraft carriers.[12] By contrast, the Kriegsmarine only had its two Scharnhorst class capital ships, with two more battleships still being fitted out. Clearly this overwhelming disparity of force meant that the Kriegsmarine couldn't possibly challenge the Royal Navy for control of the seas. Effectively, the outbreak of war had ended any long-term goal of sea control, which may just have been possible if it had run its course. That left sea denial as a strategic option.

In terms of a naval war with Britain and France, this meant that while the Kriegsmarine's limited resources would be spread thinly – more so than in a more limited war with France alone – Britain was wholly dependent on her sea lanes. So, as in World War I, a policy of commerce raiding could well bear fruit. In that previous war, though, the German battle fleet had been confined to the waters of the North Sea. This time round, the OKM expected its larger surface ships to join in the campaign in the Atlantic.

So, the three armoured cruisers of the Deutchland class, *Deutschland* (renamed *Lützow*), *Graf Spee* and *Admiral Hipper*, the two battlecruisers *Scharnhorst* and Gneisenau, and eventually *Bismarck* and *Tirpitz* would all be used as commerce raiders.[13] Despite the scarcity of ships, however, things weren't as bleak as they might have been. First, the Royal Navy had global commitments, and much of its naval strength was deployed in the Mediterranean or in the Far East. Second, while Germany's capital ships were brand new, most of the Royal Navy's battleships were veterans of World War I. So, even though the Royal Navy enjoyed a huge numerical advantage, ship for ship the Kriegsmarine had the edge. The British were aware of this, a knowledge that was reflected in their own naval strategy against Germany. This would involve a 'distant blockade', to bottle the Kriegsmarine up in the North Sea and deny it access to the Atlantic.[14] With the British Home Fleet now at its traditional wartime base of Scapa Flow in Orkney, it was ideally placed to do just that. Raeder and Schniewind had to come up with a way of breaking this blockade so that they could set about the business of sea denial in the Atlantic.

This policy was enshrined in the SKL's *Directive No. 1 for the Conduct of the War.*[15] Written on 31 August 1939 and promulgated secretly throughout the fleet, it stated: 'The Kriegsmarine is to carry out commerce warfare, and it will be aimed primarily at England.' Even at that late hour, as Hitler was poised to invade Poland, he still hoped that Britain and France would back down and not honour their alliance with the Poles. So, while commerce raiding was to be prepared for, and would start the moment Britain declared war, this was not to be an all-out naval campaign of the kind waged by the Kaiser's U-boats in the previous war. Instead, international niceties would be observed, such as avoiding attacks on passenger liners, calling on victims to abandon ship before she was sunk, and making sure potential targets weren't flying the flag of a neutral country. This would soon change, but for the moment, at least in theory, these rules would apply.

THE EARLY SORTIES

At least, as the war clouds gathered, Grossadmiral (Fleet Admiral) Raeder had the foresight to send most of his commerce raiders to sea. On 3 September 1939, the *Panzerschiff Admiral Graf Spee* was loitering in the mid-Atlantic, while far to the north her sister ship *Deutschland* was doing the same off the southern tip of Greenland.[16] Both ships had slipped out of Germany in late August, before the British Home Fleet could intercept them. So too did 21 U-boats – four-fifths of the Kriegsmarine's available U-boat fleet. At 12.30 that day, on board the *Admiral Graf Spee*, Kapitänleutnant Langsdorff was smoking a cigar on his bridge when the radio operator appeared and handed him a signal. It was the intercept of an uncoded British transmission, which said quite simply 'Total Germany'. This clearly meant that war had been declared. This was confirmed a little later by another signal from the SKL, which read: 'Hostilities with Britain to be opened forthwith.' So, this was it. The two German ships got under way, and began the business of waging war.

In fact, the two ships achieved very little. *Deutschland* was hindered from attacking Allied shipping for three more weeks, as Hitler hoped the British would negotiate a peace once Poland was conquered. She was also hampered by a scarcity of shipping and bad weather, and in her seven-week operational cruise she only sank one British freighter, and seized one neutral one and sank another. She eventually returned home by way of the Denmark Strait, arriving back in Gotenhafen on 17 November. Kapitänleutnant Langsdorff was more successful. The *Admiral Graf Spee* cruised off the West African coast and then in the Indian Ocean, sinking a total of nine British merchant ships.

Eventually, though, a number of British and French hunting groups closed in on her, and on 13 December the *Admiral Graf Spee* was brought to battle off the South American coast, at the mouth of the River Plate. There, three British cruisers forced the more powerful German ship to run into Montevideo in Uruguay. When forced to return to sea to avoid internment, Langsdorff chose to scuttle the *Admiral Graf Spee* rather than lose his crew in a battle against what he thought were superior British forces. This was the first serious loss for the Kriegsmarine during the war and it emphasised the unpleasant truth about commerce raiding: once they broke out into the Atlantic, any commerce raider, however powerful, was on its own.

By then the second phase of raiders had left port. During the autumn of 1939, the battlecruisers *Scharnhorst* and *Gneisenau* were busy undergoing sea trials and crew training. However, early on 22 November they slipped out of Wilhelmshaven and headed north.[17] The bad winter weather helped them avoid British patrols as they passed through the gap between Shetland and Norway, then turned towards the north-west, aiming for the north of Iceland. In his flagship *Gneisenau*, Admiral Wilhelm Marshall planned to use the poor visibility to help him sneak through the gap between Iceland and the Faeroe Islands. That evening, however, the storm abated, and dawn on 23 November brought clear skies and calm seas. Still, their progress went undetected, and as the day wore on Marshall began hoping he might actually make it through the British blockade.

Then, late in the afternoon, the German lookouts spotted a ship off their port bow. It turned out to be the armed merchant cruiser *Rawalpindi*, commanded by Captain Edward Kennedy.[18] The *Rawalpindi* made smoke and tried to evade the large German warships, and Kennedy managed to send off a sighting report. He ignored German signals to heave-to and, realising that escape was impossible, he turned to fight. It was a singularly one-sided contest. Her 6in. guns hadn't scored a hit when the *Rawalpindi* was battered by German shells. When one struck her magazine she was ripped apart, taking all but 38 of her crew down with her, including Captain Kennedy. It was now dusk, and as the German battlecruisers slowed to pick up survivors, the lookouts spotted more British ships approaching. Unaware they were only cruisers, Marshall ordered his two ships to turn away. Four days later, the *Scharnhorst* and *Gneisenau* were back in Wilhelmshaven.

Although this Atlantic sortie was a failure, others were planned for early the following year. Then, apart from the U-boat offensive, the whole commerce-raiding strategy was halted as the Kriegsmarine was ordered to prepare for another operation, which would have major strategic repercussions. Since the war had begun, Grossadmiral Raeder had been advocating the invasion of Norway.[19] Not only would this involve an amphibious invasion, in which the Kriegsmarine could play a major role, but if successful it would also give it secure bases along the Norwegian coast. This would be harder for the British to blockade, and so in theory it would make a breakout into the North Atlantic easier. The invasion began in April 1940. While both Norway and Denmark were conquered, the Kriegsmarine suffered heavy losses – three cruisers and ten destroyers were sunk in Norwegian waters, while *Scharnhorst* and *Gneisenau* were damaged. Nevertheless, Raeder declared that gaining control of Norway was worth the loss of half of his battle fleet.

Norway was still being consolidated by the Germans when Hitler launched his next offensive. It turned out that the Scandinavian operation had been little more than a prelude to the main event. On 10 May 1940, the German invasion of France and the Low Countries began, and within five days the German panzers had broken through the Allied front near Sedan.[20] As German tanks raced across France, the British and French troops in Belgium began to retreat to the south, but on 20 May the Germans reached the Channel coast, and so cut the Allied forces in two. With pressure mounting on land and from the air, the British began evacuating Allied troops from Dunkirk. While this saved the lives of more than 250,000 British and French troops, it left the Germans free to turn south and complete their conquest of France. Paris fell on 14 June, and just over a week later the French surrendered and signed an armistice.

France was divided in two – the northern part was occupied by the German army, while the south was considered a 'free zone', governed by a rump French government based in Vichy. What this meant for the Kriegsmarine was that it suddenly found it had access to a string of sizeable French ports on the Atlantic coast. These included the magnificently equipped French naval bases at Brest and St Nazaire. In consequence, in a matter of just two months the whole strategic situation had been turned on its head. Now the Kriegsmarine could move its U-boats to these new French ports, which lay within easy reach of Britain's sea lanes in the Atlantic.[21] With Norway in German hands, surface units and U-boats could use the fjords as a staging place for sorties into the North Atlantic. Once there, they now had the option of returning the same way, or of putting into the French Atlantic ports. As a result, when commerce raiding resumed, the Kriegsmarine held a much better hand.

Throughout the summer of 1940, the Kriegsmarine was held in readiness for Operation *Sealion* – the amphibious invasion of Britain. Raeder argued that after Norway the navy lacked the strength to guarantee success. This meant that airpower would be the deciding factor. So, after the Luftwaffe's failure to subdue the Royal Air Force in the Battle of Britain, the invasion forces were stood down, and the Kriegmarine was free to resume its policy of sea denial.

While the U-boats continued to wage their own hidden war in the Atlantic, the navy's surface warships could now rejoin the campaign. On 23 October, the *Panzerschiff Admiral Scheer* left Gotenhafen and sailed through the Baltic and into Norwegian waters. From there, she headed up past the Arctic Circle, then curved westwards. She slipped undetected through the Denmark Strait at the end of October, and into the vastness of the Atlantic.

So began a remarkable commerce-raiding cruise that lasted five months and took *Admiral Scheer* as far as the South Atlantic and the Indian Ocean.[22] In many ways, it mirrored the cruise of her sister ship the *Admiral Graf Spee* a year before. The difference was that the *Admiral Scheer* made it home again, retracing her old route through the Denmark Strait in late March 1941 and arriving back in Kiel on 1 April. Her first victim was another armed merchant cruiser, *Jervis Bay*, which was sunk by *Admiral Scheer*'s guns in a little over 20 minutes. The raider then headed south into the mid-Atlantic.

On 30 November, a second raider – the heavy cruiser *Admiral Hipper* – left Germany, and followed the route taken by the *Panzerschiff*, putting into Norwegian waters near Bergen before continuing on past the Arctic Circle.[23] On 7 December, she broke out into the Atlantic through the Denmark Strait, and once more the British cruisers on patrol there failed to spot her as she slipped past them. Her hunting ground was the convoy lanes between Newfoundland and the Western Approaches to the British Isles. Bad weather made it hard to find targets, but on Christmas Eve she came upon a convoy, escorted by the British heavy cruiser *Berwick*. The *Admiral Hipper* drove off her rival, but the duel bought time for the convoy to scatter. The next day, she caught and sank one of the freighters, but it was a poor consolation prize. Two days later, on 27 December, she put in to Brest.

The *Admiral Hipper* would put to sea again in early February, but this time her captain was under strict instructions to avoid engaging powerful enemy escorts. This cruise off the Azores lasted less than two weeks, after falling on a convoy and sinking seven merchant ships, as well as another – a straggler from another convoy. She returned to Brest to refuel and rearm, then returned to sea. The Kriegsmarine was keen to get her back to Germany, due to frequent British air attacks on the French ports. So, on 15 March she left Brest, avoided British patrols and safely passed through the Denmark Strait eight days later. By the end of the month, she was safely back in Kiel. Two days later, on 1 April 1941, she was joined by *Admiral Scheer*. During her 42,000-mile voyage she sank 17 Allied merchant ships and an armed merchant cruiser, which made her the most successful single German surface raider of the war.

OPERATION *BERLIN*

Towards the end of 1940, the *Scharnhorst* and *Gneisenau* completed their repairs and became available to play a part in these sorties.[24] So, early on 22 January they left Kiel and headed north through Danish waters. This time, the German battlecruisers were commanded by Admiral Günther Lütjens, who had planned the sortie – code named Operation *Berlin* – in meticulous detail. However, ice delayed his passage through the Skagerrak, as did a British sweep in the Norwegian Sea, but by the 26th the two battlecruisers were safely in the North Sea, and heading north. By the early hours of the 27th they were level with Iceland, and Lütjens made his move, heading west to pass through the Iceland–Faeroes gap. The trouble was, visibility was good – too good – and the night sky was lit by the aurora borealis. Both ships were equipped with radar, albeit not such a good set as the one carried on British ships. Still, Lütjens hoped it would give him an edge. Then, the set on *Gneisenau* broke down.

As dawn approached, a radar contact was made – probably an enemy cruiser – and Lütjens ordered his ships to turn away to the north. In fact, it was the light cruiser *Naiad*, whose radar was malfunctioning and was therefore slower than the Germans' to detect the enemy. A second contact at 08.00 forced another turn, until they were now heading away from the Iceland–Faeroes gap and back towards the Arctic Sea. At that point, the fleet commander gave up the attempt. Instead, he planned to head north and refuel from a waiting tanker, stationed to the east of Jan Mayen island. Unknown to him, this was the best move he could have made. The British were expecting him, and the bulk of the Home Fleet was at sea. This included the battleships *Nelson* and *Rodney*, and the battlecruiser *Repulse*. Collectively, they had more than enough firepower to destroy Lütjens' command.

Instead, he spent the next few days making contact with the tanker *Adria* and completing a refuelling at sea – a tricky operation given the rough seas and intense cold. Still, by 23.00 on 1 February the refuelling was complete, and the two German battlecruisers turned south again. Lütjens had decided, however, that this time he was going to try the Denmark Strait, between Greenland and Iceland. Again, his timing was perfect. By then the bulk of the Home Fleet was running low on fuel and had returned to Scapa Flow.[25] He also made his approach to the Denmark Strait late on the evening of 3 February, so his ships would be cloaked by the Arctic night. In theory, the Strait was 150 miles wide, but at that time of year pack ice off Greenland reduced it to a little less than half its full width. The crews were at Action Stations and the lookouts peered into the darkness, not just for enemy ships, but also for ice floes lying across their path. Everyone was tense and fully expecting an enemy warship to appear at any moment.

At 03.00 a radar contact was made, and Lütjens edged his ships away from it. This contact – an armed merchant cruiser – maintained its course, which suggested that they hadn't been spotted. By the time dawn broke, they were through the Strait and the danger of encountering the enemy was behind them. Ahead lay the vastness of the North Atlantic. Lütjens understood the importance of the moment. On his flagship's tannoy, and in a signal flashed to *Scharnhorst*, Lütjens announced: 'For the first time in history, German battleships have reached the Atlantic.'[26] It was true. That day, 4 January 1941, was a key moment in the Kriegsmarine's history. Not only had the two capital ships broken out into the Atlantic, but they had also done so without being detected. Now the two wolves were loose among the sheep.

The distances in the Atlantic were vast, so Lütjens' first priority was to refuel, to give him the greatest possible range of operation. Fortunately, the tanker *Schlettstadt* was waiting for him 100 miles south of Cape Farewell, the southernmost tip of Greenland. The two battlecruisers reached the rendezvous point, code named Point Black, and found the tanker waiting for them. By the morning of 6 February the refuelling was complete, and the battlecruisers parted company. With that done, Lütjens reviewed his options. The main transatlantic convoy route lay a few hundred miles to the south, running between Halifax in Newfoundland and the Western Approaches. Naval intelligence knew that the two old British battleships *Ramillies* and *Revenge* were being used to escort convoys part of the way, then return to Halifax to refuel. So, Lütjens planned to intercept these convoys well to the east of this, to avoid being drawn into a needless fight.

He reached the chosen area on 7 February, and intelligence reports from Berlin suggested an eastbound convoy was on its way.[27] In response, Lütjens split up his two ships to cover a wider area and waited for the enemy to appear. Sure enough, the next morning the enemy convoy appeared, directly between the two battlecruisers. Lütjens gave the order to close in. Both of the German ships were about 20 miles from the convoy, at the very edge of visibility. Then, amid Convoy HX106's ragged lines of 41 merchant ships and four destroyers, lookouts on the *Scharnhorst* spotted something a lot more menacing: it was a battleship – one of the two Royal Sovereign class ships based in Halifax. In fact, she was the *Ramillies*. Although a lumbering relic of the previous war, she carried eight 15in. guns – significantly more powerful than the 11in ones mounted in the German ships. When Lütjens heard the report he ordered his two ships to break off the attack.

This has sometimes been portrayed as a lost opportunity, as the odds still favoured the Germans.[28] However, the fleet commander's orders were clear: on no account was he to engage an enemy of equal strength. Thus, he had no choice. Fortunately for Lütjens, the British only spotted *Scharnhorst*, and incorrectly identified her as the *Admiral Hipper*. So, the British remained unaware that *Scharnhorst* and *Gneisenau* were at large in the North Atlantic.

The two German battlecruisers regrouped and two days later Lütjens began searching for another convoy. However, a fuel contamination problem on *Gneisenau* and the worsening weather meant a contact was becoming increasingly unlikely. In response, he pulled back north again, to another tanker rendezvous area code named Point Blue. There, on 14 February, the *Schlettstadt* and the *Esso Hamburg* refuelled the two warships, and once more Lütjens turned south.

The next few days were frustrating for him. Single ships were spotted, but at first Lütjens kept his distance from them, hoping to fall on an entire convoy. As it turned out, on reaching a point off the Canadian coast, that westbound convoy scattered and the ships continued on to their destination ports, which meant that the Germans were too far west.

Nevertheless, on 20 February they came across a cluster of unescorted ships to the west of Newfoundland, and sank five of them.[29] One, however, the *Kantara*, managed to send off a sighting report, which meant the British now knew where the Germans were. Having been told by German naval intelligence that British battleships were out looking for him, Lütjens decided to move well out of the way. He steamed away to the south and west, heading across the Atlantic towards the African coast. On 27–28 March he refuelled at another prearranged rendezvous point, then continued on to the south-east. His objective was the Sierra Leone Route, a sea lane leading from West Africa to the Western Approaches. By 8 March, Lütjens was 350 miles north of the Cape Verde islands, and lying astride the convoy route. It was there that his lookouts spotted a lone aircraft – a Walrus floatplane. This could only have come from a sizeable British warship, which meant a convoy was close by, and it was well protected.

In fact, the Walrus belonged to the battleship *Malaya*, which was escorting the northbound Convoy SL67 from Freetown.

Later that day, the lookouts on the British battleships saw the two German battlecruisers almost 20 miles away to the north-east.[30] Lütjens saw the convoy too, and her powerful escort. Once again, his orders forced him to turn away. Within half an hour, contact had been lost. The only consolation prize for the Germans was that the next day, 9 March, they came upon a lone British merchant ship, which they sank as they steamed past. Two days later, they reached another rendezvous point and refuelled from the two tankers waiting there. This time, Lütjens took them with him, to help him widen his search area. His plan was to have another go at the sea lanes off Newfoundland, hoping that by now the British battleships had moved somewhere else.

He was only half right. The battleships *Ramillies* and *Revenge* were still based in Halifax, and were protecting eastbound convoys as far as the mid-Atlantic, where cover could be provided by land-based aircraft and the rest of the Home Fleet.[31] The battleships *Rodney* and *King George V* had also been sent to the area, and were patrolling the area off the Newfoundland Banks. Further to the north, the Home Fleet commander Admiral Tovey was in *Rodney*'s sister ship *Nelson*, waiting off Iceland in case Lütjens tried to make a run back through the Denmark Strait. So, if Lütjens made one wrong move, his ships could easily sail into a trap. At first, everything went his way. On 15 March, he came upon another dispersed westbound convoy and sank six merchant ships. The following day, he encountered more of them, and ten more freighters were sunk.

These actions attracted the attention of the battleship *Rodney*. She appeared just as dusk was approaching, and Lütjens immediately turned his two battlecruisers away. *Rodney* carried nine 16in. guns, and so had the firepower to wreak havoc on the German force. Once again, though, Lütjens ordered his ships to turn away, and contact was lost as night fell. So, for the third time in five weeks, the German battlecruisers avoided a fight. It was now clear that the British were throwing a lot of resources into protecting their convoy routes. Lütjens duly headed away to the east, hoping to have better luck in the mid-Atlantic. Then, on 17 March, SKL ordered him to break off his cruise and make for Brest.[32] Clearly, Grossadmiral Raeder had fresh plans for both the battlecruisers and the fleet commander. On 18–19 March, the *Scharnhorst* and *Gneisenau* refuelled at sea for the last time, and Lütjens detached his two tankers so they could make their own way home when the chance arose. Then he set a course for *Brest*.

Initially, everything went smoothly. Then, on 20 May, the two German warships were spotted by a Swordfish biplane flying an air search mission from the British aircraft carrier *Ark Royal*. She was part of Vice-Admiral (V. Adm.) Somerville's Force H, which was normally based in Gibraltar. Somerville was ordered north to join in the search for the German task force, and set off in the battlecruiser *Repulse*, accompanied by the *Ark Royal* and two cruisers. The sighting was made when Lütjens was roughly 750 miles west-south-west of Brest, and 600 miles from Cape Finisterre, at the north-western tip of Spain. That meant the German battlecruisers were a little over a full day's sailing from their destination. Somerville's Force H was 160 nautical miles to the south-east, which was just too far away to launch an air strike. Only by increasing speed could his carrier get into position to launch her planes before dark.

The trouble was, the Swordfish that spotted the two German ships had a broken radio.[33] This meant that it had to fly back to the *Ark Royal* before it could report the sighting. In the meantime, the wily Lütjens turned away to the north to try to fool the airmen into thinking that he was actually heading back to the Denmark Strait. Then, under cover of the night, he turned east towards Brest. The British, however, weren't prepared to give up the chase. Force H thundered northwards at top speed, while off Iceland Admiral Tovey in *Nelson*, now reinforced by the battleship *Queen Elizabeth* and the battlecruiser *Hood*, set off to the south, hoping to meet Lütjens somewhere to the west of Ireland.

By then, it was too late. The Germans were just out of reach. On the evening of 21 March, a Lockheed Hudson of Coastal Command's 220 Squadron confirmed the worst: the German battlecruisers had been spotted just 170 miles west of Brest, heading towards the French coast. They were now well within range of German land-based air cover, and any chance of intercepting them had evaporated. The following morning, 22 March, *Scharnhorst* and *Gneisenau* arrived in Brest, as German fighters circled overhead. So, Operation *Berlin* came to an end. It was the most successful Kriegsmarine commerce-raiding operation of the war. In the two-month cruise, the two German warships had sunk or captured 22 Allied ships, displacing 115,622 tons.[34] It was a remarkable achievement, and Lütjens was feted as Germany's new naval hero.

LOOKING TO THE FUTURE

If this weren't achievement enough, the operation also achieved its main strategic goal. For those two months, the British had been forced to divert convoys, or keep hundreds of merchant ships waiting in friendly ports until the German threat had been dealt with or went away. These Atlantic convoys were like a giant conveyor belt, transporting vital war supplies, foodstuffs and troops along the sea lanes. Everything worked according to a tight schedule and, like modern air travel, any delay had a knock-on effect on other passages. So, as convoys were held back or diverted, the whole gigantic system began to falter. As a result, hundreds of thousands of tons of supplies never got through, and troops bound from Canada to Britain or from Britain to the Middle East had to remain cooped up in their troopships. This was 'sea denial' in action. Operation *Berlin* had done exactly what Grossadmiral Raeder wanted. Now, if he could repeat the operation, and this time add the new battleship *Bismarck* to the Atlantic task force, then he might cause irreparable damage to that maritime conveyor belt.

To do so, however, relied on several elements falling into place. First, it presupposed that *Bismarck* could successfully break out into the North Atlantic, ideally with at least one other warship sailing in consort with her. The heavy cruiser *Prinz Eugen* was the obvious choice.[35] This sister ship of the *Admiral Hipper* was ready for operations, and while her range was less than that of the battleship, she would still prove a useful addition to the force. The next element was that the German warships in French ports – most notably the *Scharnhorst* and the *Gneisenau* – were ready for action. The *Admiral Hipper* was another possible addition to the force. Then, once *Bismarck* and any consort successfully reached the North Atlantic, the two battlecruisers would also have to break out from Brest and then rendezvous with *Bismarck* at a prearranged spot somewhere in the Atlantic. The one element that was already decided was the name of the fleet commander: there was absolutely no question that Günther Lütjens was the man for the job.

It was clear that fortune had smiled on the fleet commander. The sighting by *Naiad* might easily have led to the bulk of the Home Fleet catching the German force before the operation had properly started. Then, at every turn, Lütjens seemed to second-guess the British moves, and managed to keep out of harm's way. Even the three encounters with battleship-armed convoys could have ended in damage to one or more of his battlecruisers, but in each case his swift reaction by turning away avoided any such outcome, while the sighting by the Swordfish from *Ark Royal* might under different circumstances have resulted in the launch of a carrier strike. Instead, a faulty wireless set meant this never happened. Finally, thanks to Lütjens' expert planning, the system of placing tankers at key points around the North Atlantic worked to perfection. Now it was time to repeat the operation on a larger scale.

Soon, however, the grand plan began to unravel. The Admiralty asked the Royal Air Force for their help in neutralising the threat posed by this assemblage of German warships. While *Bismarck* and *Prinz Eugen* were in the Baltic, and therefore out of range, Brest was only 160 miles from airfields in the south-west of England. The Kriegsmarine was acutely aware of this, and although both battlecruisers needed a refit before they were ready for sea, the Germans were keen to send them as soon as possible, and if necessary to return them to Germany by way of the Denmark Strait. It turned out, though, that *Scharnhorst* needed a more extensive refit than previously thought, and so it would be June before she could leave the French port. *Gneisenau*, by contrast, would finish her refit in early May, and so would be available for the next big sortie.

RAF Coastal Command had tried and failed to hit the battlecruisers when they first arrived in Brest. Then, reports from the French Resistance indicated that they were both undergoing refits, and so would be there for several weeks.[36] This bought the RAF time to plan the operation properly. If they'd known, they would have been heartened by the news that although the Kriegsmarine had requested extra air defences and fighter cover for the port, the Luftwaffe had done nothing about it. So, while the flak there was heavy, and Luftwaffe fighter squadrons were based nearby, a bombing attack was dangerous, but not wholly suicidal. Thus it was that from late March, heavy nightly raids were launched with the intention of 'carpet bombing' the harbour, but none of these resulted in a direct hit to either battlecruiser, which had been moved into dry dock for extra protection. Despite this, the bombing raids caused a chain of events that would completely disrupt the Kriegsmarine's plans.

During one of these attacks, a bomb landed in the dry dock next to *Gneisenau*, but failed to explode. The next morning, the dock was flooded, causing the battlecruiser to move 1,300ft out into the harbour, leaving her vulnerable to attack by aircraft-launched torpedoes. On the evening of 6 April, four twin-engined Bristol Beauforts of 22 Squadron of Coastal Command launched an attack on the battlecruiser.[37] Only one of the four planes was able to make a torpedo run, but it struck the *Gneisenau* on her starboard side, resulting in heavy flooding. Moments later, the Beaufort was shot down, but the damage had been done and *Gneisenau* now had to limp back into the dry dock for urgent repairs. The pilot, Flying Officer (Fg Off.) Ken Campbell, was later awarded a posthumous Victoria Cross for his efforts.

As a result, it was now unlikely that *Gneisenau* would be ready in time to take part in any joint operation with the *Bismarck*. In fact, four nights later she took four direct bomb hits in another bombing raid, and this time the damage was so severe that it was clear she would be out of action for months. Common sense might have dictated that any new joint sortie would best be left until these repairs had been completed, but didn't take into account the vulnerability of Brest to air attacks. Accordingly, the OKW decided that once the battlecruisers had been repaired in Brest, they would then make a break for a German port together with *Hipper*.

Meanwhile, Raeder was left with *Bismarck* and *Prinz Eugen*. Should any venture wait until *Tirpitz* was ready to join them, and possibly even the two battlecruisers and second heavy cruiser? Or, should he seize the initiative and launch another Atlantic sortie right away, to maintain pressure on the British sea lanes? Thanks to Fg Off. Campbell, his options were now limited.

Chapter 3

The Home Fleet

SCAPA FLOW

The Orkney Islands lie off the north of the British mainland, separated from the rest of Scotland by the dangerous tide-ripped waters of the Pentland Firth. The largest of this archipelago of islands is simply called the Mainland, where the main town of Kirkwall is situated, a place of charming streets dominated by a beautiful Viking-age cathedral. The Mainland lies in the middle of the archipelago, dividing the North Isles on one side and the South Isles on the other. The South Isles form a sort of natural circle, enclosing a large natural anchorage about 10 miles across and 8 wide. This virtually land-locked body of water is known as Scapa Flow. With only two navigable entrances to the west and south, it forms a large and readily defensible anchorage. Elsewhere, the low brown-and-green islands enclose it, like a protective mantle.

Shortly before World War I, Scapa Flow was chosen by Admiral 'Jackie' Fisher as the wartime base for the British Grand Fleet.[1] It was ideally placed to coordinate the distant blockade of the German coast, and as a base from which the fleet could sortie if its German counterpart put to sea. It was from Scapa that Admiral Jellicoe's dreadnoughts steamed off to fight the Battle of Jutland, and it was there in 1919 that the vanquished German High Seas Fleet was brought, and interned. While peace ended this major naval presence, a small naval base was retained there during the inter-war years. Then, in 1939, as the clouds of war were gathering, the British Admiralty ordered the Home Fleet to Scapa, as the naval strategy employed in the last war was considered just as effective in a new one. So, once again, Scapa Flow became a major wartime anchorage, and a home to hundreds of ships and tens of thousands of men.

Some of them loved the place – the tranquillity, the natural beauty and the mellow landscape are easy to fall in love with.[2] Others found Scapa a living hell. To them, it was the end of the earth, a bleak and cold spot where the wind always blew, and winters were often cold, wet and stormy. Jellicoe's successor, Admiral Beatty, called Scapa 'the most damnable place on earth', vastly preferring the gaiety of a big city and a lively social scene. Most of the sailors who served on ships based in Scapa during the two world wars probably agreed with him. The shore facilities there were limited – the navy supplied a theatre, a cinema, a few bars or canteens and sports fields, but it was nothing compared to Portsmouth, Plymouth or Chatham. There were few women, and most of them were wearing uniforms. There was little else to do but stay cooped up on your ship and wait for something to happen. In May 1941, that wish was granted.

When the war began, this battle fleet swinging at anchor in Scapa Flow had been christened the Home Fleet in 1932, and was the direct successor of the Grand Fleet of World War I.

The defences of Scapa Flow were woefully inadequate –
a point driven home early on 14 October 1939 when the
U-boat *U-47* penetrated its makeshift defences and sank the
old battleship *Royal Oak* – an attack that claimed the lives of
834 of her crew, many of whom were boy seamen.[3] The fleet
decamped to the West Coast of Scotland until March 1940,
by which time Scapa's defences had been put in order. At first,
this meant protecting the navigable entrances using torpedo
nets and underwater listening equipment, and the smaller
ones with new blockships. Next came coastal batteries, radar
stations, flak defences, airfields and fighter aircraft. By early
March, Churchill could tell the War Cabinet that Scapa was
'80% secure'.

With its base thus reasonably secure, the Home Fleet was
free to set about maintaining its distant blockade of Germany,
by obstructing German egress from the North Sea. Then,
in April 1940, the whole situation changed. The German
conquest of Norway rendered the blockading line between
Shetland and the Norwegian coast untenable. Instead,
the Home Fleet had to maintain its patrol line between
Greenland, Iceland, the Faeroe Islands and Shetland. In the
Cold War, this would be known as the GIUK gap – the route
by which Soviet submarines could reach the Atlantic. In 1940,
it was merely the redeployment of the distant blockade. This
time, though, the rough seas and harsh conditions meant that
cruisers formed the mainstay of the patrol line, rather than
smaller warships.

The German occupation of Norway also placed Scapa
within easy range of German bombers.[4] Intermittent air
attacks first started in October 1939, but by April 1940 the
'Orkney barrage' was in place, a wall of flak designed to
protect the anchorage, using land-based anti-aircraft batteries

and the air defence firepower of the Home Fleet. It was first to be put to the test on 2 April, when it proved a resounding success.[5] By June, all of Scapa's defences were complete. As a result, the anchorage remained immune from German attacks of any kind for the rest of the war. This went some way to neutralising the advantage handed to the Germans by their conquest of Norway. So, from that summer, and for the rest of the war, British reconnaissance aircraft and submarines routinely patrolled the Norwegian coast, looking for German warships.

In theory, the proximity to German-occupied Norway could have been a major problem. However, by the summer of 1940 the 'Orkney Barrage' had been tried and tested. The wall of flak thrown up during the barrage meant that no German aircraft could penetrate it. With no land to the east, radar stations could pick up approaching German bombers as they crossed the North Sea, and the fleet and its shore-based defenders would be ready for them. In addition, there were four airfields on Orkney – two run by the Fleet Air Arm and two by the Royal Air Force. They were all well provided with fighters, and these, together with nearby airfields in Caithness, meant that any large-scale Luftwaffe attack would be repulsed with potentially heavy losses. In fact, once the effectiveness of all this was demonstrated, German air attacks ceased completely. Instead, fighter-bombers based in Orkney and Caithness conducted regular sorties against German coastal shipping in Norwegian waters.

The other advantage of this secure anchorage was its location. While the homesick crews might complain about being stationed far from the fleshpots of London, or even Portsmouth or Plymouth, in strategic terms Scapa Flow was the perfect place for the Home Fleet. Orkney was far from the Luftwaffe airfields in France and the Low Countries, whereas the naval bases on Britain's south coast were just a few minutes' flying time away. To reach Scapa Flow, any German sortie from the Skagerrak would have to traverse the North Sea and reach the Atlantic by way of the Norwegian Sea and the Greenland–Iceland–Faeroes–Shetland gap. Scapa Flow was much closer to the Skagerrak than these southern bases, and virtually on the doorstep of these northern sea entrances into the Atlantic. In terms of 'sea control' it was perfect – the fleet there acted as the stopper to a bottle. Any German sortie would have to run the gauntlet of the fleet before it could threaten the Allied convoy routes. So, regardless of the grumbling of the seamen, Scapa Flow remained the wartime base of the fleet.

THE DISTANT BLOCKADE

When in Scapa Flow, the fleet flagship swung at its mooring just off the island of Flotta, where an underwater cable ran out from the island to the mooring buoy.[6] This carried a secure telephone line, which ended in a green telephone sitting on the desk of the fleet's commander-in-chief and provided a direct line that ran straight to the Admiralty in Whitehall, allowing the admiral to talk to both the War Cabinet and Prime Minister Winston Churchill. This meant that any intelligence reports reaching the Admiralty could be conveyed to the Home Fleet within a few minutes. If the flagship were at sea, then both the admiral and the fleet commander had to use the much less secure medium of encoded radio signals, which were, of course, vulnerable to interception by the enemy. In the events that unfolded in May 1940, these lines of communication played a vital part in the drama.

The stated aim of the Home Fleet was the defence of British home waters, and the vital maritime supply routes leading to British ports. However, as the war played out, various areas were devolved into separate commands. The coastal waters of the English Channel and the English east coast were administered separately, as the lighter forces stationed there fought their own private war, protecting coastal convoys and harassing enemy ones. The Western Approaches to the British Isles – those sea lanes to British ports – were controlled from Plymouth, and later from Liverpool. That, then, left the Home Fleet free to concentrate on its main job: the containment of the German Kriegsmarine within the North Sea, and the destruction of enemy warships attempting to break out into the Atlantic.

During the Napoleonic Wars, Britain maintained a close blockade of French-held ports on the European mainland, whereby any French sortie from Brest, Toulon or the Baltic would be met by a British fleet. Clearly, however, this strategy was less effective in an age of submarines, radio transmissions and long-range guns. So, the notion of a distant blockade was devised, involving a blockade being established further from enemy-held ports, but within range of friendly naval bases. The result was the same. In World War I, the naval blockade of Germany was the single most effective tool in the Allied arsenal. Imperial Germany relied heavily on maritime imports for its raw materials and foodstuffs. In November 1914 the British declared the North Sea a 'War Zone', and ships suspected of heading to enemy ports or even of carrying cargo bound for Germany were seized.[7] Even neutral ships were stopped and inspected, despite a slew of complaints.

Blocking off the English Channel was easy enough – a job given to the Dover Patrol. Sealing off the top of the North

Sea was a little more difficult. The Northern Patrol operated between the Norwegian coast and Orkney, and proved highly effective at stopping virtually all foodstuffs and war materials reaching Germany. By 1916, this had resulted in growing food shortages in Germany, and by the end of the war the German people faced starvation, a major factor in the cessation of the conflict. In 1939, the situation was very similar, and the same blockade tactics were employed. Hundreds of small patrol craft, such as requisitioned trawlers, were pressed into service, but this time, rather than a full naval blockade, this was called 'British Contraband Control'. Once again, Orkney became the base for the northern part of this blockade, and within weeks hundreds of tons of war materials were confiscated from German-registered or neutral ships.

Nazi Germany responded by imposing its own economic blockade, using mines to disrupt British coastal convoys, and U-boats to harry convoys in the Western Approaches.[8] Soon, both sides were feeling the effects of shortages. Then, in the spring of 1940, the capture of Norway and the Fall of France changed everything. Now, the Northern Patrol had no firm anchor on the Norwegian coast. Now, German U-boats could use French Atlantic ports, and reach their patrol areas in half the time. So, a new strategy was needed. This involved the stepping up of convoy efforts, helped by the increasing unofficial support of the USA. It also meant abandoning the existing patrol line and moving it back, out of easy reach of Norwegian airfields.

This required the re-establishment of a patrol line running between Denmark and Iceland, Iceland and the Faeroes, and the Faeroe Islands and Shetland, Orkney and the Scottish mainland.[9] Of these, the Pentland Firth south of Orkney and the gap between Orkney and Shetland were easily covered by small patrol craft, destroyers and aerial patrols. The three more distant gaps were more of a problem, one that was addressed with the use of all-weather small ships such as ocean-going trawlers, corvettes and destroyers, supported by heavy and light cruisers. The distant blockade was just as effective – although the distances involved were greater and more ships were needed to do the job.

This business was actually made a little easier in April 1940 when the Germans invaded Denmark. At the time, Iceland was a sovereign nation but was united to Denmark under the rule of the Danish crown. In consequence, Iceland was considered neutral. However, following the German invasion of Denmark the British sent troops to occupy Iceland, after the Icelanders refused to join the Western Allies. So, from May 1940, Iceland was controlled by Britain, until July 1941, when it was transferred to American control.[10] Although officially Iceland remained neutral throughout the war, its government actively cooperated with the Allies, and in 1944 it declared its independence from Denmark. As a result of this, the Allies gained vital air and naval bases on the island, which rendered the distant blockade of Germany far more effective. Now, British warships could put in there to refuel or shelter from storms, and search aircraft could range far out into the Arctic Sea.

While smaller craft maintained the distant blockade from Greenland to Orkney, larger warships – mainly cruisers – also patrolled the same waters, ready to intercept any German warships attempting to break out into the North Atlantic. While a cruiser armed with 6in. or 8in. guns lacked the firepower to stop a *Scharnhorst*, *Gneisenau* or *Bismarck*, they could use their radar to shadow them and thereby help larger British ships intercept the enemy. That was where naval intelligence came in. The Admiralty relied on a whole range of sources – from signal intercepts, Enigma decryptions, spies, resistance cells, patrolling submarines and search aircraft – to let them know when a German breakout was imminent, whereupon the commander-in-chief of the Home Fleet would send a powerful force to intercept the enemy.

This of course demanded the timely acquisition of suitable intelligence, and a certain amount of forewarning. It took roughly 30 hours for a battleship to cover the 800 miles from Scapa Flow to the Denmark Strait between Greenland and Iceland. It took half that to reach the Iceland–Faeroes gap. So, not only did the fleet need advance warning, but its commander also had to predict which of these routes the German warships would take. That meant that the green telephone was crucially important, as were the search and photo reconnaissance planes that might spot the enemy on their way towards the Atlantic. Meanwhile, the Home Fleet's capital ships – the battleships, battlecruisers and aircraft carriers – swung at anchor in Scapa Flow, or conducted training exercises, while their crews waited for that all-important signal that would galvanise them into action.

TOVEY'S FLEET

On 2 December 1940, on a cold and windy day in Rosyth, Admiral Sir Charles Forbes hauled down his flag as commander-in-chief of the Home Fleet and handed over both his command and his flagship *Nelson* to Admiral Sir John Tovey.[11] The new fleet commander had just returned from the Mediterranean, where he'd served as second-in-command of the Mediterranean Fleet, under Admiral Cunningham. The following day, *Nelson* sailed for Scapa Flow, where Tovey was better placed to control his fleet and deal with any German sorties. The first of these – the breakout of the *Scharnhorst* and *Gneisenau* – came soon after the New Year, and Tovey was caught on the wrong foot by his opponent Admiral Lütjens. As we've seen, the two German battlecruisers evaded all British attempts to intercept them, and after a successful Atlantic cruise they made it safely into Brest. This was undoubtedly a trying experience for Tovey, but he was determined that if his chance came again, he would bring the enemy to battle.

Tovey had a powerful fleet at his disposal, and on paper it looked like he had everything he needed to do just that. The trouble was, many of his ships were fairly old, and some even dated from the previous war. When he took command, *Nelson* and *Rodney* were the most modern battleships in the navy, and both of them were 13 years old.[12] With a top speed of just 23 knots they were far too slow to catch the new generation of German capital ships like *Scharnhorst* or *Bismarck*. Still, if they did manage to, they carried nine 16in. guns in three triple turrets, and their hulls were well armoured. If they could actually bring these German warships to battle then they had a good chance of destroying them. The nine other battleships in the navy were all of World War I vintage.[13] In fact, in 1916 five of them fought in the Battle of Jutland. Another Jutland veteran, the *Royal Oak*, had been sunk in October 1939.

What made them useful was that they all carried eight 15in. guns apiece. Some of the Queen Elizabeth class had been modernised, and with decent fire control systems and modern radar they still proved themselves useful. During 1940, several of them had seen action in the Mediterranean – in fact, most of them had seen service with the Home Fleet earlier in the war – and by the spring of 1941 all five were either serving with the Mediterranean fleet or were undergoing repairs.

By 1941, the four remaining battleships of the Royal Sovereign class were relegated to second-line duties such as escorting convoys or shore bombardment. With a top speed of just 23 knots – and most were now slower than that – they were of little or no use as front-line warships. So, that left Tovey with just two ageing but well-armed battleships to confront the most powerful warships in the German fleet.

Less well armoured were his battlecruisers. When it was first dreamed up before World War I, the idea of the battlecruiser made some sense: it was a ship that was as well armed as a dreadnought battleship but as fast as a cruiser. In effect, it was a sort of super cruiser, designed to hunt down enemy cruisers. This was achieved by doing away with decent armour, a sacrifice that resulted in the loss of three British battlecruisers at Jutland. The trouble was, with such a powerful armament the temptation to use battlecruisers to fight other equally powerful warships was simply too great. The Germans had a less unbalanced design and so they only lost one battlecruiser as a result of the battle. While Jutland should have marked the end of the battlecruiser experiment, new ones were already under construction, with the result that although earlier ones had been scrapped soon after World War I, these new battlecruisers were still in service in 1941.

The *Renown* and *Repulse* entered service soon after Jutland.[14] Both carried six 15in. guns, in three twin turrets, but their main armoured belt was just 6in. thick – less than half that of the fleet's new dreadnought battleships. Still, their 15in. guns meant they were still considered useful, and during the inter-war years another 2–3in. of armour was added to protect the ships' most vulnerable parts – their magazines and engine rooms. Other modifications were made, too, so that by 1941 they were still considered effective warships, particularly because they had a top speed of 30 knots. Thus it was that in the spring of 1941, *Renown* was the flagship of Force H, based in Gibraltar, while *Repulse* formed part of the Home Fleet.

Then there was the *Hood*.[15] She had been laid down four months after Jutland, the first of a class of four powerful battlecruisers, although all the others had been cancelled while still on the stocks. She was launched in August 1918, three months before the end of World War I, and finally entered service in 1920. She was a large and beautiful ship, 860ft long, armed with eight 15in. guns, in four twin turrets. Her elegant lines and impressive size meant she was perfect for 'showing the flag', and for almost two decades she did exactly that. If any warship could be seen as the floating symbol of the Royal Navy, and of the might of the British Empire, it was the *Hood*. During her career, she had been seen by millions of people and was probably the best-known warship in the world.

When World War II began, *Hood* was attached to the Home Fleet, although the following summer she was briefly attached to Force H, for the bombardment of the French fleet based at Oran in North Africa.[16] In early 1941 she joined the hunt for the *Scharnhorst* and *Gneisenau*. By then, though, she was more than two decades old and was showing her age; her value as a floating advert for the Royal Navy meant she hadn't undergone the extensive modifications that the other two battlecruisers went through. So, although she now carried slightly more modern secondary guns and anti-aircraft weapons, and a fire control radar, her main armament was the same as it had been when she first entered service 20 years previously. Just as importantly, she carried the same armour, too. She had a respectable 12in. armoured belt, but her main deck was only protected by 1–3in. of armour, with just 2in. of steel plate over her magazines. Still, with a speed of 32 knots, the *Hood* was one of the few British capital ships fast enough to overhaul the *Scharnhorst* or the *Bismarck*.

Then, in January 1941, just weeks after Tovey took command, the battleship *King George V* joined the Home Fleet. The first British battleship to enter service in a decade and a half, and the namesake of what would become a class of five, the arrival of *King George V* marked a turning point for Tovey's battle fleet.[17] Now it had some real teeth. The second battleship in the class, the *Prince of Wales*, would join him in May. Each of them carried ten 14in. guns, in two quadruple turrets fore and aft, and a third twin turret superimposed behind the larger forward turret. This strange configuration was due to the limits of the various inter-war naval treaties, which also explained why the British had left it for ten years before ordering these new capital ships. However, they were well protected, with a 14–16in. main belt, and 5–6in. deck armour. They could also make 28.5 knots, which gave them a fighting chance of intercepting *Scharnhorst* and *Bismarck*.

They had issues, though. In the Kriegsmarine, a new capital ship would go through a rigorous set of sea trials, followed by an equally lengthy period of crew training. The British couldn't afford that luxury; with *Bismarck* and *Tirpitz* nearing completion, these new battleships were needed right away. So, after cursory sea trials they were sent to join the fleet, and the crew had to learn on the job. By the time the *Bismarck* sortied, the *King George V* was fully operational. In fact, in April 1941 Tovey shifted his flag into her.

The *Prince of Wales* was more of a problem. In August 1940, she was nearing completion in Birkenhead when a German air raid struck Merseyside and she was badly damaged.[18] This delayed her completion, but she still sailed for her trials on schedule, in January 1941. However, two of her three main turrets were not functioning, and only half of her crew were on board.

The real snag was that her newly designed quadruple turrets didn't work.[19] They were still having serious teething problems, and as the sea trials continued, civilian workmen continued to try to get them fixed. Still, on 31 March she was officially declared 'complete', and handed over to the Royal Navy. Several key tests hadn't been carried out, but the Admiralty were so keen to get her operational that these had been waived. By then, she was in Scapa Flow, where working-up exercises continued through April and May, and the work on her faulty turrets continued. It wasn't until 26 April that Vickers-Armstrongs – who built her guns – finally approved the work, and she could begin her gunnery trials. Even then, a group of Vickers-Armstrongs technicians stayed on board to iron out a long list of last-minute hitches. They were still on board her when she steamed off to fight the *Bismarck*.

Despite the issues, one thing that gave British warships like the *Prince of Wales* an edge over the Germans was what we now call radar, although in 1941 the British still called it Radio Direction Finding (RDF).[20] While the Germans had their own Seetakt sets, these were neither as effective nor as efficient as the British system. Also, by 1941 the British had a range of different sets, used to detect both aircraft and surface targets, and to help direct the guns. For example, in May 1941 *Prince of Wales* carried Type 281 early warning radar, which could detect approaching aircraft over 100 miles away. Various other sets were used to control the fire of the ship's main guns and her anti-aircraft batteries. *King George V* had a similar suite of electronics. Even older ships like *Rodney* and *Hood* carried radar – a Type 279 air warning set in *Rodney*, and a Type 284 fire control radar in *Hood*. This all helped the British search for the enemy, and hit them once they were within range.

The other big advantage Tovey enjoyed over his German rivals was the aircraft carrier. It was the British who first perfected this type of warship during World War I – in fact, in 1917 the first successful carrier landing took place in Scapa Flow. The big fleet carriers of 1939–40 were formidable weapons of war, capable of carrying a mixed bag of fighters and multipurpose bomber and torpedo planes. Although most carried the antiquated Fairey Swordfish as their main strike aircraft, this biplane was still effective.[21] Affectionately known as 'Stringbag', the Swordfish could carry a torpedo or bombs, or simply act as a reconnaissance plane, which made it extremely versatile, albeit slow and with a limited strike range. Still, in December 1940 both the fleet carrier and the Swordfish demonstrated their effectiveness at Taranto in southern Italy when they put most of the Italian battle fleet out of action.

So, all things considered, these fleet carriers were powerful naval assets. The trouble was that there simply wasn't enough of them. Two had been lost in 1939 and 1940, which, apart from two light carriers serving overseas, only left *Ark Royal* and *Furious*. Then, in 1940, the first two Illustrious class fleet carriers entered service. A third – *Victorious* – joined the fleet in the late spring of 1941. However, in May 1941 *Ark Royal* was in service with Force H in Gibraltar, and *Furious*, *Illustrious* and *Formidable* were in the Mediterranean.[22] That just left *Victorious*. She departed the Vickers-Armstrongs yard in Tyneside in April 1941, and in mid-May, after her sea trials, she joined the Home Fleet, accompanied by a ship's company and airmen who were both inexperienced and whose training was still incomplete. Still, she was all there was, and Tovey had little option but to press her into service, ready or not.

As well as these capital ships, Tovey had at his disposal a powerful force of cruisers and destroyers. The cruisers were his 'eyes and ears', whose main job was to maintain the patrol line running between Greenland and Shetland.[23] They consisted of 8in. gun heavy cruisers and 6in. gun light cruisers, but in the event of a German sortie both cruiser types had the same job. They lacked the firepower and armour to take on a German capital ship, but they had radar, and radios. So, once the enemy were spotted they could shadow them and send Tovey regular reports, which would allow him to dispatch his capital ships to intercept the enemy. This of course was a dangerous game: one false move and they could be blown apart by heavy German guns.

As for the destroyers, their main role was to protect larger warships from enemy U-boats. They could also join the patrol line, though, and by May 1941 most of them were fitted with a search radar. This meant that they could actually augment the cruiser patrols, making sure nothing slipped through the British net. Also, when the need arose and in the right circumstances, they could carry out high-speed torpedo attacks. On the downside, their effectiveness was reduced by their limited range and their inability to operate effectively in extremely rough seas. The first problem was solved by the proximity of refuelling bases in Iceland, but the latter was entirely dependent on the weather.

So, in summary, Admiral Tovey's Home Fleet comprised an assortment of ships. He had a few battleships and battlecruisers, both old and new, most of which had some form of limitation to them – be it age, speed, crew experience or persistent technical problems. His one carrier was a great asset, but her raw air crew needed time to learn their job. These were the ships that would have to take on the *Bismarck* if she tried to make a sortie. Supporting them was an equally varied selection of cruisers and destroyers, whose main role was to locate and shadow, not to fight. That was the job of Tovey's capital ships. Above all, though, the whole thing centred around intelligence reports. Once Tovey knew the Germans were making their move, he could do something about it. Until then, he simply had to remain at anchor in Scapa Flow and wait for that green telephone to ring.

Chapter 4

Preparations

DETAINED IN HAMBURG

In Hamburg, as the bulk of *Bismarck*'s crew rejoined their ship after Christmas leave, they found her a hive of activity. Stores were being loaded on board, filling her with everything from 15in.shells and powder charges to potatoes, razor blades and toilet paper. Finally, on 24 January 1941, Kapitän Lindemann reported to Berlin that *Bismarck* was ready for active operations.[1] The plan was to sail her through the Kaiser Wilhelm Canal to Kiel, but the narrow waterway (now the Nord-Ostsee-Kanal) was blocked by a merchant ship, an ore carrier that had been sunk during an Allied bombing raid. Therefore, the *Bismarck* remained in dock, and her crew were able to enjoy the dubious wartime delights of Hamburg for a few more weeks as salvage divers worked to clear the canal.

Meanwhile, at a nearby berth on the Blohm+Voss shipyard, a new U-boat was being fitted out.[2] She was the *U-556*, a Type VIIC boat, and was due to be commissioned into service in early February. Her commander was Kapitänleutnant Herbert Wohlfarth, a veteran U-boat commander with 21 sinkings to his name, and seven war patrols. In the U-boat service he was nicknamed 'Parsifal', after the hero of Arthurian legend, medieval poetry and a Wagner opera who never stopped searching for the Holy Grail. While the U-boat was being prepared, he and his men were busy planning their U-boat's commissioning ceremony, which was set for early February. Every day, they kept hearing the *Bismarck*'s band practising on the quayside above them. So, when they learned the *Bismarck*'s sailing had been delayed, and with their own big day approaching, Wohlfarth hatched a plan.

There has long been a tradition, called *Patenschaft*, of towns and cities 'adopting' or 'sponsoring' a warship or regiment. Wohlfarth and his officers therefore decided to adapt this for their own ends, drafting a certificate of sponsorship between *U-556* and the *Bismarck* and ageing it by ripping and burning its edges. This document declared: 'We *U-556* (500 tons) hereby declare before Neptune, the ruler of oceans, seas, lakes, rivers, streams, ponds and rivulets that we will assist our big brother, the battleship *Bismarck* (42,000 tons), in every situation, in water, underwater, on land and in the air.'[3]

It was dated 28 January. The U-boat commander even added two cartoons – one showing Parsifal deflecting enemy aircraft and torpedoes from the battleship using his sword and shield, and the other showing *Bismarck* being towed home by the tiny U-boat. Wohlfarth then visited Kapitän Lindemann and presented him with the certificate of adoption. Lindemann was highly amused, and had it framed before hanging it up in the battleship's wardroom. In return, Wohlfarth achieved his goal: *Bismarck*'s band played at the U-boat's commissioning ceremony just over a week later, on 6 February.

Although the intention was that the ship should sail by 5 February, two days before this date the sailing was cancelled because the thick layer of winter ice in the canal was delaying the clearance work. In fact, the job of clearing the canal continued throughout February and into March. The other option – moving the battleship to the Baltic around the top of Denmark's Jutland peninsula – was deemed too risky by Naval High Command. So, the waiting continued.

There was another problem, too. *Bismarck* had returned to Hamburg for minor repairs following her sea trials, but the extreme cold had also caused issues in her engine room, damaging some of her pressure gauges and the electrical lines to her boiler room ventilators. Until these had been repaired, she couldn't go to sea. In the end, they were fixed by the middle of February, but of course the canal was still blocked. Kapitän Lindemann was furious. At the end of February, he wrote in the ship's war diary: 'The ship has been detained in Hamburg since 24 January. Five weeks of training time at sea have been lost!'[4] Not one to sit idly by, Lindemann made sure that the time was used to conduct training and battle drills in Hamburg harbour.

Finally, on 5 March, word reached the men that the canal had been cleared. Immediately, Lindemann ordered the ship to prepare to sail. Then, as Müllenheim-Rechberg described it: 'On 6th March, we cast off from the wharf at the Blohm & Voss yard, and steamed out into the Elbe, and once again headed downstream. As the familiar silhouette of Hamburg slowly sank astern, I had the feeling that our absence from the beautiful Hanseatic city would be for longer.'[5] In fact, the *Bismarck* would never return to her birthplace.

Forty miles downriver lay the town of Brunsbüttel, and the western entrance to the Kaiser Wilhelm Canal. *Bismarck* steamed down the wide, slow river, watched by groups of onlookers on the riverbank. It would have been hard not to feel a surge of pride as this beautiful and powerful ship made her stately way past.

By noon, the battleship had reached Brunsbüttel, and at 12.24 she dropped anchor off the western entrance to the canal. Kapitän Lindemann planned to begin his transit of the canal the following morning, which would allow him to make the whole journey in daylight. So, all that afternoon and the next, Luftwaffe Bf 109 fighters flew overhead, while an icebreaker and two blockade breakers (*Sperrbrecher*) were anchored close by, as protection against an attack by British torpedo bombers.

At 08.22 the next morning, *Bismarck* raised anchor and, nudged by two tugs, she gingerly entered the canal. Although it had been enlarged, the canal was designed for Great War-era dreadnoughts, not the largest battleship in the world. In consequence, progress was slow, and as dusk approached the battleship was still inside the canal, at its eastern end. Lindemann wisely ordered her to be tied up for the night, as the final and hardest part of the transit – the passage through the Kiel-Holtenau lock system – lay just ahead. Lindemann was right to be cautious. At 08.45 the following morning, as the *Bismarck* approached the lock system, she grounded on the southern bank of the canal.[6] It hadn't been dredged deeply enough. It took an hour to free her, under her own power but assisted by a tug. She then passed through the locks without further incident, and that afternoon the battleship dropped anchor in Kiel fjord.

WORKING UP

On the morning of 9 March, more tugs eased the *Bismarck* into the largest dry dock at the Deutsche Werke shipyard so that her underside could be inspected for any damage caused during her grounding. This allowed Lindemann to repaint the ship's hull. Then, on 14 March the battleship was refloated and a tug towed her round to the Scheerhafen, the main naval quayside near the eastern entrance to the canal. *Bismarck* was berthed on the commodious North Mole, where a small mountain of stores was waiting for her. The next two days were spent loading these, along with ammunition, fuel, fresh water and other necessities, including two crated-up spotter aircraft. While all this was going on, the ship's gunnery department busied themselves with calibrating and aligning their batteries, ready for the combat training that was due to begin the following week. Others in the crew were ordered to continue the repainting of the ship, so that by the time she started her working up she would look her best.

So it was that on the morning of 17 March *Bismarck* cast off and headed up the Kiel fjord towards the Baltic Sea.[7] Ahead of her was the blockade runner *Sperrbrecher 36* and the old pre-dreadnought battleship *Schlesien*. An Imperial Naval veteran of Jutland and an inter-war training ship, the *Schlesien* was now used as an icebreaker. That March there was still ice in the western Baltic, and so she now led the way – a German battleship of a bygone era, followed by the most modern battleship afloat.

Their destination was Gotenhafen (now Gdynia), a suburb of Danzig (or Gdansk), 340 miles to the east. *Bismarck* dropped anchor off the port on the afternoon of 17 March.[8] This would be their base for the next two months as the crew of *Bismarck* honed their battle skills and the ship was prepared for her first operational sortie. The naval term for this thorough period of crew training, weapons drill and damage control exercises was 'working up' – using these drills to bring the ship and her crew to the peak of efficiency. The advantage of doing so in Gotenhafen was that it was beyond the range of British bombers. What's more, the entrance to the Baltic was effectively sealed off by minefields and naval and air patrols, so effectively the enclosed sea was safe from predators. This meant that all the *Bismarck*'s crew had to worry about was perfecting their skills.

A day after their arrival, *Bismarck*'s sister ship *Tirpitz* also arrived off Gotenhafen. She was still conducting sea trials, and so on 19 March her commander, Kapitän Topp, invited Lindemann over for dinner. During the meal, Topp passed on some important information.[9] Topp had hoped to sortie alongside *Bismarck*, but according to what he was told by the Naval War Staff, this wouldn't be happening. Instead, *Tirpitz* would complete her sea trials and then undergo her own extensive working up in the Baltic. This was what Lindemann expected. What came next was more of a bombshell. At headquarters, Topp had been told that in any case, a joint sortie was out of the question since *Bismarck* would be making her own first operational voyage earlier than had been intended. Lindemann had been instructed to have *Bismarck* ready for active service by the end of May. This meant that if the report were true, she would have to be ready three or four weeks earlier – the end of April.

In response, Lindemann called his officers together and demanded that they hasten the working up. This involved conducting almost continual drills and exercises, something that all of the ship's officers accepted as necessary since they knew this was crucial if their battleship were to carry out her mission effectively. For the most part, the working up centred around her armament, against surface and air targets, so that the battleship would be fit to sail out into the Baltic, sometimes alone and at other times in company with other ships. The battleship's main guns were therefore fired – the blast coming as something of a shock to some of the inexperienced recruits – and the secondary guns were tested, too, while aircraft flying from nearby airfields flew by the ship at a variety of heights, towing targets for the ship's anti-aircraft guns to blast away at.

In other preparations, the Arado Ar floatplanes were launched and recovered, until the aircraft handlers could do their job perfectly. Once in the air, these planes were used to spot the fall of shot of the *Bismarck*'s main guns, radioing the results back to the ship's gunnery team, who would correct their aim until their shells were falling around the target. The crews of these aircraft also flew in search patterns, until they felt confident that they could spot an enemy convoy on the high seas and shadow it until the *Bismarck* could steam over the horizon to intercept the enemy.

On 17 April, they were joined by the heavy cruiser *Prinz Eugen*, commanded by V. Adm. Brinkmann, an old naval academy classmate of Kapitän Lindemann.[10] She displaced almost 17,000 tons, and was armed with eight 8in. guns. The Naval High Command were planning for the two warships to make their operational sortie together, so it made sense that they should get used to operating as a team. The cruiser was remarkably similar in appearance to *Bismarck* – so much so that she resembled a scaled-down version of the battleship. This was a design feature that would pay dividends during their later joint operation.

Kapitänleutnant von Müllenheim-Rechberg provided a useful account of this working up period:

> We conducted more high-speed trials and endurance runs, and tried out our hydrophone gear... The most important thing now was intensive testing of our batteries. Practice firing for the instruction of the fire control officers and gun crews alternated with carrying out projects for the Gunnery Research Command for Ships [a Kriegsmarine research body], an organisation that ran its own trials on new ships with a view to improving the ordnance of various ship types. For me, as a gunnery officer, these tests were exciting but for the crew they just meant drill and still more drill. Battle practice in the daytime, battle practice at night! The men did not complain however; they were in the swing of things, and were becoming more and more anxious for our first operation to get under way.[11]

In fact, Lindemann deliberately cut short the Gunnery Research Command's evaluation programme, ending it on 2 April. This allowed him to concentrate on bringing his ship and crew up to full operational readiness. During one of these gunnery exercises – a sub-calibre shoot for the 4.1in. heavy flak guns – the *U-556* surfaced nearby, and Wohlfarth flashed a signal to the *Bismarck*'s bridge, asking permission to fire off a few rounds first, using his 3.46in. deck gun.[12] Permission was granted and, to the delight of the onlookers, the U-boat's gun crew hit the target float with their second round, then kept pounding it. Graciously, Lindemann signalled: 'I hope you'll be as successful in the Atlantic, and earn the Knight's Cross as well.' Wohlfarth flashed back: 'I hope we may both earn the Knight's Cross, in joint action together.' The U-boat then chugged away, leaving the *Bismarck*'s gun crews free to demolish what was left of the target.

As well as the *Prinz Eugen*, which took part in several joint gunnery drills with *Bismarck*, the battleship also conducted exercises with the 25th U-boat Flotilla, a training flotilla based in Danzig, which supervised the torpedo training of newly commissioned U-boats. It was for this reason that the *U-556* had been in the area. The flotilla's presence was of benefit to Lindemann since it allowed the *Bismarck*'s hydrophone operators to practise detecting the sounds of approaching submarines and torpedoes, and for the communication staff to work together with the U-boats that might soon be guiding the battleship towards a British convoy. Another vital skill was refuelling at sea. With no friendly bases in the North Atlantic, both *Bismarck* and *Prinz Eugen* would have to rely on tankers for their fuel. Accordingly, the tanker *Bromberg* was assigned to them, so that both ships could practise refuelling at sea.

One of the crucial parts of a ship's working up was the training of her crew in damage control. That meant repairing damage to the ship and her weapons or propulsion systems, to make sure she could still fight, and it also involved dealing with any fire and flooding. During one of these drills, held in the after steering compartment, seaman Herbert Blum asked his officer if he and his shipmates could play dead, as if the compartment had been knocked out.[13] The officer agreed, and told them to put their caps on back to front and lie on the deck. Afterwards, Blum remembered the lieutenant telling him that 'the chances of getting a hit there are a hundred thousand against'. Almost exactly a month later, those long odds would come home.

For now, however, it was all part of the training. It was important that if an officer or senior rating were killed the rest of their crew would know what to do. Senior officers would therefore appear, telling the crew that their turret or working space had been knocked out, or that their officers had, and the survivors would have to keep on fighting the ship. As von Müllenheim-Rechberg put it: 'The damage done to the *Bismarck* would be presented as realistically as possible: electrical breakdowns by removing fuses, fires by using some bombs, gaseous fumes by using tear gas, and so forth. In the case of damage that could not be portrayed, "damage notices" would be posted in the relevant parts of the ship.'[14] In the main electrical control station, Stabsoberfeldwebel (Senior Non-Commissioned Officer) Oskar Bahro kept telling his team of electricians: 'If I become a casualty, you must keep everything going exactly the same way, regardless of your grade!'

After each drill or battle exercise, the crew would be gathered on the quarterdeck and Lindemann and his senior officers would discuss what had happened, what had gone wrong, and what the crew needed to do better the next time. The aim was to point out mistakes, but to be thoroughly objective, and to make sure they weren't repeated. Throughout all this, Kapitän Lindemann remained unruffled, and was quick to praise those who deserved it. In this way, the crew of the *Bismarck* were rapidly being brought up to the peak of their proficiency. As Lindemann put it in the ship's diary: 'All our time was taken up in training. Heavy emphasis was placed on how the men would perform in the upcoming operation. The men seem to have come to recognise for the first time the magnitude of our mission, which they still don't know, but easily guess.'[15]

All this time, though, tension on board the *Bismarck* was building. The crew knew perfectly well that after their training was over they'd be sailing on their first operational sortie. Rumours abounded, and when they proved unfounded, new ones circulated in their place. They didn't know when it would happen, or where they would go, but it didn't take much to guess that it would be soon, and would probably involve a raid into the North Atlantic. What they were sure of, however, was that with every day of drills and exercises, they were getting better prepared for any challenge the Kriegsmarine – or the Royal Navy – could throw at them. Even Kapitän Lindemann was in the dark, as despite the report from Kapitän Topp of the *Tirpitz*, and requests from naval headquarters that he complete his training sooner than previously directed, he had no firm confirmation of just when he'd be required to lead his ship into enemy-held waters.

Lindemann had other problems, too. These exercises had revealed a few minor defects in the battleship's engines.[16] A ring on the middle shaft coupling was broken, there were problems with the steam line casings, and saltwater had got into one of the turbines. These were all relatively unimportant, and given the ship was brand new they were even to be expected. Still, Lindemann wasn't pleased, and he made sure that everything was completely rectified before the training programme had run its course. This was achieved on 13 April, when *Bismarck* put in to the quay in Gotenhafen for four days to take on more stores and ammunition, during which time the engineers fixed the engines. So, by the end of April – a month ahead of schedule – Lindemann was finally able to declare to the Naval High Command that his ship was ready. Soon, her readiness would be put to the test.

OPERATION *RHEINÜBUNG*

On 2 April, as *Bismarck* was in the midst of her working up, the Kriegsmarine's *Seekriegsleitung* (Naval War Staff) issued a preparatory order that specifically mentioned *Bismarck*, and her role in the coming sortie.[17] This was an operational directive, spelling out what would be expected of the battleship. It began by covering the earlier sorties into the Atlantic, claiming that they had achieved 'important tactical results', and had also 'demonstrated what important strategic effects a similar sortie could have'. Before going into specifics, it stated the strategic aim of the enterprise: 'We must not lose sight of the fact that the decisive objective in our struggle with England is to destroy her trade. This can be most effectively accomplished in the North Atlantic, where all her supply lines come together.' It emphasised this again by saying: 'Gaining command of the sea in the North Atlantic is the best solution to this problem', but added that the Kriegsmarine lacked the resources to achieve this. It also noted: 'We must strive for local and temporary command of the sea in this area, and to gradually, methodically and systematically extend it.'

So, that was the plan – not just to sortie into the Atlantic as a commerce raider, but also to temporarily achieve control of the area. That was a tall order, even for a battleship as powerful as the *Bismarck*. The strength of the British Home Fleet meant that if she lingered, *Bismarck* invited being brought to battle and overwhelmed by sheer weight of numbers. Therefore, what the *Seekriegsleitung* really meant was that by being at large in the North Atlantic, *Bismarck* could attack convoys and disrupt or divert the progress of others. It would also tie down enemy ships, which would be vitally needed in other theatres. Taken together, this amounted to gaining a temporary control of the area, but it still fell far short of the High Command's lofty strategic goal.

The *Seekriegsleitung* then got to the crux of the operation. Having initially said it would prefer *Bismarck* to sail in company with the *Tirpitz*, it added that this wouldn't be possible yet. So, as an 'intermediate step', *Bismarck* would be used to lure escorts away from convoys, allowing other warships to attack them. In other words, *Bismarck* would serve as a decoy. It continued:

> At the earliest possible date, which it is hoped will be during the new-moon period of April, the *Bismarck* and the *Prinz Eugen*, led by the Fleet Commander, are to be deployed as commerce raiders in the Atlantic. At a time that will be dependent on the completion of the repairs she is currently undergoing, *Gneisenau* will also be sent into the Atlantic.[18]

As we have seen, the addition of either the *Scharnhorst* or the *Gneisenau* was thwarted by developments in Brest, where they were currently based. So, in the end, *Bismarck* and *Prinz Eugen* would make the sortie on their own.

These operational orders differed from the ones for Operation *Berlin*. For that operation, *Scharnhorst* and *Gneisenau* had been forbidden to attack heavily escorted convoys. Now, though, the mission was to attack any promising convoy, even if it were escorted by a battleship. Clearly, the *Seekriegsleitung* had a low opinion of the older British battleships that formed the bulk of these heavy escorts. It did, though, inject a note of caution: 'However, the objective of the battleship *Bismarck* should not be to defeat in an all-out engagement enemies of equal strength, but to tie them down in a delaying action, while preserving her own combat capability as much as possible, so as to allow the other ships to get at the merchant vessels of the convoy.'[19]

This meant that the German force commander Admiral Lütjens had to walk a tightrope, enticing the heavier enemy warships away from the convoy, leaving it exposed to attack by the *Prinz Eugen*, while not getting into a major fight himself. Success would depend on *Bismarck*'s speed and armour, and on Lütjens' nerve. A lot could go wrong. As if to underline the need for caution, the *Seekriegsleitung* added: 'The primary mission of this operation also is the destruction of the enemy's merchant shipping; enemy warships will be engaged only when the objective makes it necessary, and it can be done without excessive risk.'[20] This single sentence, or rather Lütjens' interpretation of it, would soon spare the lives of up to 1,500 British sailors, in the closing stages of the Battle of the Denmark Strait.

This operational order came from the *Seekriegsleitung*, and the pen of its director, V. Adm. Otto Schniewind. However, he was also the chief-of-staff, and therefore Grossadmiral Raeder's right-hand man. So, despite the curious wording of it, the plan represented the wishes of the German Naval High Command. Compared to a similar document issued before Operation *Berlin*, which precluded the deliberate engagement of enemy capital ships, these instructions offered more leeway, and thus incurred greater risk. This showed that both Raeder and Schniewind were willing to up the stakes in their naval campaign, in the hope of winning an even greater reward in terms of the number of enemy merchant ships sent to the bottom.

The operation also had a name – Operation *Rheinübung* (Rhine Exercise). The previous sorties by the cruiser *Admiral*

Scheer (October 1940–April 1941) and the two battlecruisers *Scharnhorst* and *Gneisenau* (January–March 1941) had been reasonably successful, despite the relative lack of firepower and armour of the ships involved. Clearly, then, the *Bismarck* was better able to take care of herself if she got into a fight, and this represented the Kriegsmarine's best counter to the new British tactic of using battleships to escort convoys if they thought a German sortie was imminent. So, while the emphasis of the operational orders was still one of evading trouble, and the preference was to reach the Atlantic undetected, this operation would require considerably more subtlety than previous ones. It would also rely heavily on the judgement and intuition of the force commander.

It was for this reason that the Naval High Command only had one choice when it came to filling this key post: Admiral Lütjens. The fleet commander for Operation *Berlin*, Lütjens already had a successful breakout into the Atlantic under his belt, and was a man whose cool judgement and analytical mind were perfectly suited to the challenges expected in Operation *Rheinübung*. Also, his orders after the Berlin operation meant that he was already waiting in readiness to command a similar sortie. So, Lütjens was given his orders, while Lindemann and Brinkmann were told to have their ships ready by 26 April.

The fleet commander had his misgivings about the operation – the two ships had different roles and requirements, and didn't make a good pairing, as the sister ships *Scharnhorst* and *Gneisenau* had.[21] Thanks to her smaller fuel tanks, the *Prinz Eugen* had much less of a range than the *Bismarck*, and so couldn't stay at sea as long. It would also be hard to coordinate convoy attacks with the two ships. Furthermore, the long summer nights were fast approaching, which would make slipping past the British blockade undetected even harder. Lütjens planned to discuss these problems with Raeder, but first he had to deal with a last-minute setback. At 03.00 on 23 April, a magnetic mine detonated close to the starboard side of *Prinz Eugen* as she steamed through the Fehman Belt, 50 miles from Kiel.[22] The damage to her hull was minor, but it would take at least 12 days to repair, back in Kiel. So, Operation *Rheinübung* was postponed.

Three days later, on 26 April, Admiral Lütjens travelled to Berlin to discuss the operation with Grossadmiral Raeder and V. Adm. Otto Schniewind. It was the perfect chance to air his misgivings about the operation, but there is no evidence that he did. Instead, all the fleet commander managed was to suggest waiting until *Tirpitz* was ready to accompany him, or the battlecruisers in Brest had been repaired. Raeder rejected the idea – for him, speed was essential in light of the rapidly lengthening days. There was another reason, too. As part of Hitler's inner circle of advisors, he knew that Operation *Barbarossa* – the German invasion of the Soviet Union – was planned to start in mid- to late June. He feared that if Operation *Rheinübung* were delayed, Hitler would cancel the operation, so that *Bismarck* could be used in the Baltic instead.

So, a new date was set for 16 May[23] and Lütjens was told to sort out the details of the operation – his plans for the breakout into the Atlantic and the arrangements for logistical support from tankers, weather ships, minesweepers and reconnaissance vessels, and from both the Luftwaffe and the U-boat fleet. It was a complex operation, and back in their headquarters in Kiel the fleet commander and his staff set to work. Meanwhile, in the nearby Deutsche Werke shipyard, work on the *Prinz Eugen* was coming along splendidly. On 6 May, she left the dry dock and headed back to Gotenhafen, arriving there the following afternoon. She was once more ready for service, although she had managed to miss all the excitement that had gripped the port the day before.

Meanwhile, during the last days of April, Kapitän Lindemann concentrated on getting the *Bismarck* ready for active service. Then, on 1 May, he received a call from Lütjens' office warning him that the German Führer Adolf Hitler intended to visit the port in four days, to tour both *Bismarck* and *Tirpitz*. Last-minute training schedules were therefore abandoned as Lindemann and Topp had their men clean and paint the two battleships and prepare their best uniforms. On 5 May, Hitler arrived in Gotenhafen, where he was met by Admiral Lütjens.[24] He began his tour by boarding the tender *Hela*, which brought the visitors out to the *Bismarck*, which was anchored in the roads. The crew lined the upper decks, and as he clambered on board Hitler was greeted by Kapitän Lindemann and his senior officers. The ship's band struck up the national anthem, then the German warlord began his tour of inspection.

He was accompanied by GFM (Generalfeldmarschall/ Field Marshal) Keitel and his Kriegsmarine and Luftwaffe aides; Hitler, by his own admission, was no naval expert, but he had an intense interest in military technology. So, in the after gunnery control room he listened with rapt attention as Lt Cardinal explained the workings of the ship's fire control system. The analogue computer on board was able to calculate firing solutions for the ship's great 15in. guns, capable of hitting targets 18.5 miles away while the ship was travelling at full speed. Clearly, Hitler was impressed. Next, he listened to an optimistic presentation by Lütjens on the successes of Operation *Berlin*, and the potential of future raids into the North Atlantic. When Hitler questioned the risk posed by the Royal Navy's superior numbers, the fleet commander replied: 'The *Bismarck* is superior to any British battleship. Her firepower and protection is so outstanding that there is no need for fear.'[25] Hitler seemed to be satisfied.

Next came lunch, served in the wardroom. Due to Hitler's dietary requirements, this was a one-course vegetarian affair – a simple vegetable stew. Then Hitler addressed the assembled ship's officers. He spoke of the persecution of Germans in Romania, and his belief that the USA wouldn't enter the war. Rather courageously, Lütjens disagreed with the Führer, voicing the unspoken concerns of many of the officers gathered there. Still, the incident was overlooked, and moments later Hitler re-embarked on the *Hela* for the short trip back to the quayside, and a quick tour of the *Tirpitz*, which was tied up there. Lütjens accompanied him and saw Hitler off before returning to Kiel and his planning office.

A week later, on 12 May, the fleet commander returned to Gotenhafen and embarked on his new flagship.[26] Once again, he was greeted by Lindemann, his officers and the ship's band. This time, though, he was led to his own suite of cabins, while his extensive staff of 65 officers and men were shown theirs, as well as the fleet operations offices housed in the battleship's after superstructure. By that time, *Tirpitz* had sailed off to continue her sea trials and *Prinz Eugen* had arrived. So, the task force was fully assembled.

On 14 May, a slight delay was caused by the malfunctioning of one of *Bismarck*'s two deck cranes, causing the ship to return alongside for repairs, which took two days. Finally, on 16 May, Lütjens reported that his force would be ready for operations in two days' time.[27] In return, a message arrived from Raeder, giving him permission to proceed with his mission. So, that was it. There would be no more delays. Operation *Rheinübung* would begin on 18 May.

Chapter 5

Through the Baltic

'MUSS I DENN'

It was time. Four days earlier, both Lütjens and Lindemann had received the coded message 'Marburg 5724'.[1] This meant that the *Seekriegsleitung* expected *Bismarck* to pass through the Great Belt between the Danish islands of Funen (Fyn) and Zealand (Sjælland) on the night of 18–19 May. Admiral Lütjens, whose staff had been embarked with him, had carefully read and re-read his orders and studied his charts. He now thoroughly understood his mission and had considered the many imponderables, the most important of which was the reaction of the British Home Fleet. Also, in the areas where he had complete initiative and freedom of action, he'd already figured out what his best course of action might be. He was now as ready as any flag officer could be on the eve of such a major undertaking.

The day before, leave had been cancelled for the two ships and all the last-minute preparations had been carried out. This included the taking on of fuel. On *Bismarck*, this was preceded by the fuel bunkers being cleaned out.[2] Von Müllenheim-Rechberg explained the procedure:

> A Petty Officer and a seaman, armed with a fresh air pipe to enable them to breathe, and a safety lamp, had to go into each bunker and clean out the sludge. They collected the muck in buckets, which were then passed from hand to hand, via the upper deck, to barges made fast alongside ... The dirtiest work was done by Polish forced labourers, with whom the language difference made communication difficult. But after 24 hours the job was done, and the bunkers were spanking clean, and ready to take on a new supply of fuel. The Polish workers were rewarded with schnapps and cigarettes.

Next, the ships began to take on water, stores, ammunition and fuel, so that everything would be ready for departure.

Finally, on the morning of 18 May 1941, it was time to put it all in motion. Of course, Lütjens wasn't the only senior Kriegsmarine officer to wake up with a sense of purpose that morning. While he had operational control of the venture, overall control still rested in the hands of Grossadmiral Raeder in Berlin, and strategic direction lay with Admiral Otto Schniewind of the *Seekriegsleitung*, who was also based in Berlin.[3] Then, while in northern waters, Lütjens and his two ships would come under the control of Generaladmiral (Grand Admiral) Rolf Carls and his Group North, based in Wilhelmshaven. Once *Bismarck* and *Prinz Eugen* broke out into the North Atlantic and passed an invisible line running west of the northern tip of Scotland, Lütjens and his ships would move into the area controlled by Group West based in Paris, which was run by Generaladmiral Alfred Saalwächter. However, these commands were largely administrative ones. Once at sea, Lütjens would be in sole operational command.

That morning, the two ships were berthed alongside the quayside in Gotenhafen.[4] After breakfast, the fleet commander had a quick meeting with his staff, and with Kapitän Lindemann. Then, shortly before 10.00 he and his senior aides walked along the quay to the *Prinz Eugen*. V. Adm. Brinkmann met them at the gangway and accompanied Lütjens as he conducted a quick inspection of the ship. Lütjens also chatted with Brinkmann's officers before he accompanied his fleet commander ashore, then headed to the *Bismarck*. There, at 10.45, a conference was held on the battleship. Generaladmiral Saalwächter was present, having flown in to Gotenhafen the previous evening. Also present was Lütjens' chief-of-staff Kapitän Netzbald, who had supervised the detailed planning of Operation *Rheinübung*. Naturally, captains Lindemann and Brinkmann were there too, and listened as Netzbald outlined the plan for the next few days. As he was speaking, however, the tannoy announced the battleship was preparing for departure, so the conference was kept short.

The two captains already had their sailing orders, but Netzbald went through them again. The ships would pass through the Great Belt, then continue on through the Kattegat and Skagerrak, and so out into the North Sea. They would then turn northwards, following the Norwegian coast, heading for the Korsfjord (Krossfjord) near Bergen. There, their fuel would be topped up by a waiting tanker. Under cover of darkness, the two ships would continue their journey up the Norwegian coast, until they passed the Arctic Circle. Netzbald outlined the other elements – the destroyer escorts, the minesweepers and the Luftwaffe cover that would be supporting them during the voyage – and finished by emphasising that at sea all ships would need to maintain radio silence. This meant that all signals between the two warships would have to be by lamps or flags. Then he handed over to Lütjens.

The fleet commander had little to add at that stage, save for the possibility that if the weather allowed it, he might refuel at sea, from a tanker already in position beyond the Arctic Circle – a decision he would make when he reached Norwegian waters.[5] He also stated his preference for the Denmark Strait as a route through the British blockade. This, however, might also change, depending on circumstances. A few other points were raised, including the use of aircraft, but essentially the aim of this conference was to make sure both captains knew exactly what was expected of them. Finally, Lütjens stressed that the nature of their mission would be kept secret from the crews until the ships were safely out at sea. The meeting concluded, the conference broke up.

Saalwächter and his staff went ashore, Brinkmann returned to his ship, which was also bustling with activity, and Lütjens and Lindemann headed to the *Bismarck*'s bridge. The sky was overcast that morning, which boded well for what would, after all, be a journey that emphasised stealth and avoiding detection. Then, at 11.30, Lindemann gave the order to cast off the lines, and the battleship eased away from the quayside, watched by the Generaladmiral and his staff.[6] As they looked on, the ship's band on the quarterdeck opened up, playing a tune selected by the bandmaster called '*Muss i denn*'. A folk song, written in 1827 by Friedrich Silcher, it was a song of love and leaving, and was later popularised by both Marlene Dietrich and Elvis Presley (as 'Wooden Heart'). During the war, it was adopted by the Imperial German Navy as a song played on the departure of a warship on a long and arduous voyage. The Kriegsmarine used it too, but for such a secret mission the playing of it was something of a security oversight. As Müllenheim-Rechberg put it:

> I must admit that I was more than a little surprised by this musical advertisement that Rheinübung had begun. I think it highly doubtful that either our Fleet Commander or our captain knew we were to have this musical programme. In all likelihood, it did not occur to any responsible officer that such a thing would happen, and therefore nothing was done to stop it. The bandmaster, aware that our departure was imminent, probably just automatically chose that song without giving the matter another thought.[7]

However, it quite effectively told any spies who overheard it that *Bismarck* and *Prinz Eugen* weren't merely going to sea for another exercise. This was the real thing.

Operation *Rheinübung* was now officially under way, but in fact it didn't begin with a long voyage at all. Instead, the two warships went out into the Baltic, and conducted routine exercises for a few hours, in an attempt to make it seem like a normal day. Then, early in the afternoon they returned to the roadstead and dropped anchor before finishing topping up with fuel and stores, and bringing the last batches of extra personnel on board. On the *Bismarck*, these supernumeraries included the fleet commander's staff of 65 officers and men, and a prize crew of 80 seamen, whose job it was to guard any prisoners and to board any merchant ships captured intact in the mid-Atlantic.[8] In all, a total of 2,221 officers and men were aboard the battleship when she finally sailed from Gotenhafen.

One incident of note during this process was that while refuelling, a fuel line leading from the tanker to the *Bismarck's* fuel valves ruptured, and pumping had to be cut short to prevent even more fuel oil spilling over her decks. This meant that *Bismarck* was 200 tons short of her fuel capacity. However, neither Lütjens nor Lindemann felt this was overly important. After all, they planned to refuel in either Norway or at sea, beyond the Arctic Circle. Late that evening, under cover of dark, *Prinz Eugen* prepared to depart, and at 21.18 she recovered her anchors. V. Adm. Brinkmann headed north-east to pass the sandy Hel peninsula (now Mierzeja Helska), guarded by a battery of three huge 16in. guns. He then turned his ship to the west, steaming slowly down the Pomeranian coast, but keeping out of sight of land. Again, the two warships didn't leave together, in order to confuse any spies in the port. So, it was 02.00 on the morning of 19 May when the *Bismarck* finally recovered her anchor and followed the same route towards Danish waters.[9]

THE *GOTLAND*

The voyage down the Pomeranian coast was uneventful, and a cloudy sky and unsettled weather helped reduce the risk of being observed. That morning, after the crew had eaten breakfast, Lindemann addressed them over the ship's loudspeakers. The rumour had been flying around for weeks and pretty much everyone on board knew they were going on their first operational sortie. Now their captain confirmed it. He told them the plan was to break out into the North Atlantic and spend several months attacking Britain's trade routes, sinking and capturing enemy merchant shipping. This announcement effectively ended any remaining uncertainty about what was expected of the ship and her crew, as Müllenheim-Rechberg noted: 'Their apprehension about the unknown was replaced by certainty. Below, the gentle vibration of the engines reminded them of the tremendous power that made their ship a deadly weapon.'[10]

At 11.30, the two warships rendezvoused off the white cliffs of Cape Arkona.[11] This was the northern tip of the island of Rügen, 190 miles south-west of the Hel peninsula. The *Bismarck* had already been joined by two German destroyers, the *Z-16 Friedrich Eckoldt* and the *Z-23*, under the command of Korvettenkapitän Friedrich Böhme, a veteran of the destroyer battles fought off Narvik the previous year. As the destroyers took station on either side of the battleship, two other small warships, *Sp-13* and *Sp-31* – both blockade runners or *Sperrbrecher* – took up position ahead of them. On Lütjens' command, this powerful force got under way again, and shortly after noon a trio of Luftwaffe fighters appeared. These and others would continue to fly over the task force for the rest of the day. From Cape Arkona it was 75 miles to the start of the Fehmarn Belt, where *Prinz Eugen* had been damaged by a mine almost four weeks earlier.

That then led to the Great Belt (or *Langelädsbaelt*). Waiting for them off its entrance was another destroyer, the *Z-10 Hans Lody*, the flagship of the 6th Destroyer Flotilla, which had just sailed from Kiel. The flotilla commander, Kapitän Alfred Schulze-Hinrichs, was on board, to take command of the destroyers during the critical passage through the Baltic. *Z-10 Hans Lody* took station astern of the formation at 22.30, just as the warships entered the entrance to the narrow channel.

The Great Belt was 85 miles long and the transit through it was expected to last until dawn. They were exactly 24 hours behind the schedule requested by the 'Marburg 5724' signal, thanks to the problem with the crane, but at least *Bismarck* and *Prinz Eugen* were on their way. As a security measure,

the Kriegsmarine had ordered the suspension of all maritime traffic through all three of the Danish 'belts' that night, so their progress went unobserved.

As dawn broke on 20 May, the ships emerged from the channel into the wider waters of the Kattegat.[12] The two blockade runners were detached, having completed their job of safely leading the way through the channel. By 04.50 they were passing Rosnaes, where the Kattegat opened out into a waterway some 50 miles across. Shortly afterwards, the destroyer *Z-10 Hans Lody* sounded its air alarm. Aircraft had been spotted approaching from the west, over the Jutland peninsula. The fear was that these were British reconnaissance aircraft or, worse, enemy bombers. It turned out to be a false alarm. This was merely their fighter escort for the day arriving – the Luftwaffe had simply forgotten to tell the

Kriegsmarine when and where it would appear. The transit of the Kattegat thus continued.

Unlike the previous day, it was a bright, clear morning and the sun was out; it would have been a pleasant cruise were it not for the increased risk of the task force being spotted and identified by observers on the neutral coast of Sweden, or among the increasing number of Danish and Swedish fishing boats that they passed once the task force drew north of the little island of Anholt. As Müllenheim-Rechberg remembered it: 'They seemed to be everywhere, these little white craft with their chugging motors, some of them bobbing up and down beside us. Not only that but steamers from all sorts of countries were passing through the Kattegat.'[13] While the Germans were able to restrict maritime traffic in Danish waters, they could do nothing about shipping off the neutral coast of Sweden, or the activities of local fishing boats. There was always the likelihood that some of these vessels would radio the news of their passing to others, and word of the German naval force would eventually reach London.

On their port side lay the low-lying coast of the Jutland peninsula – part of German-occupied Denmark. To starboard lay Sweden, a neutral country. Despite her status, the intelligence section of the German Naval High Command felt that this neutrality had been damaged by the German invasion of Denmark and Norway the previous spring, and that the Swedes were likely to pass on any intelligence information they had to the British. For this reason, Lütjens decided to keep as far from the Swedish coast as he could, to reduce the risk of being observed. However, this action didn't take into account any encounter with other neutral ships, or Swedish warships.

By noon, they were passing the island of Laeso on their port side. Beyond this the Kattegat narrowed, until it ended at Skagen, the northernmost tip of Denmark's Jutland peninsula. Opposite it, 40 miles away on the Swedish side of the channel, was the city of Gothenburg. Past the line between the two, the Kattegat turned into the Skagerrak, the mouth of the Baltic that lay between Denmark and Norway. So far, their progress had been uneventful. This was about to change.

Shortly before 13.00, they spotted a warship ahead of them, off the starboard bow. It turned out to be the Swedish light cruiser *Gotland*. She was a slightly odd warship that had been built during the early 1930s and combined the roles of light cruiser and seaplane carrier.[14] As such, she had two twin 6in. turrets, but behind her after turret was a small flight deck, equipped with a catapult. She carried six British-built seaplanes. This odd hybrid was patrolling off Gothenburg when the German task force appeared.

Gotland's captain, Angren, duly ordered the sighting to be reported to the naval headquarters in Gothenburg. Then he turned his ship around and shadowed the German task force as it sailed northwards towards the Skagerrak. On board the *Bismarck*, Admiral Lütjens sent his own signal to Group North's headquarters in Wilhelmshaven, reporting the sighting, adding that the battleship's B-Dienst section had detected radio signals being sent from the Swedish cruiser.[15] In other words, Lütjens was sure that the Swedish navy now knew *Bismarck* was at sea, and therefore it was possible that the news would also be passed on to the British. The *Gotland*, meanwhile, settled on a parallel north-westerly course to that of the Germans and continued to shadow them for an hour, until she finally turned away at the entrance of the Skagerrak.

To add to the Germans' security problems, a formation of Swedish aircraft also passed them at noon, while patrolling their side of the Kattegat. Their commander also sent off a sighting report of a very large warship, a cruiser and three destroyers, steering a northerly course. Ten to 12 aircraft were flying over the German force. The German fleet commander had every reason to be concerned about these two sightings, and a third at 15.45, when the *Gotland* made another report: that in the Skagerrak the German force had held a north-westerly course until it was lost from view.

Back in Gothenburg, Angren's two signals had been decoded, then passed up the chain of command to the Swedish Admiralty in Stockholm. A copy was duly passed to the Swedish intelligence service. While officially it was of little importance to the Swedish authorities, there were several Swedes in positions of authority who had no love for Nazi Germany. One of these people was Överstelöjtnant (Lt Col.) Petersén, head of the Swedish secret service. He read a copy of the first signal from the *Gotland*, and noted it in his log.

He then very deliberately passed it to his chief-of-staff, Maj. Örlkn (Major) Egon Törnberg. He was half Norwegian, and ever since the German invasion of Norway the previous April had done what he could to help the British. Petersén was almost certainly well aware of this, and of his deputy's link with Kommandør (Commander) Roscher Lund, the military attaché in Sweden of the Norwegian government in exile, which was based in London. Sure enough, Törnberg arranged an urgent meeting with Lund and passed on a copy of the signal. The next link in the chain was Captain Henry Denham, the British naval attaché in Stockholm.[16] In April 1940, Denham had been the naval attaché in Copenhagen when the Germans invaded Norway. He had got out by way of Norway and Finland, and was now performing his old job in the Swedish capital. On the evening of 20 May 1941, he suddenly found himself at the centre of a spy drama.

Denham was having dinner in a nearby restaurant on the Riddargatan when Kommandør Lund appeared and asked to speak to him. Although they routinely met twice a week, this was the first time that the Norwegian had broken protocol and demanded an urgent and unscheduled meeting. Denham was sure the Germans were bugging his phone and keeping his flat under observation so, rather than talk either there or in the very public restaurant, Denham and Lund cycled to the British embassy, half a mile away. There, Denham ushered Lund into his office and closed the door. Once inside, the Norwegian handed over a transcript of the Gotland signal. It didn't mention that the source was the Swedish cruiser, but it did state that two German 'battleships' and three destroyers had just been sighted off Marstrand, heading towards the north-west.

Once Lund had gone, the British naval attaché drafted a signal to the Admiralty in London. It repeated the report, and Denham labelled it 'Most Immediate'. It was transmitted shortly before 21.00. This was the first word the British had that *Bismarck* had sailed from Gotenhafen.[17] This intelligence, together with a subsequent sighting from southern Norway, was enough to convince First Sea Lord Admiral of the Fleet Sir Dudley Pound that this was an actual operational sortie, and that the *Bismarck* was leaving the Baltic. On this evidence, he went on to activate the British Home Fleet based in Scapa Flow, and so started the chain of events that would ultimately lead to the Battle of the Denmark Strait, and the pursuit of *Bismarck* across the North Atlantic.

THROUGH THE SKAGERRAK

Meanwhile, Admiral Lütjens realised that even if the British learned that his force had sailed, he still had the initiative, and was determined that the mission would continue. He also had more important concerns than the mere possibility that the Swedes had reported his presence to the enemy. As Generaladmiral Carls said in his reply to Lütjens' signal to Group North that afternoon: 'I do not think the danger of being compromised by a Swedish warship is any greater than from the already present, systematic enemy surveillance of the entrance to the Baltic.'[18] This raised a very valid point. The Skagerrak was blocked by German minefields, which funnelled any approaching ships into clearly defined lanes. While this made it easier for the Germans to patrol the entrance to the Baltic, it also made it easier for British submarines to keep these channels under surveillance. The same submarines could also launch torpedo attacks at high-value targets – and none was more valuable than the *Bismarck*.

Still, when the task force headed off towards the north-west steering a course of 300°, the *Gotland* was left behind, as she stayed resolutely inside Swedish territorial waters. The danger now was from British submarines, which were known to patrol the Skagerrak.[19] With this in mind, the task force took basic precautions. First, the escorting destroyers formed an anti-submarine screen around the larger ships, with *Z-10 Hans Lody* in the lead, then *Z-16 Friedrich Eckoldt* to port and *Z-23* to starboard. Overhead flew six Messerschmitt Bf 110 twin-engined fighter-bombers, while a pair of Heinkel He 115 seaplanes scouted in front, looking for the telltale white wake of a submarine periscope. Ahead of them lay the start of the belt of protective minefields. Waiting for them there, at a prearranged rendezvous point, were the small vessels of the 5th Minesweeping Flotilla, commanded by Fregattenkapitän Rudolf Lell.

So far, everything had gone smoothly, apart from the encounter with the *Gotland* and the Swedish aircraft. Then *Z-10 Hans Lody* sounded the alarm. Their lookouts had spotted a solitary aircraft far ahead of them – possibly a British reconnaissance plane. Clearly, it couldn't come too close because of the fighter cover over the German task force, but there was now a good chance they'd been spotted. The British made regular flights over the Skagerrak to check on shipping movements and today their timing couldn't have been worse for the Germans. It soon disappeared, however, leaving the skies free, apart from German aircraft. Still, it was disconcerting for Lütjens. Ahead of them lay the main passage through the minefield, the minesweeper flotilla and a cluster of merchant ships, waiting to pass through the cleared channel.

Admiral Lütjens regarded these merchant ships as another possible security risk – some of them would undoubtedly report their presence by radio, allowing the British to pick up the transmission.[20] So, he decided to forge his own path. Lell and his five minesweepers were ordered to take position ahead of the task force and to clear a fresh path through the minefield several miles to the north of the main channel. This was a fairly straightforward task for them, albeit a dangerous one. Around 16.00 they began the transit of the minefield at a steady speed of 17 knots. Everything went smoothly, and by 17.15 they were through. The minesweeping flotilla was dismissed, and the task force turned on to a new heading of 270°, or due west. There was still a risk of encountering an enemy submarine so everyone remained vigilant, particularly the hydrophone operators.

In fact, at one stage that evening the operator on the *Prinz Eugen* detected what he thought was a contact to port, but nothing developed and the task force swept past. At 17 knots, they were much faster than any British submarine, and so the only real threat was from one that lay directly in their path. Accordingly, they continued to zigzag, to reduce the chances of a lurking submarine being able to launch a torpedo spread, and gradually the mountains of southern Norway loomed into view ahead of them.

At 21.00, they reached the start of the Kristiansand minefield's swept channel. The formation changed, with *Z-10 Hans Lody* leading, followed by *Prinz Eugen*, *Bismarck* and *Z-16 Friedrich Eckoldt*.[21] The *Z-23* brought up the rear. Speed was kept at 17 knots, but in case a mine was accidentally triggered, all of the ships had their damage control teams standing ready and kept their watertight doors closed. It took an hour to work through the minefield. On board the *Bismarck*, Müllenheim-Rechberg and some of his fellow officers settled down in the wardroom to see a film, *Spiel im Sommerwind* (*Play in the Summer Wind*), a romantic comedy released in 1938. They were up on deck, though, as darkness fell, to take in the scenery as they left the minefield.

Sunset that evening was at around 22.00, and as they drew closer to the coast near Kristiansand the sun began to fall behind the mountains. Müllenheim-Rechberg described the scene: 'The outlines of the beautiful, austere landscape, with the black silhouette of its mountains raised against the red glow of the sky, enabled me to forget for a moment all about the war.'[22] As the sun set, they cleared the swept channel, and the destroyers took up their usual positions again, ahead and on each side of the larger ships. Now they were in open water, Lütjens ordered their speed to be increased to 27 knots and the task force surged forwards, heading around the southernmost tip of Norway. Until darkness fell, half of the flak guns on *Bismarck* had been manned, with the crews taking turns about to stand anti-aircraft watches. Now, for the next six-and-a-half hours, night would protect them from British aircraft.

WATCHERS ON THE SHORE

Meanwhile, as the task force approached the channel to the next minefield off Kristiansand, the ships were clearly visible from the shore. In Vestervien, a western suburb of Kristiansand, a group of young Norwegians were making their way along the shore to a bar and restaurant out of town to celebrate the launch of Viggo Axelssen's new boat, the previous one having been commandeered by the German authorities.[23] Unknown to most of his friends, Axelssen was a member of the Norwegian Resistance. He worked for a local ship's chandlery and so had easy access both to the harbour and to the port office. There, he learned useful snippets of intelligence, such as the position of the Kristiansand minefield, as well as the channel through it. He also reported shipping movements through the swept channel – usually coastal convoys. He hoped this information would allow British submarines to lie in wait.

Normally, Axelssen sent his reports once a week, by way of another Resistance member who lived near Flekkefjord, some 60 miles to the east.[24] Axelssen himself had no contact with the radio operator. Instead, his encrypted messages were passed to Arne Moen, a local bus driver and good friend, who smuggled them to Flekkefjord hidden in a secret compartment in his bus engine. From Flekkefjord, the messages were passed on to London. While the Germans knew there was a Resistance cell in the area, and a radio transmitter somewhere near Flekkefjord, they hadn't found them. Nevertheless, each transmission represented a huge risk.

At one point, as dusk was approaching, the group stopped to admire the view. In front of them, the wide channel fringed by a patchwork of islands led to the lighthouse on Oskøy, 5 miles away at the mouth of the bay. Beyond that was the open sea of the Skagerrak. As they watched, a group of ships appeared, heading towards the minefield. Axelssen recognised them for what they were – a task force of German warships. One of the group had an old-fashioned spyglass with him, which Axelssen borrowed and used to make out two large ships, led by smaller destroyers, with aircraft flying above them. Clearly, this was important – a major German task force leaving the Baltic and heading west. He realised that this news couldn't wait.

So, when his friends reached the town, Axelssen claimed he had something to deal with at work and that he would join them shortly. He scurried off, wrote out a short message in code and went round to see the bus driver Arne Moen. He was in luck – he was due to make an evening run to Flekkefjord. Axelssen handed over the note and went back to the party. In this manner, later that evening the message reached Gunvald Tomstad, the man with the radio transmitter. He usually took his transmitter deep into the woods before he sent his signal but, sensing the urgency, he realised that this time was different and with the help of another Resistance man erected the equipment in his barn and sent the signal immediately. This meant that it reached the Admiralty in London shortly before midnight. Little did he know that a second, similar message was already there, courtesy of Captain Denham in

Stockholm. Now there was no room for doubt – a powerful German task force was at sea, in Norwegian waters.

Back out at sea, 8 miles south of Kristiansand, the three destroyers threaded their way through the minefield, then increased speed to 27 knots. At 22.15 they altered on to a new heading of 286° – or west-north-west.[25] This meant that they had passed the southernmost tip of Norway near Lindesnes and were curving up slightly, to clear the westward bulge of the coastline. They were out of the Skagerrak now, and in the North Sea. Midnight came and went, and shortly before 02.00 on 21 May the task force made another turn towards the north. They were now steering 327°, or north-north-west. A little later, in accordance with Admiral Lütjens' standing orders, the ships cleared for action. Who knew what might be waiting for them as dawn broke.

In fact, the fleet commander had every reason to be cautious. During the night, several messages were transmitted to the flagship, either from Group North in Wilhelmshaven or Naval High Command in Berlin. The first of these, received a little before 01.00, said that the British were looking for two large warships and three destroyers.[26] That was reassuring because it suggested the British Admiralty had no idea what the warships were, or where they were heading. Before 02.00, as the task force drew level with Stavanger, Berlin sent a copy of a report on a reconnaissance flight over Scapa Flow. Apparently, a little after noon the previous day, an aircraft carrier, three battleships or battlecruisers and several cruisers had still been in the anchorage. This meant that the chances of an encounter off the Norwegian coast were slim, and perhaps Lütjens relaxed slightly as a consequence.

Still, when dawn came at around 04.30, Admiral Lütjens, Kapitän Lindemann and dozens of lookouts scanned the horizon in search of enemy ships or aircraft. It was empty. So, they steamed on, by now steering a fraction west of north, keeping roughly parallel to the Norwegian coast. This was decision time for the fleet commander.[27] His original plan called for a refuelling stop near Bergen, which was fast approaching. However, he had already expressed that he favoured his alternate plan – continuing on into the Arctic Sea, and a rendezvous with a tanker beyond the Arctic Circle. We don't know why he returned to the original plan and decided to put in to the Korsfjord near Bergen.

He may, perhaps, have been swayed by another message, intercepted by the B-Dienst section on board *Prinz Eugen* at 06.40 that morning.[28] This reported that an overheard and decoded British signal had said they were looking for a German naval task force heading northwards up the Norwegian coast. Minutes later, the radio office on *Bismarck* received another message, this time from Berlin. It told a similar story: the British were looking for two German battleships and three destroyers, heading north. So, apart from the misidentification of the *Prinz Eugen*, Lütjens now knew that the British were looking for him, and knew roughly which way he was heading. In response, he gave the order that would send his task force turning towards the coast and the fjord that led towards Bergen.

Chapter 6

Sojourn in Norway

THE KORSFJORD

It was 07.00 on the morning of 21 May 1941. Admiral Lütjens had made his decision. The German task force would put in to the Korsfjord, near Bergen. As his order was signalled from the flagship to the other warships, a cluster of specks appeared off *Bismarck*'s port beam.[1] They were aircraft, but thanks to the bright sun nobody knew whether they were friendly or not. In fact, these were four RAF Bristol Blenheims from 254 Squadron on a reconnaissance patrol off the Norwegian coast. Since dawn, a pair of Messerschmitt Bf 109s had been circling over the task force, and it was one of these that first spotted the aircraft. They disappeared, though, and nobody knew whether or not they'd sighted the ships.

By then, the force had turned to starboard and was approaching the mouth of the Korsfjord. One of the advantages of this particular part of the Norwegian coast was that it had two entrances – this southern one and then a second one, above Bergen. Lütjens liked the flexibility that gave him, and the fact that he had the chance to use the coastal islands as cover as the task force headed north that evening. His plan was to lie low for the day in the Korsfjord and to top up their fuel tanks – something that was particularly important for the *Prinz Eugen*, whose tanks were running low after her voyage from Gotenhafen.

Initially, the Korsfjord ran towards the north-east, but after a few miles it opened out into a larger body of water that ran northwards towards Bergen. The long, hilly island Fjell lay to port, while to starboard was the Norwegian mainland. Other small islands lay dotted around the fjord, while small inlets lay off either side, the largest of which, on the north-east, led to the Norwegian city of Bergen. Müllenheim-Rechberg described how the rocky cliffs of the Norwegian coast appeared first, followed a little later by a barren, mountainous landscape.[2] As they entered the Korsfjord itself, picturesque houses could be seen, lit by the bright morning sunlight.

According to Lütjens' wishes, the ships now split up, with *Bismarck* heading into the Grimstadfjord on the eastern side of the Korsfjord, a little south of Bergen, while the *Prinz Eugen* and the destroyers continued northwards before dropping anchor in Kalvanes Bay, off the north-eastern side of Fjell, a few miles to the west of Bergen.

The *Bismarck* dropped anchor at 09.00, the ship protected by the narrowness of the small inlet, augmented by a couple of supply ships, which were ordered to anchor near the entrance to the inlet to protect the German battleship from torpedo attack.[3] Then they set about the business of waiting out the day. It was the same in Kalvanes Bay, where *Prinz Eugen* and the three destroyers had dropped anchor. Again, with no torpedo nets available it was up to the destroyers to form a protective shield around the cruiser, as did the German tanker *Wollin*, and two *Sperrbrecher* and more supply vessels.

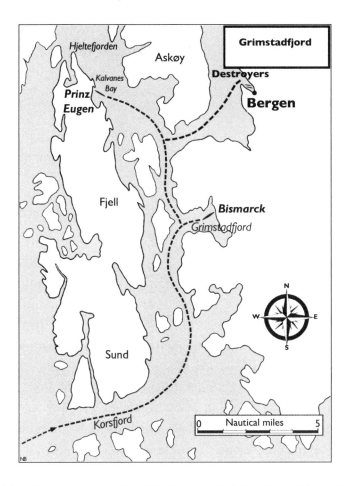

The plan was to use the *Wollin* to refuel the *Prinz Eugen* first, and then the *Bismarck*. The cruiser had used up a quarter of her fuel during the voyage north and needed this replenishment if she were to operate effectively in the North Atlantic. The destroyers were low on fuel, too, but as they weren't leaving Norwegian waters, their needs were less urgent. Accordingly, that forenoon and early afternoon, the *Prinz Eugen* took on fuel oil until her tanks were fully replenished.

Strangely, while the *Wollin* should have dropped down to the Grimstadfjord and done the same for *Bismarck*, neither

Lütjens nor Lindemann considered this particularly urgent, as the battleship's tanks were still around 90 per cent full.[4] Presumably – and the real reason may never be known – Lütjens planned to refuel the battleship from one of the tankers stationed in the north-western fringes of the North Atlantic. There was certainly time to do it in the Korsfjord – the fleet admiral planned to remain there all day and leave under cover of darkness. Instead, the *Wollin* remained at anchor in Kalvanes Bay. Perhaps the reason was that the fleet commander had realised that the British now knew where he was.

That morning, Lütjens gave the orders that both the *Bismarck* and *Prinz Eugen* should change their camouflage schemes.[5] Both ships carried what was known as a Baltic scheme, whereby the plain light-grey hulls were broken by two-colour black-and-white chevrons. Darker grey at the bow and the stern gave the illusion that the ship was shorter than it actually was, to confuse enemy rangefinders. This was augmented by false white waves at the fake bow and stern. Then, on the upper deck, at the ends of the focsle and quarterdeck of both ships, there was a black swastika inside a white circle. These were aircraft recognition patches, to spare the ships the ignominy of being bombed by their own air force. During the sojourn in Norway these were covered over with tarpaulins, but once at sea they were painted over in grey.

Then, on both *Bismarck* and *Prinz Eugen*, working parties were sent over the side to paint over the chevrons. This took most of the morning, but eventually it was done. The dark grey at the bow and stern were gone, too, but the bow wave remained. One final touch was the painting of the turret tops in a slightly darker grey. The result was a pair of ships whose appearances were better suited to the grey seas and grey skies of the North Atlantic than the waters of the Baltic Sea. This was the colour scheme the *Bismarck* wore when she sailed from the Grimstadfjord and would keep throughout the operation. That task done, the crews settled down to enjoy the rest of the long, sunlit afternoon.

THE BLUE SPITFIRE

Meanwhile, 320 miles to the south-west, a pair of Spitfires was taking off from RAF Wick, in the north-east tip of Scotland.[6] A year before, the Supermarine Spitfire fighter had been the mainstay of Great Britain's air defence during the Battle of Britain. These Mark III aircraft, however, were different. Rather than sporting a green-and-grey camouflage scheme, they were painted light grey-blue all over, to merge with the sky. They belonged to the Photo Reconnaissance Unit (PRU), and carried cameras rather than guns – four of them mounted in their fuselage, designed to take overlapping pictures of targets on the ground. These little planes had a range of 1,500 miles, and with a top speed of over 300mph they could also outpace most enemy fighters they ran into.

Their job was to locate the German task force that had been reported by Denham and Axelssen. One PRU Spitfire flown by Flying Officer (Fg Off.) Frank Greenhill was to reach the Norwegian coast near Stavanger and fly around it as far as Oslo. The other, flown by Fg Off. Mike Suckling, was to head north towards Bergen. Greenhill drew a blank and only spotted small patrol boats and merchant ships during his sweep. Suckling's sweep was proving fruitless, too, until he began approaching Bergen and flew up the Korsfjord. There, 27,000ft below him, was a large warship – probably a cruiser – surrounded by several merchant vessels.[7] The time was 13.15. His cameras clicked away at it, but also below him, Suckling noticed enemy fighters. So, he flew on, and was rewarded with the sighting of another cruiser in nearby Kalvanes Bay. He continued his probe of the fjord and then turned for home.

Back in a corner of the bleak airfield at Wick sat the PRU technical building. Once Suckling had landed, the cameras were unclipped from his Spitfire and taken straight to the darkroom there. Earlier in the war, this had been centralised, and film was sent south for development and analysis. Now, a two-tier system had taken its place and each PRU base had its own photographic laboratory where the prints were developed within an hour of the plane landing. These were then taken to an initial analysing team, who pored over them and made an evaluation. If the photographs revealed something of critical importance, then they would be studied in more detail and the negatives would be flown south for further examination. This meant that important or time-sensitive discoveries – such as the presence of major German warships – could be acted on without any unnecessary delay.

Suckling landed a little before 15.00, and within two hours the ships had been identified as a Bismarck class battleship in the Grimstadfjord and an Admiral Hipper class heavy cruiser in Kalvanes Bay.[8] The Admiralty were fairly certain they were the *Bismarck* and the *Prinz Eugen*. So, their next problem was what to do about this sighting. The immediate step was to inform Admiral Tovey in Scapa Flow. Then, RAF Coastal Command were contacted and asked to organise an air attack on the two anchorages. That evening, a force of 12 Hudson and six Whitley twin-engined bombers from 222, 269 and 619 Squadrons were sent from RAF Wick, carrying a mixture of 500lb bombs and flares.[9] However, when they reached the Bergen area two hours later they found the Korsfjord was blanketed in a layer of fog.

Only two of the Hudson bombers therefore actually managed to identify their target areas, and blindly dropped their ordnance into the murk below them, in the vicinity of Kalvanes Bay. The problem was, the weather conditions were changing. A strong wind had sprung up from the south-west, bringing rain, low cloud and poor visibility with it. The fog over Bergen was more of a local phenomenon – the region was well known for it. However, it was enough to hide the German task force. Worse, though, was to come. Back in Britain, a second, even larger, air attack was being coordinated.[10] This would have involved up to 30 two-engined bombers from RAF airfields in Caithness and Orkney – a mixture of bomb-carrying Hudsons and torpedo-armed Beauforts. Also prepared to join them were seven torpedo-armed Albacores from 828 Squadron, Fleet Air Arm.

However, by the evening of the 21st the rain and low cloud had swept in and the skies were completely overcast, with a cloud base of just 100ft. As a result, the mission was cancelled, which meant that nothing could be done until the following morning.[11] Even then, meteorologists predicted that the bad weather over Bergen was set to continue for up to 24 hours. So, there was nothing for it but to wait until dawn and then send off PRU aircraft and Coastal Command search planes in the hope of finding the Germans still anchored near Bergen, or else locating them somewhere in the Norwegian Sea. It was a tense night for the British, particularly for Admiral Tovey, who had to make his naval dispositions without any real idea of where the two German warships were, or which way they were heading.

A LAZY AFTERNOON

Back in the Grimstadfjord, the on-duty flak crews of the *Bismarck* had heard the sound of Suckling's aircraft and the anti-aircraft watch had been sounded.[12] However, the aircraft hadn't been spotted; the two Bf 109 fighters flying over the battleship remained unaware of the intruder, so the battleship's flak guns remained silent. It was only afterwards that the sound of the Spitfire's engine was heard over Kalvanes Bay and the alarm was raised. This, though, was the only thing to disturb what turned out to be a lazy, sun-kissed afternoon. Many of the crew took the opportunity to sun themselves on the upper deck, while a few tried their hand at fishing.[13] The battleship lay quite close to the north-eastern shore of the small inlet and her crew could spy Norwegian civilians standing outside their houses, staring at the largest vessel ever seen in their little bay.

It was an idyllic scene and the sailors were amused when they saw a little rowing boat put out from the shore, with a German soldier at the oars. As he reached the battleship he called up, saying he had run out of tobacco and begging the sailors for some cigarettes. Within minutes, several buckets had been lowered down, filled with enough cigarettes and tobacco to keep the soldier smoking for a year. Then the men went back to their sunbathing. The scene, however, was not without its detractors. A machinist heard another engineering technician say idly: 'Frightful, when you think in a week everyone sunning here on board today could be dead.'[14] Fortunately for the two engineers, they survived the week's events. Most of their shipmates were not so lucky.

Clearly, word of the *Bismarck*'s arrival had spread throughout the area. A little after noon, Maj. Otto Schneider, an army doctor based in Bergen, received a telephone call, telling him that the *Bismarck* was anchored less than 4.5 miles away, in the Grimstadfjord.[15] His brother served on board, and so he and two companions negotiated the use of a fast motorboat, which took them out into the Korsfjord, then down into the inlet to the south. Later, he described what he saw there: 'After a short fast ride we turned into a bay and saw a bewitching sight. Before us, the *Bismarck* lay like a silver-grey dream from *A Thousand and One Nights*. In spite of her mighty superstructure, gun barrels and armour, her silhouette was a thing of beauty, almost as though it were worked in filigree.'

Once alongside, he met his brother Adalbert and was invited aboard. Otto had been exhilarated by his speedboat ride, saying it did 32 knots. He was amazed when his brother told him *Bismarck* was just as fast, if not a little faster. Korvettenkapitän Adalbert Schneider was *Bismarck*'s chief gunnery officer, in charge of her main armament. He was evidently proud of his ship, and her abilities.[16] 'We're stronger than anything faster, and faster than anything stronger,' he boasted. He added, 'Nothing can really happen to us.' In the wardroom, where Otto was invited for lunch, he found a similar mood of optimism. One officer claimed that up to now their voyage had been 'a pleasure cruise'. However, the officers seemed a little more apprehensive when discussing what might happen next, when they tried to break out into the Atlantic.

Afterwards, Adalbert took Otto to his cabin, where he showed his brother a recent picture of his three daughters, and together they wrote joint postcards to friends and family, which Otto promised to mail home from Bergen. Kapitän Lindemann had graciously allowed Otto to remain on board while they sailed that evening, and agreed to put him ashore in the pilot boat when the *Bismarck* reached the open sea. This allowed the two brothers to spend some time together. Otto was also able to watch the battleship's crew prepare to sail. As a gunnery officer, Adalbert had no immediate duties and so the brothers were able to watch the departure, while talking about family, the war and their plans for the future.

Adalbert continued to reassure Otto that the *Bismarck* was as safe as she was powerful, but his brother was not wholly convinced. As *Bismarck* reached the northern mouth of the Korsfjord, Otto went to the bridge to thank Lindemann for his kindness.[17] They shook hands, but the doctor thought that Lindemann looked pale, and with hindsight he felt he seemed pensive. Still, the pilot boat came alongside; then Otto stepped aboard and waved farewell to his brother before the battleship was swallowed up in the darkness. It was the last time Otto Schneider saw his brother alive.

SLIPPING AWAY

When Lütjens learned of the mysterious aircraft he must have realised that his task force had been detected. He would have worked out that a reconnaissance plane would return to base, and any photographs it had taken might well reveal the location of his ships. That in turn meant that by the evening, the British were likely to launch a bombing raid on his two anchorages. It took three hours to refuel the *Prinz Eugen* from the *Wollin*. By that time, the fleet commander had decided that he couldn't linger in his pleasant anchorage. So, the refuelling of the *Bismarck* was cancelled, and the *Wollin* remained in Kalvanes Bay. Lütjens had other options:

the tanker *Weissenburg* was already at sea, lingering beyond the Arctic Circle, near Jan Mayen island; and other tankers were deployed off the southern tip of Greenland, or further south in the North Atlantic.[18] As a result, he felt he could accept the risk of not topping up *Bismarck's* fuel tanks in Norway while he had the chance.

This decision made, he spent the afternoon poring over charts or consulting with his intelligence staff. The indications from Group North were that the British Home Fleet were still at anchor in Scapa Flow. Recent photographs had been flown to Bergen, then shipped down to him. The same fuel constraints meant that his rival Admiral Tovey would only make his move when he had firm information about *Bismarck's* whereabouts. Thus, his greatest threat at the moment came from an air attack in Norwegian waters, or from British submarines patrolling off the coast. However, this could all change when the British reconnaissance plane reported its findings. So, the sooner his task force put to sea, the better.

At 19.00 that evening he gave orders for his ships to prepare to sail.[19] Thirty minutes later, at 19.30, the *Bismarck* raised her anchor and headed out of the Grimstadfjord into the main channel to the west. She steamed northwards and met the three waiting destroyers off the channel leading to Bergen. As the *Bismarck* passed Kalvanes Bay the *Prinz Eugen* came out and joined her. Then, in line astern, the task force threaded its way out of the channel leading towards the open sea. The line was led by *Sperrbrecher 13*, followed by *Bismarck*, then *Prinz Eugen* and *Sperrbrecher 31*. Astern of them came the three destroyers. Given the high risk of a British air strike, all of the crews were at anti-aircraft stations, and the lookouts scanned the sky ahead of them for signs of enemy bombers.

After passing Kalvanes Bay the line of ships entered the Hjeltefjorden, a 30-mile-long channel that led off to the north-north-west.[20] The task force sailed up the fjord at 17 knots, with the long, thin chain of islands on their port side shielding them from the open sea. If the British planes came, they would appear over this line of islands. However, the transit of the fjord continued without incident. At 20.00, the escorting Luftwaffe fighters had to break off, but by then they were far enough away from their old anchorage that the risk of air attacks had diminished. The Bergen pilot boat guided them through the channel past Herdla, where a German-manned battery on their starboard side guarded the approaches to Bergen. There, the fjord widened slightly into the Fedjeosen. It was a peaceful evening, despite the worsening weather, and the fog had lifted sufficiently to allow the officers grouped on the quarterdeck to see the wooded islands as they slipped by.

During this transit, Korvettenkapitän Rechberg, in charge of the flagship B-Dienst unit, brought an intercept to the bridge. It told Lütjens that the British Coastal Command aircraft were actively searching for him.[21] While this was worrying, it justified his decision to leave the anchorage. He was still one step ahead. As the line of ships passed the skerries fringing the island of Fedje, the *Bismarck* heaved-to for a moment, to drop Dr Schneider off in the pilot boat. The pilot was then detached and the warships headed out into the Norwegian Sea.

It was now dark, and as the destroyers took up position ahead and to the sides of the larger ships, they headed out towards the north-west at 20 knots, steering a zigzag course.[22] As the land fell away astern of them they noticed the wind had strengthened to a Force 4, and the sky was overcast. This was ideal since it made detection by enemy aircraft virtually impossible. It was then that Lütjens signalled Group North, asking for a fresh update on the Home Fleet in Scapa Flow – information that would help him decide which route he would take into the North Atlantic. Shortly before midnight, the staff navigator declared they were past the bulge in the coast to the north, and so the warships turned north. They were now heading deeper into the Norwegian Sea, towards the Arctic Circle.

It was then that lookouts saw a glow in the darkness astern of them.[23] It seemed to be coming from the Norwegian coast, somewhere close to Bergen. This was followed by a signal from Group North, which reported that five British aircraft had been sighted 6.2 miles north of Bergen, flying south. They had dropped bombs and flares over Kalvanes Bay, where the *Prinz Eugen* had been just a few hours before. While this wasn't the major bombing raid Lütjens had expected, it was clearly a prelude to it. The British were merely throwing in what was available that evening. Had they remained in the Korsfjord, the task force could have expected a much larger air attack there the following morning. The fleet admiral must have quietly congratulated himself on his sense of timing.

He was now safely back at sea and heading northwards towards the latitudes of the Faeroes and then Iceland. It was time to prepare for the breakout into the North Atlantic. One final message from Group North had told him that as of that afternoon, the major warships of the Home Fleet were still in Scapa Flow. That suggested that he had a reasonable chance of slipping through the British blockade without running into any enemy battleships. That must have been a reassuring thought. Little did Lütjens know, however, that at roughly the same time his force had turned north after leaving the Norwegian coast, V. Adm. Holland's flagship *Hood*, accompanied by *Prince of Wales* and six destroyers, had sailed from Scapa Flow and were at that moment speeding towards Iceland, with orders to intercept *Bismarck* and bring her to battle.

Chapter 7

Move and Countermove

THE GREEN PHONE

Early on 21 May, while Admiral Lütjens was approaching Bergen, Admiral Tovey was in his spacious cabin on board the *King George V*, swinging at her mooring off Flotta, in Scapa Flow. At 08.00, in the adjacent office, the green telephone rang.[1] It was answered by Commander (Cdr) Ronald Paffard, a supply officer and Admiral Tovey's secretary. He immediately called in the admiral's chief-of-staff, Commodore (Cdre) Patrick Brind. Known as 'Daddy' for his paternal nature, Brind was an experienced officer who first saw action at Jutland. He immediately understood the importance of the call. It was the Admiralty's intelligence section, passing on the information from Captain Denham's signal, sent from Stockholm the previous night. Two large German warships had passed through the Kattegat the previous afternoon, heading towards the north-west. Brind didn't need to glance at the chart to guess the importance of the news. As he knocked on the door of the admiral's cabin he already had a shrewd idea of what those two warships were, and where they were heading.

Once he'd heard Brind's report, Tovey was also pretty sure that the two warships were the *Bismarck* and *Prinz Eugen*. Recent intelligence reports had told him that both ships had just completed their training period in Gotenhafen and that preparations were being made for them to leave the Baltic port. An increase in German air activity – patrols over the North Sea and Norwegian Sea, and high-altitude reconnaissance flights over Orkney – all suggested something was about to happen. Then there was the news from the French Resistance that new battleship moorings were being prepared in Brest. It all pointed to one thing: the *Bismarck* was coming out. Cdre Brind agreed. The report from Denham might be wrong, or the German ships might just be on a training exercise, but Tovey really didn't think so. This was what he'd been waiting for.

First, however, he had to be sure. The Admiralty had already requested that the RAF conduct an aerial reconnaissance of the Norwegian fjords. That meant the PRU unit based in Wick. Before Tovey examined his options, he therefore gave Brind a series of orders – things that could be done right away. First, he put the fleet on short notice to sail.[2] Signal flags fluttered up the foremast of the flagship, and across the anchorage captains ordered their engineers to flash up boilers, and cancelled leave. Next, Tovey ordered Brind to call in Captain Wilfed Patterson, the ship's commanding officer, who confirmed the flagship was fully armed, stored and ready for sea. That left his other major units – the battlecruiser *Hood*, flagship of Tovey's second-in-command V. Adm. Lancelot Holland; the new battleship *Prince of Wales*; and the equally new aircraft carrier *Victorious*. Tovey wasn't too concerned about *Hood* – he knew Captain Kerr ran a well-ordered ship. He was more worried about the two newcomers.

For this reason, the admiral called his own staff officers into his day cabin, as well as V. Adm. Holland and Captain Kerr from the *Hood*, and Captain Leach from the *Prince of Wales*. *Victorious* had sailed from Scapa that morning to conduct exercises to the west of Orkney, so she would have to wait. On that calm and sunny day, as the routine of the anchorage continued, Tovey stayed in his day cabin, conferred with Holland and worked out his plan. Meanwhile, two PRU Spitfires were flying towards Norway and one would soon pass over the Korsfjord. Meanwhile, the routine of the anchored fleet went on as usual. Visits still continued to other ships, or to the naval bases and facilities at Lyness and Flotta. Ship's boats and drifters still plied around the anchorage, carrying mail to or from the ships, along with patients on their way to the shore hospital or naval dentist, sports teams to football or rugby games, and officers with fishing rods or golf clubs. Only the two admirals and their staffs spent the day waiting, planning and organising.

Then, in mid-afternoon, a call came through from the RAF airfield at Wick, 26 miles to the south, on the Scottish mainland. It broke the news that two warships had been spotted near Bergen – a Bismarck class battleship and a Hipper class cruiser. This was the news Tovey had been waiting for. He already knew that Coastal Command had been sending out search planes, but this was the first sighting of the missing warships. That gave him something to work with. Undoubtedly – as the PRU report said – these were the same large warships spotted in the Kattegat the previous day. So, Tovey knew where the enemy were. He now had to work out what the Germans intended to do, and how to stop them.

While a small RAF bomber force had been gathered to attack these warships, Tovey had little faith in them achieving very much. The weather was proving fickle, and a front of overcast skies and poor weather was moving in from the south-west. This meant that by the time a larger force had been gathered, the low cloud had rendered flying impossible. It also prevented any further PRU flights taking off. By late afternoon, the same conditions had settled over Orkney. However, this didn't stop Captain Leach of the *Prince of Wales* going ashore for a spot of fishing at the start of the Dog Watches (16.00), accompanied by two brothers, both officers on the battleship. A ship's boat landed them at Scapa Pier, where they waited for a taxi to whisk them off to the nearby Loch of Kirbister. Fortunately for the fish, they'd barely reached the loch when another car arrived and a breathless midshipman told the captain that the battleship had just received the signal 'raise steam without dispatch'. So, they raced back to the pier, where the ship's launch took them back on board.

The engineering officer had everything under control, so Captain Leach changed back into his uniform and waited for the inevitable summons to the flagship. Sure enough, the flag signal came at 19.40 and the captain's gig set off for the *King George V*, as did the admiral's barge from the *Hood*. Precedent demanded that V. Adm. Holland board first, so Leach and his crew waited in the lee of their sister ship before coming alongside the accommodation ladder. At 20.00, after being welcomed by Captain Patterson, the two officers walked aft to the admiral's cabin, where Tovey, Holland, Kerr and Brind were already waiting. Without further preamble, Tovey broke the news and announced his decision:[3] Holland would take the *Hood* and *Prince of Wales* to sea that evening, accompanied by six destroyers. Their job was to intercept the *Bismarck* and bring her to battle.

During the afternoon, Admiral Tovey had considered the task facing him and then made his decision. The first issue was figuring out what the Germans were doing there. They could just be escorting a convoy to Bergen, which explained all the merchant ships in the area. They might be heading further north, to establish a base near Trondheim or even Narvik, beyond the easy range of British bombers. They might even be part of a German force assembling to launch an invasion of Iceland. All of these were moves that could have far-reaching consequences for the Home Fleet. The most dangerous possibility, though, was that the two warships were planning to break out into the North Atlantic. This, then, was the contingency that Tovey had to plan for. At all costs he had to prevent the Germans from entering the vastness of the Atlantic, where they would be much harder to find, and where every Allied convoy would be a potential target.

The question was, which route would the Germans take to get there?[4] The presence of British airfields in Shetland, Orkney and the north of Scotland meant that it was unlikely they would break out by the two more southern avenues, between Orkney and Shetland, or Shetland and the Faeroes. Air patrols saw to that. They were also too close to Scapa Flow, which made it relatively easy for the Home Fleet to intercept the enemy as they passed through the gap. That, then, left the two more northerly routes – the Denmark Strait between Greenland and Iceland, and the route between Iceland and the Faeroes. The first was 175 miles wide, but at that time of year the coast of Greenland was still girded by pack ice, a floating barrier of ice that extended roughly 80–90 miles

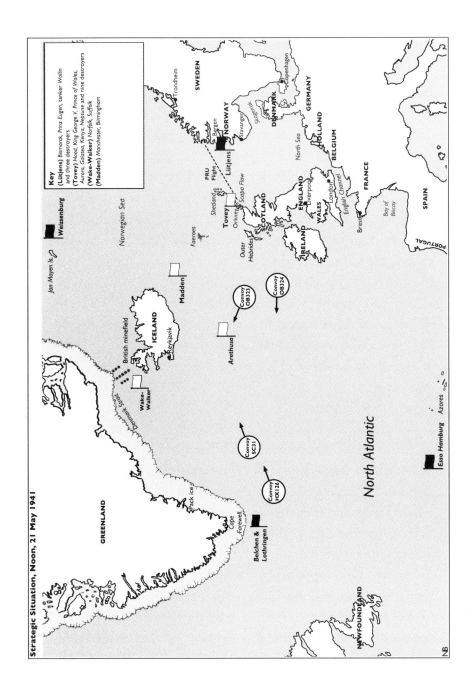

out from the coast. That reduced the navigable waters of the Denmark Strait by half.

In April 1941, the British 1st Minelaying Squadron had also laid a minefield off the north-west corner of Iceland, which extended out into the Denmark Strait. This effectively reduced the navigable channel to just 50 miles – a space that could be patrolled by a pair of cruisers. Between January and March, a double belt of mines had also been laid in the Iceland–Faeroes gap, working out from the coastal waters of both islands. That reduced the 240-mile-wide gap to a more manageable 140 miles, although problems with the premature detonation of mines suggested these fields weren't as effective as the Admiralty had hoped.[5] Still, a squadron of cruisers stationed in this gap should be able to spot any German warships trying to pass through their patrol line. Tovey already had cruisers covering both gaps. He just needed to make sure they were ready for the Germans when they came.

Two days previously, Tovey had sent the heavy cruiser *Suffolk* from Scapa to the Denmark Strait, to reinforce the cruiser *Norfolk*, which was flying the flag of Rear Admiral (R. Adm.) Wake-Walker.[6] The day before, the light cruiser *Arethusa* had also been sent north, to join the light cruisers *Manchester* and *Birmingham*, which were patrolling the Iceland–Faeroes gap. Tovey ordered both *Arethusa* and *Suffolk* to refuel in Hvalfjord, the British base outside Reykjavik, so they were fully 'topped up' before joining the patrol lines. He'd also requested a stepping up of air patrols from Iceland, the Faeroes and Shetland. This dealt with Tovey's first line of defence – his early-warning tripwire. Now he had to make sure it was supported by warships that were capable of actually bringing the *Bismarck* to battle.

Late that afternoon, he decided to send V. Adm. Holland in the *Hood* to the waters off Iceland, accompanied by the *Prince of Wales*.[7] This was done with some reservation, because the brand-new battleship was clearly not fully ready to fight. Workmen were still labouring on her gun turrets and her largely inexperienced crew were still learning their jobs. However, Captain Leach insisted that she was ready for action. In fact, without any other battleship apart from his own flagship, Tovey had little option but to include her in Holland's force. So, both ships were ordered to put to sea as soon as possible. Cdre Brind had already set the departure in motion by ordering the six destroyers to sea, to wait in the Pentland Firth. Now it was the turn of the two capital ships.

It was about 21.30 when Holland and his captains returned to their ships.[8] The crews had all been fed and the men were settling down for a quiet night at anchor. On board *Prince of Wales* Captain Leach called his senior officers to his cabin, told them the plan, then ordered the ship to prepare to sail. Minutes later, the tannoy announced, 'Special sea dutymen, close up at the double'. This could only mean one thing. All thoughts of a quiet night were abandoned as the seamen pulled on their coats and rushed on to the upper deck, ready to slip the ship's mooring. Half a mile away, the same thing was happening on board the *Hood*. Soon, both ships were skirting around Flotta and into Hoxa Sound, where they passed through the defensive boom. With the *Hood* leading, the two great warships, barely visible in the overcast night, slipped out of Scapa Flow. Just in case of trouble, both crews were at Action Stations.

Then, after the destroyers had formed an anti-submarine screen around them, Holland ordered the force to head west, out towards the open Atlantic. Shortly before midnight, they passed out of the Pentland Firth, picked up speed and set a course for Iceland. Holland's instructions were clear: his ships were to head to Hvalfjord, where if possible they would refuel. Then his capital ships were to take up a position to the south-west of Iceland, where they could intercept the *Bismarck* if she entered the Denmark Strait. However, if the Germans came the other way they could also seal off the Iceland–Faeroes gap. This meant waiting there until a sighting was made by one of the two patrol lines. Accordingly, the two capital ships rushed on into the night, while at the same moment, 260 miles to the north-east, *Bismarck* and *Prinz Eugen* were also at sea, with their own escort of three destroyers, making their way northwards from Bergen. Soon, both forces would be on a collision course.

THE SHELL GAME

That night, on board the *Bismarck*, Admiral Lütjens faced his own dilemma. He had to break out into the North Atlantic, and ideally do it without being detected. The latest aerial reconnaissance report from Scapa Flow showed that the capital ships of the Home Fleet were still in the anchorage. Of course, this had been taken before the *Hood* and *Prince of Wales* had set off towards Iceland. He now had to decide which of the three main routes to take to reach the Atlantic. Ideally, he also hoped to do it without being detected.

His dilemma was a lot like the age-old cups and balls routine made famous by magicians, and which tricksters turned into a con that they called the 'shell game'. In this fraudster form, a ball was hidden beneath three cups and, in front of a watching audience, the cups were switched round repeatedly, before a watcher was asked to say which cup now contained the ball. In reality, the ball was moved out from one cup and placed in another one *after* the watcher had chosen what he thought was the right cup.

Now Lütjens had to perform a similar sleight of hand, and hope the British chose the wrong cup. It was a trick he'd pulled off before: during Operation *Berlin* he played the shell game to perfection, enticing the British by probing the Iceland–Faeroes gap, and then doubling back around Iceland to reappear in the Denmark Strait. This time round, he had to choose the right cup in which to hide his ball. While the German naval command favoured the Iceland–Faeroes gap, Lütjens had successfully used the Greenland–Iceland gap during Operation *Berlin*, and clearly preferred this route.[9] It lay further from Scapa Flow, and if the Home Fleet's capital ships were still there then he would probably make it through before they could intercept him. Enemy cruisers were likely to be patrolling both of the gaps, but they posed no real threat to the *Bismarck*. He had already ruled out the third option – the Faeroes–Shetland gap – as it lay even closer to Scapa, and was regularly patrolled by British search planes.

The bad weather might help screen him, but it was still too great a risk. So that reduced his three cups to just two. Interestingly, back in Berlin, Grossadmiral Raeder had briefed Hitler on Operation *Rheinübung*, but apart from minor quibbles about maintaining American neutrality, the German leader had no objections to the operation. Raeder, though, had to confess that he had no real control over it; Admiral Lütjens, the man on the spot, had full control over what happened. So, while Raeder might have preferred one route over another, the ultimate decision lay with the fleet commander. During the early hours of 22 May the German ships therefore headed north, while the coast of Norway gradually fell away to the east.

By now it was pretty clear that the more southerly of the three routes was no longer an option – they'd gone too far north – but apart from telling Kapitän Lindemann, Admiral Lütjens preferred to keep his plans to himself, though of course that didn't stop the crews of both warships trying to guess where they were heading. At around 04.00, the three accompanying destroyers were detached and ordered to head in to Trondheim.[10] Where the capital ships were going was no place for destroyers – they lacked the range to operate that far from home. That left *Bismarck* and *Prinz Eugen* very much on their own. As dawn broke on 22 May it was clear that the weather had deteriorated during the night. This suited Lütjens perfectly as it made detection less likely. This was clearly an important consideration, as at 11.00 a radio message from Group North in Wilhelmshaven informed him the RAF had bombed the Korsfjord – an action that confirmed that the British definitely knew he was in Norwegian waters.[11]

That changed things slightly. The likelihood was that the Home Fleet would assume he was trying to break out into the Atlantic, and Admiral Tovey would deploy his ships accordingly. Lütjens still thought he had a head start – he had no idea *Hood* and *Prince of Wales* had sailed – and this may well have influenced his decision. If he headed through the Iceland–Faeroes gap, the breakout attempt would take place that evening and during the night of 22–23 May. If he opted for the Denmark Strait, it would take place the following night – 23–24 May. If Tovey had led the Home Fleet to sea that morning, he might just be in place to block either passage in time to stop Lütjens. However, the Denmark Strait was

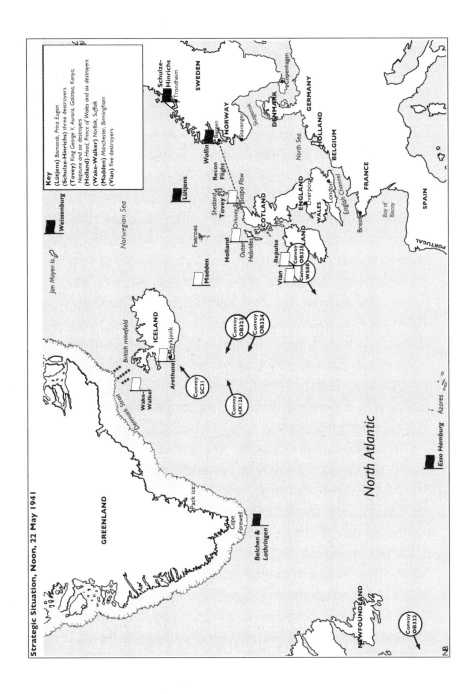

Strategic Situation, Noon, 22 May 1941

Key
(Lütjens) *Bismarck, Prinz Eugen*
(Schulze-Hinrichs) three destroyers
(Tovey) *King George V, Aurora, Galatea, Kenya,*
Neptune and six destroyers
(Holland) *Hood, Prince of Wales and six destroyers*
(Wake-Walker) *Norfolk, Suffolk*
(Madden) *Manchester, Birmingham*
(Vian) five destroyers

sufficiently far enough away to make this a race the Germans stood a good chance of winning.

As the day wore on the two German ships drew further away from the Norwegian coast. By mid-afternoon they were beyond the range of friendly air cover; only long-range reconnaissance aircraft could patrol that far out into what had now become the Arctic Sea. They were also beyond the reach of British air patrols. Had they been in range, and if a British aircraft had seen them, it would have reported that the two ships were making 24 knots and were now steering towards the north-west, on a course that would lead them directly around the northern coast of Iceland. The only break in the routine came at 12.37, when a periscope was sighted.[12] The two ships went to Action Stations again, increased speed and started zigzagging. In fact, no Allied submarines were in the area. It was a false alarm. More importantly, at 16.00 they entered a bank of light fog, which completely cloaked them throughout the last hours of daylight. On board *Bismarck*, the fleet meteorologist Dr Heinz Externbrink suggested this favourable weather would continue as they rounded the coast of Iceland.[13]

He was right. Shortly after 18.00 the fog became thicker, and visibility dropped to less than 1,300ft. For Lütjens, it was perfect weather. The following day he would be within range of British search aircraft operating from airfields in Iceland. This would serve as the ideal shield, cloaking his two ships as they sped towards the Denmark Strait. In fact, it was so thick that as darkness fell *Bismarck* and *Prinz Eugen* had to switch on their searchlights and all navigation lights so they could keep track of each other in the fog-laden darkness. Best of all, shortly after 23.00, the radio room on board *Bismarck* received a signal from Group North.[14] It reported two key pieces of information. First, that radio intercepts suggested that the German force had not been sighted. This implied that Lütjens' rival Admiral Tovey was still in the dark over which of the three cups to look under. It added that there was still no sign that the British were even trying to intercept him.

The best news from Wilhelmshaven, however, concerned a reconnaissance flight over Scapa Flow. Earlier that day, the high-level flight revealed that four battleships and an aircraft carrier were still in the anchorage, together with numerous smaller ships. Lütjens was well aware of Tovey's strength. That meant that *Hood, Prince of Wales, King George V* and one other battleship or battlecruiser were still in port. So too was the new carrier *Victorious*. He had won the race. With only a cruiser screen expected in the Denmark Strait – one that could easily be brushed aside – there was nothing to stop him breaking out into the Atlantic. Little did he know that this report was wildly inaccurate. *Hood* and *Prince of Wales* were already well on their way to Iceland, and in fact at that moment they were just 450 miles to the south-west of him. Low cloud over Orkney that day, and possibly the presence of two dummy battleships made of wood and canvas, had outfoxed the Luftwaffe airmen. That evening, Lütjens must have felt very content indeed.

At dawn the following morning – 23 May – Dr Externbrink's prediction proved correct. The fog continued, as did the rough weather, blowing in from the south-east, but veering easterly. It was the perfect weather for a breakout. At this point Lütjens had another decision to make. He could alter course to the north and refuel from the tanker *Weissenburg*, waiting for him off Jan Mayen island, 260 miles to the north, which would delay his transit of the Denmark Strait for a day. Or he could press on, hoping to pass through the narrow channel before Tovey's capital ships arrived to block his route. Some armchair historians have criticised the German fleet commander for not 'topping up' from the tanker *Wollin* in the Korsfjord, or the *Weissenburg* in the Arctic Ocean. However, Lütjens still had two tankers ahead of him, the *Belchen* and *Lothringen*, stationed off the southern tip of Greenland, so refuelling this early in the mission wasn't imperative.[15] More importantly, based on the intelligence he'd been given, he thought that if he pressed on, he'd win the race through the Denmark Strait.

So, the German ships maintained their course and speed. By noon, the *Bismarck*'s navigator, Korvettenkapitän Wolf Neuendorf, announced that they were now due north of Iceland. That meant that the huge ice-clad land mass of Greenland lay off their starboard bow, fringed by its thick lifebelt of pack ice. He calculated that they would enter the northern mouth of the Denmark Strait that evening, at around 17.00.[16] This would herald the start of the British minefields and the waiting British cruisers. Meanwhile, for the next six hours or so, the crew had nothing to do but rest before what most suspected would be a challenging night. However, as Müllenheim-Rechberg noted: 'In the afternoon visibility increased to 50 kilometres, but before long intermittent heavy snow caused it to vary considerably between one point on the horizon and another.' Still, by now Lütjens was committed, and his ships steamed on towards the Denmark Strait.

TOVEY'S RESPONSE

Back in Scapa Flow, Admiral Tovey was still in the dark. Since that photograph taken by Fg Off. Suckling in the early afternoon of 22 May, he had had no news of the German ships. It was unlikely they were still anchored near Bergen, but he needed hard information before he could commit his last reserves – the battleship *King George V* and the aircraft carrier *Victorious*. When the carrier returned to Scapa following a series of exercises, Tovey signalled her, asking Captain Henry Bovell whether he thought she was fully ready. After all, the air crews were largely inexperienced, the carrier was new, its aircraft had only embarked on her a few days before, and she was laden with crated-up fighters, bound for the Mediterranean.

Bovell was clearly keen to take part in the coming operation, but he was a professional, so deferred the decision to Cdr Herbert Ranald, his flight operations officer, and his senior squadron commander, Lieutenant-Commander (Lt Cdr) Eugene Esmonde, a veteran of the Taranto raid – the Fleet Air Arm's finest hour.[17] The three officers conferred and agreed that although the crews were inexperienced, *Victorious* was the only carrier in Scapa Flow, and the air crews were at least keen to play their part. So, Tovey agreed to add *Victorious* to his force. Still, though, the carrier and flagship remained at anchor throughout the 23rd, as the admiral waited for news of the enemy. And therein lay the real problem. With low cloud blanketing Norway, there was little chance of spotting anything until the weather cleared.

The bad news had begun for Tovey that morning. A phone call revealed that of the 18 bombers that flew from Wick the previous evening, only two had managed to drop their bombs over the target area, and even then it was shrouded in murk. That morning, every reconnaissance flight had been forced to give up due to the low cloud. It made for an extremely frustrating day on board the flagship. Had *Bismarck* and *Prinz Eugen* sailed? Tovey was now pretty sure of their identity – intelligence reports confirmed they had sailed from Gotenhafen five days before. Were they still in the Korsfjord? Every few hours, Cdr Frankie Lloyd marked the admiral's chart, showing the *Bismarck*'s 'furthest on position' from the sighting in the fjord the day before. That was based on the distance the battleship could have steamed since the sighting. Every four hours the circle expanded by 100 miles. It was all deeply worrying.

His break came through a phone call with Captain Henry St John Fancourt, the commanding officer of *Sparrowhawk* – the naval air station at Hatston, on the outskirts of Kirkwall.[18] It was largely a training base, and home to squadrons from carriers in Scapa Flow. However, it also was home to a squadron of Albacore torpedo bombers. That morning, Fancourt flew them up to Sumburgh in Shetland, 100 miles closer to Bergen, just in case the weather cleared and they had a chance to launch an attack. The Norwegian coast, however, remained blanketed in fog. While this put off Coastal Command's search planes, it didn't deter Cdr Geoffrey 'Hank' Rotherham. He was Fancourt's second-in-command, but he was an experienced observer and had a reputation for both skill and daring. 'Hank' persuaded Fancourt to give him a go at finding *Bismarck*. If anyone could in these conditions, it was Rotherham.

Fancourt did, however, have certain stipulations. After all, he was placing a plane and crew in jeopardy. First, he had to clear the mission with both Admiral Tovey and Air Marshal Sir Frederick Bowhill, the head of Coastal Command. Rotherham planned to use an American-built Martin Maryland twin-engined bomber. Part of 771 Squadron, she was used by the Fleet Air Arm as a target-towing plane, and belonged to Coastal Command. With approval given by both Tovey and Bowhill, Fancourt's final stipulation was that it had to be an all-volunteer crew. Within minutes, Rotherham had three volunteers for the three-crew plane – the acting commander of 771 Squadron, Lt Noel Goddard RNVR (Royal Navy Volunteer Reserve), and Leading Airmen Armstrong and Milne. At 16.30, the four men took off, with Goddard at the controls.[19] With a cruising speed of 248mph the Maryland made the crossing in just over an hour. This was tricky flying: even at 80ft they couldn't see the sea, and after each of three attempts Goddard headed back into the clouds, despite advice from Coastal Command to fly at 200ft, in order to keep below German coastal radar and to avoid enemy fighters.

On the last dip down to sea level the experienced Rotherham noticed the wind had changed, and altered course slightly to compensate. Then, after 70 minutes, they reached their estimated landfall and he asked Goddard to drop down to the sea again, for another look. The plan was to reach the Norwegian coast off Marstein, a rocky island marking the entrance to the Korsfjord. As they dropped down below 100ft the clouds parted for a moment, and they saw the rock with its lighthouse dead ahead of them.

Miraculously, the clouds there were at 150ft, and Goddard flew just below them, as the men scanned the Korsfjord below them. They looked into Grimstadfjord and Kalvanes Bay, but found them empty, apart from a few merchant ships. They pressed on to Bergen itself, flying over the roofs of the town, and drawing flak from the German defenders. They were hit, but no real damage was done. On the way out Goddard even flew up the Hjeltefjorden – the likely exit the German ships might have taken. Nothing. It was clear by now that the birds had flown.

After leaving the Norwegian coast, they headed due west, as Rotherham and Armstrong tried to radio a sighting report on the Coastal Command network. There was no reply. Then they tried calling the control tower at Sparrowhawk, using the frequency used for target-towing exercises. They got through, but for good measure Rotherham had them fly straight to Sumburgh in Shetland, the nearest friendly airfield. As soon as they touched down at 19.45 he ran to the tower to call in a report, only to find a message from Cdre Brind on board the *King George V*. His transmission had got through, but Brind wanted a full report to pass on to Tovey. This done, the plane was refuelled and they headed back to Orkney. By then, though, Tovey had the information he needed. While the report was a negative one – the German ships had gone – at least the admiral now had something to work with. He could make his move.

Earlier that afternoon, he had been dealing with the scattered units of his fleet.[20] *Norfolk* was in the Denmark Strait, while *Suffolk* was refuelling in Hvalfjord in Iceland. He therefore ordered the *Suffolk* to join the *Norfolk* immediately, giving Wake-Walker two heavy cruisers with which to patrol the entrance to the Denmark Strait. Similarly, he ordered *Arethusa*, which was also refuelling in Iceland, to head east at full speed and join the patrol line of cruisers blocking the Iceland–Faeroes gap. Finally, he sent a signal to the battlecruiser *Repulse*, which was in the Clyde, where a convoy was forming up. She was ordered to refuel, then head north at full speed to rendezvous with the Home Fleet either in Scapa Flow or at sea, somewhere to the west of Orkney. As it happened, Captain William Tennant of the *Repulse* received his new orders at 22.00 that evening, as he was steaming past the island of Islay. He would rendezvous with Tovey at 07.00 the following morning (24 May), to the north-west of the Outer Hebrides.

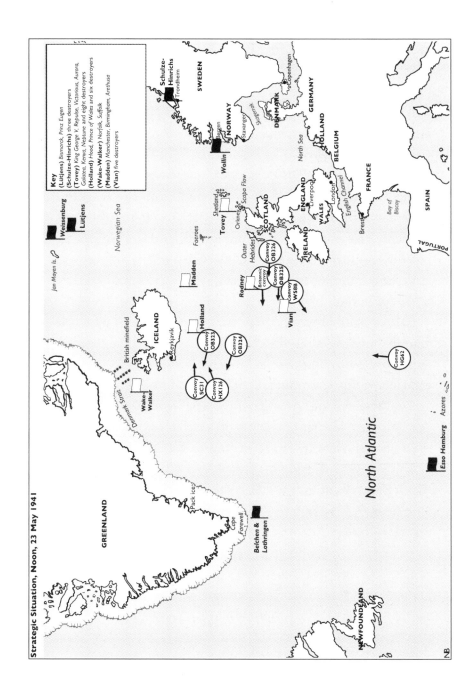

Strategic Situation, Noon, 23 May 1941

Key
(Lutjens) *Bismarck, Prinz Eugen*
(Schulze-Hinrichs) three destroyers
(Tovey) *King George V, Repulse, Victorious, Aurora,*
Galatea, Kenya, Neptune and eight destroyers
(Holland) *Hood, Prince of Wales* and six destroyers
(Wake-Walker) *Norfolk, Suffolk*
(Madden) *Manchester, Birmingham, Arethusa*
(Vian) five destroyers

Those deployments out of the way, Tovey was free to deal with his main force. That evening, *King George V* and *Victorious* were already at short notice to sail, and just before 21.00 the long-awaited order was flashed out by signal lamp.[21] The two ships would put to sea at 22.15, accompanied by the light cruisers *Aurora, Galatea, Hermione* and *Kenya*, plus six destroyers – *Active, Inglefield, Intrepid, Lance, Punjabi* and *Windsor.* Tovey still had no idea where the German ships were, but he had to presume the worst – they were about to attempt to break out into the Atlantic. His plan was therefore to place this powerful force – the bulk of the Home Fleet – to the south of Iceland. That way they could intercept any breakout attempt, whether the Germans headed through the Denmark Strait or the Iceland–Faeroes gap.

That night, Tovey's force duly slipped past the opened boom and headed out into the Pentland Firth. After picking up *Repulse* at 07.00 the next morning, they would then alter course slightly towards the east-north-east, and head out into the vastness of the Atlantic. By then, though – even before the Home Fleet steamed out of Scapa Flow – contact had been made with the enemy. Admiral Tovey knew where the enemy were, and R. Adm. Wake-Walker's two cruisers were busy playing cat and mouse with a German battleship and her powerful consort.

Chapter 8

The Denmark Strait

FIRST CONTACT

Being a lookout on an open-topped bridge was often an unpleasant duty. It was particularly so that evening on board *Norfolk*, as the British heavy cruiser loitered off the northwest corner of Iceland. It was freezing cold, intermittent icy rain showers soaked everyone on the bridge, and the lookouts were forced to keep as sharp an eye out for ice floes as they did for the Germans.[1] Huddled in his duffle coat, wearing his senior officer's cap pulled down tight, was R. Adm. Frederic Wake-Walker. The somewhat dour 58-year-old commander of the 1st Cruiser Squadron was sipping a cup of cocoa and peering into the fog swirling off the Icelandic coast. He had been in the navy since he was 15, had seen service in the last war, and was an expert in torpedo warfare.

In April 1940, as the rear admiral running Dover Command, he coordinated the evacuation from Dunkirk. When his flagship, the destroyer *Keith*, was sunk under him, he continued supervising the evacuation from a motor torpedo boat. Wake-Walker was therefore a determined man, and he knew his job. What's more, on the evening of 23 May 1941 he was a man with a very clear mission: his task was to spot any German ships trying to slip through the Denmark Strait. He was then to shadow them and send reports back to Admiral Tovey. He wasn't there to fight the *Bismarck* – only to help other, more powerful, warships to bring her to battle.

When the *Bismarck* first began her sortie, Wake-Walker's flagship *Norfolk* was heading north to the Denmark Strait to relieve her near sister-ship *Suffolk*, commanded by Captain Robert Ellis.[2] When the flagship arrived there Ellis and his men had been on patrol there for 11 days in cold, miserable weather. *Suffolk* was low on fuel. So, on 18 May – the day *Bismarck* left Gotenhafen – *Suffolk* was ordered to break off and head for Hvalfjord in Iceland in order to refill her oil tanks. She made the passage at night, and the following evening she returned to her station, by which time *Norfolk* had arrived to keep her company. Wake-Walker's flagship had refuelled in Hvalfjord before she took up station, so now both cruisers were fully 'topped up' and ready for business.

On 22 May, while *Bismarck* and *Prinz Eugen* were in Bergen, Wake-Walker took the *Norfolk* in to Isafjorður, where a new British radar station was being set up on the bleak rocky headland on its northern side, from which it could sweep the approaches to the Denmark Strait. It wasn't operational yet – work had only just started – but Wake-Walker inspected it, and being a keen amateur botanist, he also seized the opportunity to look out for local wild flowers. The following morning, *Suffolk* also edged into the fjord and Wake-Walker asked Ellis to join him and Captain Alfred Phillips of the *Norfolk* so that they could discuss the patrol.[3] He shared the latest intelligence reports – the fact that *Bismarck* had left the Korsfjord – and added that he expected that she and her consort, a heavy cruiser, would make for the Denmark Strait. Ellis returned to his ship, and minutes later the flagship ordered her to put to sea.

The plan was for *Suffolk* to move to within 15 miles of the Greenland pack ice and patrol the entrance of the Denmark Strait, cruising on a north-easterly course, then reversing course every three hours. In daylight, this meant that *Suffolk*'s lookouts would be able to spot any enemy ship entering the western side of the Strait. These lookouts had a vital role to play – any delay in sighting *Bismarck* could lead to the cruiser being ripped apart by the battleship's guns. To help them, *Suffolk* also carried a Type 273 search radar, which in theory could detect large surface ships at a range of up to 18 miles.[4] In practice, 13 miles was more realistic. *Norfolk* carried a similar set, but while the one on *Suffolk* could be turned to make it more effective, and covered everywhere apart from astern of the ship, *Norfolk*'s set was fixed and had a more limited 150-degree arc, ahead of the cruiser.

So, while *Suffolk* cruised off the pack ice, *Norfolk* took up position about 15 miles south of her, further out into the Strait. That afternoon, as the cruisers began their patrol, a thick freezing fog clung to the Icelandic coast, extending 30 miles out into the Strait. Still, the minefields would seal off the eastern side of the Strait. Everywhere else visibility was good – as much as 20 miles; Ellis and his men could even see the glaciers of Greenland in the distance. The sea was relatively calm, although meteorological reports suggested the fog over Iceland would spread and thicken a little during the evening. So, if *Bismarck* and her consort made a run through the Denmark Strait that evening, Wake-Walker was confident his men would spot them.

The lookouts and radar operators on the two cruisers weren't the only ones looking for the Germans. Almost 500 miles to the south-east, seamen on board the light cruisers *Arethusa*, *Birmingham* and *Manchester* were also at full alert.[5] So too were the men on board the smaller vessels of the Northern Patrol, cruising the same waters, or those between the Faeroes and Orkney. The airmen of Coastal Command, too, were doing the same, now that the low skies had lifted slightly, and patrol aircraft were active between Iceland and Orkney. To the west of Scapa Flow, Tovey and his Home Fleet were at sea, eagerly waiting for the first sighting report. Similarly, V. Adm. Holland's force was well on the way to the Denmark Strait, ready to seal it off. So far, however, there was no sign of the enemy.

The afternoon wore on. On board *Suffolk*, Captain Ellis was thankful that during the ship's refit in Greenock the previous year the cruiser's bridge had been 'Articised', i.e. enclosed and provided with heating. While bridge lookouts still looked through its windows with binoculars, others wrapped in duffle coats and woolly hats remained outside, stamping their feet to keep warm and peering into the distance. While Ellis was delighted with his new radar, he was aware that it didn't cover astern of him, and funnel smoke also helped obscure the view behind the bridge. So, on the south-western leg of his patrol he knew he was largely blind – a situation that required him to station extra lookouts in the stern superstructure. So, on that leg he veered over towards the middle of the Strait, close to the edge of the bank of fog. That way, if he were taken by surprise, he could hide his ship in the murk. His job was to spot the enemy, not to fight them.

18.00 marked the changing of a watch – the end of the First Dog and the start of the Last Dog Watch. Unlike the other five watches in the naval day, these lasted two hours rather than four – the idea being to make the total number of watches an odd number, so helping to vary the crew's watchkeeping routine. In fact, Ellis had been changing his lookouts every hour that afternoon – it paid to keep them sharp and keyed up. That Last Dog Watch, his scheme paid off. At 19.00, an hour after the start of the watch, Able Seaman Alf 'Ginger' Newall took up his position as the after starboard lookout, stationed just outside the bridge. By 19.20 he had been at his post for 20 minutes, and in that time he'd noticed that the fog had become patchy and seemed to be spreading closer to the ship.[6] Over towards Greenland the distant horizon had become obscured, too, and visibility was dropping as dusk crept in. Then he tensed, raised his binoculars and peered through them again.

His job was to sweep the starboard side of the *Suffolk*, from her beam to dead astern. He must have made that same sweep dozens of times that evening, and seen nothing. The cruiser was heading towards the south-west, on the return leg of her patrol. That meant her radar wasn't going to pick up anything behind her. So, it was up to Ginger and his shipmates to detect anything coming up astern of them. He was getting bored of looking at empty sea and sky, and at 19.22, after another sweep of the empty horizon, he lowered his binoculars to his lap and rubbed his eyes. When he opened them again he spotted something – a ship emerging on the haze-filled horizon. Then, as he peered through his binoculars, he saw another one emerge behind it. He immediately called out to the officer of the watch: 'Bearing Green One Four Oh – two ships!' On the bridge, everyone turned to look along that bearing – over the starboard quarter of the cruiser. Now there was no doubt. Ginger had spotted the *Bismarck*.

A GAME OF CAT AND MOUSE

On board the *Bismarck* that evening, the tension increased as the two German ships approached the northern end of the Denmark Strait. Officially, the Strait began at a line running between Straumnes, the north-western tip of Iceland's Westfjord peninsula, and Cape Nansen in Greenland, roughly 200 miles away to the north-west. Until 18.00 that evening, *Bismarck*, followed by *Prinz Eugen*, had been running due west, towards the coast of Greenland and its girdle of pack ice. Earlier, a fresh meteorological report from Group North suggested that the poor visibility might continue, with rain, low cloud and patchy fog. However, the visibility improved during the day, although patches of snow tended to hinder the job of the lookouts.[7] It was also freezing, and as the ships steamed on towards that invisible line in the sea, fragments of ice in the water tinkled against their metal hulls.

They were making 25 knots now, and ahead of them the crews saw the line of blue-white pack ice fringing the Greenland coast. Then, beyond it, due west, the ice-covered glaciers of Greenland itself appeared, clear against the late afternoon sky. As Müllenheim-Rechberg put it: 'I had to resist the temptation to let myself be bewitched by this icy landscape longer than was compatible with the watchfulness required of us all, as we steamed at high speed through the narrowest part of the strait.'[8] The *Bismarck*'s FuMo23 radar – one each on top of the forward and after superstructure – swept the surrounding waters as they went. In theory, it could

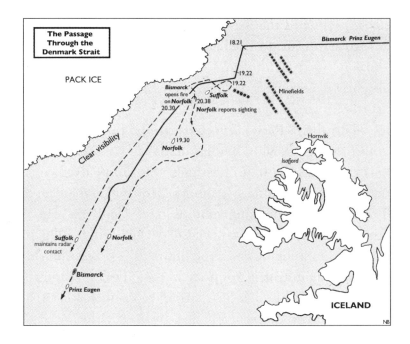

detect an enemy ship at 13.5 miles. In practice, though, for ships smaller than battleships, a range of 6 miles was more realistic. The ship's SB hydrophones also provided another form of warning, as the operators listened for the sound of ships' propellers.

At 18.11 the alarm bells sounded – enemy ships spotted to starboard.[9] A moment later, however, everyone relaxed. The lookouts had spotted icebergs rising out of the pack ice, and the cold air and tense atmosphere had led to the imagination of one lookout playing tricks. Still, it was now clear that they were approaching the outer edge of the pack ice. So, at 18.21, Lütjens ordered his ships to turn to port and follow a course towards the south-south-west. By then, he reckoned he was safely past the line of the British minefields and as close to the western side of the channel as he could sensibly go. A half-mile astern, *Prinz*

Eugen followed the flagship, and together they entered the Denmark Strait. Just before 19.00 they found ice floes had broken off from the pack ice and the ships had to zigzag slightly to keep clear of them – something that helped keep everyone on their toes.

Müllenheim-Rechberg noted that off to port there was a thick wall of fog, while immediately to their right were broken pieces of pack ice. It was freezing cold and the visibility ahead of them was crystal clear, but that haze on the southern horizon meant that the lookouts could only see a few miles ahead of them. Patches of fog appeared, too, between the fog bank and the pack ice. Then, at 19.22, the alarm was sounded.[10] The crews of both ships were already at Action Stations, standing alternate watches, which meant that most people were already at their posts. The alarm had been sounded by the hydrophone operator, who had picked up the sound of twin propellers off their port bow. Müllenheim-Rechberg was at the battleship's after gunnery director, but even with its powerful rangefinding equipment he couldn't see anything. Then the radar picked up the contact too. Something was definitely out there.

The radar contact revealed a ship, possibly an enemy cruiser, heading south-south-west – directly away from them – at high speed. The lookouts thought they saw a glimpse of her, but the fog made it difficult to make her out. Then, a brief rent in the wall of fog revealed her shadowy outline, fine off their port bow. It was a three-masted warship – undoubtedly a British heavy cruiser. The battleship's guns were already trained in that direction, but before they could fire, the target disappeared again. Quite sensibly, the cruiser hadn't wanted to become a target and had darted back into the fog.

On board the *Suffolk* – the three-masted warship – it seemed as if time stood still for a few moments. Everyone looked at the German ships in amazement, their outlines appearing black against the white sea, mist and ice. Captain Ellis raced out on to the starboard bridge wing and stood next to 'Ginger' Newall, looking aft through his binoculars. The two ships were about 7 miles away – he could clearly see the 'V' of the leading ship's bow wave.[11] Ellis turned to look ahead. His cruiser was just on the edge of the wall of fog, heading towards the south-west. He yelled into the bridge, calling for an immediate hard turn to port. As the ship slowly began to swing round, he kept watching the two German ships, expecting to see the flash of their heavy guns. No enemy salvo came and seconds later the fog shrouded them, and the enemy were lost from view. The *Suffolk*'s captain was in no doubt about what they were. For the first time since the PRU flight over the Korsfjord 36 hours before, *Bismarck* and *Prinz Eugen* had been spotted.

The immediate crisis over, Ellis walked back into his bridge and ordered his ship to run on a parallel course, sheltered inside the fog bank, but he reduced speed slightly. His plan was to work his way behind the German ships and then use his radar to shadow them.[12] Meanwhile, his first priority was to report his sighting.

Elsewhere, the ship was a hive of activity, having already been called to Action Stations. Half of the crew were already at their posts; the rest tumbled out of mess decks and bunks or, worse, abandoned their evening meal. In the wardroom, pre-dinner drinks had just been served, but these were abandoned as the officers began a headlong rush for the door. A midshipman, running on to the quarterdeck, spotted the two dark ships through the mist. At first he thought they were *Hood* and *Prince of Wales*, until his shipmates told him the bad news. His ship was now playing the role of a mouse, being chased by two very ferocious cats.

The first radio message went out, but due to dampness and atmospheric problems caused by the fog it only reached *Norfolk*, 15 miles away to the south.[13] That though, was enough. Not only did Wake-Walker now know what to expect, but he was also able to pass on the news to Holland and Tovey. On board *Bismarck*, the B-Dienst unit reported the enemy radio signal being sent. It was pretty easy to guess what it said. Sure enough, the translation of the plain language signal read: 'One battleship, one cruiser in sight at 20°. Range 7 miles, course 240°.' According to Müllenheim-Rechberg: 'Thereafter the hydrophone and radar bearing of the vanished enemy soon shifted astern, and the range increased.' According to the plan, *Suffolk* was dropping back and shadowing the ships using her radar. Through the coming night, the cruiser sent a string of detailed contact reports, describing every move the German ships made as they thundered southwards through the Denmark Strait.

On board the *Norfolk*, Captain Phillips was in his sea cabin when his chief yeoman knocked and entered to tell him '*Suffolk*'s got 'em, Sir.'[14] Phillips donned his coat and rushed on to the open bridge, followed moments later by Wake-Walker. Captain Phillips ordered an increase of speed to 30 knots, but as the ship was still shrouded in fog he couldn't see anything. His radar also chose that moment to break down. Repairing it was just a matter of replacing valves, but it would take at least 30 minutes. All that time, the cruiser had to rely on the skill of her lookouts and the reports coming in from the *Suffolk*. Meanwhile, *Norfolk* was surging forwards, heading towards the hidden enemy.

Away to the north, *Suffolk* had turned away in a loop to port and worked her way round to the north-east of the two enemy ships. This was a tricky manoeuvre. Just ahead of them lay the British minefield, and following the advice of his navigating officer Ellis edged the cruiser through a narrow gap between two areas of mines. This was difficult enough in clear daylight, but they were steaming fast through thick fog, and at dusk, too. Fortunately, in those northern latitudes there was still plenty of light, and somehow they passed through the mines to reach open water. Ellis then fell in astern of the Germans and began the game of shadowing them through the Strait.

Ellis was now directing his ship from over the shoulder of his senior radar operator – the most experienced one on board. It took skilled eyes and experience to detect any change of speed or course. This wasn't the type of radar modern eyes are used to, with its PPI screen, looking down from above – that was only fitted to *Suffolk* later in the war. This one was more like the heart rate monitor in a hospital – a screen showing a blip, which an experienced eye could turn into the range, bearing and speed that Ellis needed to send his contact reports. By now, the enemy were about 15 miles ahead, and *Suffolk* was clear of the fog, but beyond the range of visibility. It was clear by now that the two German ships were travelling at 25 knots and skirting the edge of the pack ice as they headed south. So, these crucial contact reports kept being sent out, and now, free of the fog, they could reach other listeners, too, on Iceland, although wireless problems meant the signals couldn't reach Holland's or Tovey's flagships.

On board *Norfolk*, the run to the north continued. Then, at 20.30, Wake-Walker's flagship broke free of the fog bank and entered clearer water.[15] Suddenly they saw the enemy ahead of them, just 6 miles away, fine off their port bow. The two ships were approaching each other at a closing speed of almost a mile a minute. Worse, as the men on *Norfolk*'s open bridge watched, they could see the *Bismarck*'s forward guns open fire, the muzzles belching orange flame. At that range it took 23 seconds for the shells to reach their target. During those key seconds Phillips ordered a hard turn to starboard, and the cruiser's rudder had begun to bite just as the shells landed. The four-shell salvo landed just off the cruiser's port quarter, and as the 15in. shells hit the water they detonated and threw up splinters that hurtled into the cruiser's aftermost turret as if her 1in. turret armour were made of butter.

Wake-Walker watched with professional interest, and later described the fall of shot as throwing up a broad wall of smoke and water 200ft high, but noted that the salvo was well grouped. One shell – highly burnished – struck the water and then ricocheted over the cruiser's bridge. He was clearly impressed. That, though, was the *Bismarck*'s only chance to demolish the British cruiser. As *Norfolk* turned, Captain Phillips ordered a smoke screen to be laid, to throw off the enemy gunners. Half an agonisingly slow minute later, the cruiser was safely back behind the wall of fog. However, *Bismarck* fired three more salvos at them, but without anything to aim at they all fell wide. Nevertheless, Phillips had almost paid a high price for his impetuous charge towards the enemy.

Away to the north, observers on *Suffolk*'s bridge saw the gun flashes through the haze ahead of them, and when nothing landed near them they realised that *Norfolk* must have run into trouble. Little did any of the British seamen realise, but this opening salvo of the campaign had damaged *Bismarck*'s ability to fight, since the shock waves from the turrets had put the forward FuMo23 radar out of action. Without it, until it was fixed, *Bismarck* would have to rely on her lookouts. This would have a dramatic impact on events the following morning: because of the issue, Lütjens ordered *Prinz Eugen* to take the lead, as her radar was still intact. This was done, albeit with a momentary risk of collision as *Prinz Eugen* surged past the *Bismarck*. Importantly, this change of position wasn't detected by either *Norfolk* or *Suffolk*. Wake-Walker's flagship had now taken station astern of the Germans, and so both British cruisers were now shadowing the enemy.

SHADOWING THROUGH THE NIGHT

On board *Bismarck*, Müllenheim-Rechberg expressed his concern about the situation: 'This sudden encounter with British cruisers came as a shock to me, especially as it was reasonable to assume that there would be other enemy ships in these rather narrow waters.'[16] He added that the thing they'd most wanted to avoid – an encounter with British warships – had taken place right at the start of the breakout attempt. Clearly that didn't bode well. However, he continued: 'I regarded it as only the opening act, and naturally we were confident that we should be able to ward off the threat. Lütjens' next moves were aimed at either shaking off our pursuers or sinking them.'

As for the pursuers, they were now shadowing *Bismarck* and *Prinz Eugen* from a reasonably safe distance of around 13 miles. *Suffolk* was to starboard, closest to the edge of the pack ice, while *Norfolk* was a few miles to port of her, skirting the edge of the fog bank. Although most of the time they couldn't see the enemy ships, sometimes the haze cleared and they could catch a glimpse of their outline – and the enemy presumably could see them. Mostly, though, they kept their distance. Thanks to radar they knew where the enemy were, whether they were visible or not. In fact, the superior radar on *Suffolk* did the job for both of them; *Norfolk*'s fixed aerial radar proved less able to deal with the snow flurries and course changes during the night. However, together the pair of cruisers – one with a better radar, the other with a more powerful radio transmitter – did exactly what had been asked of them.

By tracking the two German ships as they passed through the Denmark Strait they could let Tovey plan his strategy, directing his ships to intercept the enemy as they reached the North Atlantic. Just as importantly, it allowed V. Adm. Holland to plot a course that meant that as dawn broke, *Hood* and *Prince of Wales* would be waiting for the Germans at the southern end of the Denmark Strait. Some 600 miles to the south-east, Tovey considered himself lucky.[17] His dispositions had been made based on very little hard information, but his gamble had paid off. Holland's two capital ships were now going to be in a position to intercept the Germans early the following morning. As night fell, his ships were 300 miles to the south-east of their opponents. In case the Germans slipped past them, *King George V*, *Repulse* and *Victorious* were steaming towards a position to the south-west of Iceland where they could intercept the *Bismarck*.

Tovey, however, wasn't content with that. *Bismarck* was still a powerful ship and the 14in. guns of *King George V* and *Prince of Wales* hadn't been tested in battle. He therefore needed to improve the odds in their favour. That evening, he ordered the venerable but still powerful battleship *Rodney* detached from escort duties. She had just left the Clyde, accompanying the troopship liner *Britannic*, which was bound for the USA. *Rodney* herself was heading there for a refit in Boston. Now, Tovey ordered her north to reinforce the Home Fleet. On board *Hood*, Holland ordered his two ships to speed on towards their dawn rendezvous. *Hood* was in the lead, followed by *Prince of Wales* and four destroyers. Two more had put in to Hvalfjord to refuel. Later, one of the destroyer men remembered the moment: 'With *Hood* to support us we felt we could tackle anything … there was no beating her.' Now, for the first time in her long career, she was about to fire her guns in anger.

Away to the north-west, the pursuit through the Denmark Strait continued, with all four ships now making around 30 knots as they sped south. Dusk had fallen, but there was still a sort of half-light, which kept the lookouts on both pairs of ships peering towards the enemy. On board *Bismarck*, now behind the *Prinz Eugen*, Müllenheim-Rechberg caught occasional glimpses of *Suffolk* through the after rangefinder, which had superb optics.[18] The visibility came and went depending on flurries of snow or fog. Finally, at 22.00, Lütjens had had enough. He waited until a fresh rain squall swept in and hid the two pairs of ships from each other, then he ordered *Bismarck* to make a hard turn to port, and reverse her course.

He hoped to surprise the *Suffolk* as the battleship emerged from the rain squall.[19] However, on board *Suffolk* the manoeuvre had been detected on the cruiser's radar, and *Suffolk* turned away, making smoke. By the time *Bismarck* emerged into the open *Suffolk* had gone. Lütjens held his course for ten minutes, hoping to spot either of the enemy cruisers, but nothing was seen. So, at 22.10 he turned back on to his original course, and the battleship sped after the *Prinz Eugen*. Within half an hour *Suffolk* was back in position, as was *Norfolk*, and the shadowing continued.

There was another incident shortly before midnight, when the German lookouts spotted a Catalina flying boat, patrolling to the south-east of them, flying above the fog. Soon, however, it turned away, and it seemed likely it hadn't spotted the two enemy ships.

A little after midnight, a heavy snowstorm cut visibility down to less than a mile. At the same time, the B-Dienst signal interception unit on board the *Bismarck* reported that the British cruisers had stopped sending contact reports.[20] The assumption was that they had lost contact. *Norfolk* and *Suffolk* were still out there, following the German ships, but the snow was disrupting their radar picture. So, with no new information to pass on, Wake-Walker was waiting until the blizzard passed. However, he knew that by dawn two British capital ships would be blocking *Bismarck*'s path to the Atlantic. His cruisers had done their job. Apart from some last-minute signalling to help guide *Hood* and *Prince of Wales* towards the enemy, Wake-Walker's cruisers had played their part to perfection. It was up to V. Adm. Holland now, to finish the job.

Chapter 9

Duel at Dawn

IN HARM'S WAY

Just before 04.00 that morning, Signalman Edward 'Ted' Briggs reported for duty on the *Hood*'s bridge.[1] It was the start of the Morning Watch, and after their ship's race through the night, everyone was fired up with excitement. If the admiral's calculations were correct, then around dawn that morning they would go into action. He wouldn't admit it to his shipmates – almost none of them would – but he was afraid. He was only 27, and hadn't considered dying before. That, however, wasn't his worst fear. He was far more scared of suffering some horrible, disfiguring injury. He also wondered how he would react when he saw his shipmates being blown apart beside him. Would he panic and cower in the corner of the bridge, or would he acquit himself bravely. Like everyone else, he didn't express those thoughts, but in those long hours before dawn they were shared by just about every sailor on board *Hood*, *Prince of Wales*, *Bismarck* and *Prinz Eugen*. All of them, silently, knew their courage would soon be put to the test.

Throughout that night, *Hood* and *Prince of Wales* had steamed through the Atlantic at 27 knots.[2] The seas were becoming rougher and the four destroyers were having a hard time of it, with the seas breaking over them every time they rose out of a trough. In the navy they called it 'taking the green'. The two capital ships, by contrast, were big enough to barely notice the heavy seas, although spray and waves still broke over their bows. On board the destroyer *Electra*, those on the bridge thought the water steaming out of the capital ship's hawseholes made them look like angry, snorting dragons. At one point Holland signalled the escorts, asking if it was too rough for them. They all said no, as nobody wanted to miss the action. So, *Hood* and *Prince of Wales* steamed on, while the four destroyers struggled to keep pace with them.

At 22.00 the two ships began preparing for the coming battle.[3] Men wrote letters or listened to briefings by their officers. They collected white anti-flash hoods and mittens, designed to protect them from burns. If they talked at all, they did it in low voices, as if in a church. Above all, though, they tried to contain their fear, not letting their shipmates see how scared they actually were. Meanwhile, on the bridge of *Hood*, V. Adm. Holland and Captain Kerr talked in equally quiet tones, discussing the tactical situation. Thanks to the signals coming from Wake-Walker's cruisers they knew exactly where the enemy were, as well as their course and speed. By their calculations, at midnight the enemy were a little over a hundred miles away to the north, which meant they would probably make contact at around 14.30. That didn't suit Holland. As a gunnery expert, relying on one aged but untried capital ship and a faulty new one, he wanted to weigh the odds more in his favour.

In those latitudes it only really got dark a little after 02.00. The night was short, so dawn was expected at around 05.30. This meant that if he could speed up the rate of closure and bring the enemy to battle at sunset, the setting sun would illuminate the enemy ships, while his own would be difficult to see in the dark. So, to make this happen, at 00.12 he ordered a turn to starboard, so that his force was now heading north-north-west.[4] It was at that point that he received the latest contact report from the cruisers. The *Bismarck* had disappeared in a snowstorm, which obscured the radar picture. So, he simply had to hope the Germans didn't change course before *Suffolk*'s radar could relocate the enemy ships. This raised the possibility that the Germans might slip past him during the brief Arctic darkness. In response, five minutes later, at 00.17, he ordered another turn, this time on to a course of due north. This meant the protagonists were sailing almost directly towards each other, with a closing speed of about 43 knots.

At the same moment, he sent the signal to *Prince of Wales*, 'Prepare for Action'.[5] This was largely superfluous – both ships had been at Action Stations for more than two hours by now, and all their main guns were loaded, trained on to the likely enemy bearing, and ready to fire. Still, it meant that his six ships could hoist their battle flags – oversized white ensigns. He added in a follow up signal that he expected to make contact at any time after 01.40. There was nothing more to do now but wait. Some 300 miles to the south, Admiral Tovey knew that Holland was about to sail into battle. The previous evening, he had considered asking his second-in-command to put the better-protected *Prince of Wales* in the lead, rather than *Hood*, but had decided against it. Holland was experienced enough to make up his own mind on tactics. Afterwards, Tovey regretted not sending that signal.[6]

Holland, meanwhile, had his own problems to deal with. His headlong race towards the enemy was all very well, but since midnight the two cruisers hadn't been sending out any contact reports. As the clock ticked on, this raised the possibility that they might have lost contact with the *Bismarck* and *Prinz Eugen* or, worse, they had been surprised and sunk. The danger was that somehow the Germans had slipped past Holland's ships in the pre-dawn darkness. In fact, at 00.21, while his ships were still hidden by the snowstorm, Admiral Lütjens had ordered his ships to turn slightly to starboard, from a course of 190° to 220°. He also increased speed slightly, to 28 knots. At that southern part of the Denmark Strait the coast of Greenland fell away to the west, and so too did the ice pack. By changing course he was keeping the ice on his starboard side, and steaming down the western side of the Strait. V. Adm. Holland didn't know of this course change yet, but the possibility of it wasn't lost on him.

It was a matter of psychology. Holland was aware that Lütjens knew that he'd been spotted by the British cruisers and that they were probably sending contact reports back to the rest of the Home Fleet. If he were the German commander, Holland would expect the British to send capital ships to intercept him before he broke out into the North Atlantic. So, by keeping as far as he could to the west, he made it slightly harder for the British ships to reach him in time. However, it was just as likely that the Germans would keep on their present course, as he doubted they knew two British capital ships were on track to intercept them. His present northerly course would only bring about a battle if the enemy were where he expected them to be. So, he made a decision. If no fresh report reached him by 02.30, he'd turn his ships around and head off to the south-west. That way he might lose the tactical advantage he'd been planning, but at least he'd make sure the enemy didn't slip past him in the darkness.

There was another reason V. Adm. Holland was hoping to intercept the enemy on his own terms. Just before contact was made, he intended to turn to port, so his own ships were steaming across the path of the enemy. The Germans, according to the latest contact reports, were in line astern – one ship behind the other – and presumably *Bismarck* was in the lead. That meant only her four forward 15in. guns could bear on the British, while all eight of *Hood*'s 15in. guns and all ten of the 14in. ones on *Prince of Wales* could bear on the enemy battleship. In naval terms this was called 'crossing the T'. All of your guns could bear on the enemy, but only a few of theirs could fire back. It was a tactic that had stood the test of time, having been used by Nelson at Trafalgar and Jellicoe at Jutland. Now, Holland planned to cross the enemy's T in the Denmark Strait.

However, the clock on *Hood*'s bridge continued to tick on, and still no word came from Wake-Walker. 02.00 came and went, and darkness descended on them, but the British lookouts couldn't see any sign of the enemy. It was clear that something had gone wrong in Holland's calculations. The enemy weren't where they should have been. That meant that they had altered course. It was unlikely they'd have altered to port, as that would place them closer to the warships of the Home Fleet, so the most likely thing was that they'd altered course to starboard and were still hugging the edge of the pack ice. If that were indeed the situation, then if Holland held his present course there was a good chance he'd miss the Germans altogether. At 02.03 he therefore ordered his capital ships to reverse course, and steer 200°, or south-south-west.[7] At the same time, his three destroyers were ordered to continue on to the north, in an attempt to make contact with the enemy.

ENEMY IN SIGHT!

Now, both groups of ships were heading towards the south, on slightly diverging courses. For Holland and all the sailors in the two British ships it was a tense time. They had all been keyed up for a battle – now there was a chance there mightn't be a fight after all. Then, at 02.46, the radio receiver on board *Hood* crackled into life. It was a fresh contact report from *Suffolk*.[8] *Bismarck* and *Prinz Eugen* had changed course slightly during the night, from 190° to 220°, to conform to the gradual angling away of the Greenland pack ice. Now Holland knew where the enemy were and so he could work out how best to intercept them. As a gunnery expert, he realised that his run to the north had robbed him of his big tactical advantage. He would no longer be able to cross the enemy's T. However, he felt that his two ships had more than sufficient firepower to deal with the *Bismarck* in a straightforward gunnery duel. Still, he held that course for a little longer, waiting for more contact reports to come in.

Finally, at 03.21, he ordered another alteration to starboard, this time on to a new course of 240°.[9] This change of course meant that the paths of the two pairs of ships were now converging slightly. While a few moments before the British crews had considered the possibility that there mightn't be a battle after all, they now realised they would have to fight. However, that fight would be at least another two hours away. Just over 30 minutes later, at 03.53, Holland ordered an increase of speed to 28 knots. His four destroyers were still away to the north, and he now recalled them, ordering them to catch up at their best possible speed. This, however, meant that when contact was made, probably around dawn or slightly after, the destroyers would be too far away to intervene in the coming battle. A clash was coming – that now was fairly certain – but it would be a straightforward duel between two pairs of warships. By Holland's calculations, the enemy were a little over 20 miles away to the north.

About an hour later, shortly after 05.00, the first signs of a new dawn could be seen emerging over the eastern horizon. Earlier, Holland had hoped to use the sunset to his advantage, as it would silhouette the German ships, while his own would be harder to see. Now that position was reversed. When sunrise came, it would be the German gunners who would have the advantage. Regardless, Holland persevered and maintained his course and speed, guided by a renewed stream of contact reports coming from the two British cruisers. Minute by minute the tension was mounting. At 05.10, Holland signalled *Prince of Wales*, demanding her instant readiness for action. In response, Captain Leach went on the ship's tannoy and announced that he expected the battleship would be in action in 15 minutes.[10] To reinforce the point, the ship's chaplain then gave a short prayer, finishing with the plea to the Almighty: 'If we forget thee, do not thou forget us.' Meanwhile, on both British ships, lookouts strained to be the first to spot the approaching enemy.

Then, at 05.23, the latest radio message from Wake-Walker reported another German change of course. The Germans were now steering 170°, a little east of due south.[11] That placed the two forces on a collision course. Throughout the past two days, the British admiral had pondered how he should bring the enemy to battle. He knew that the *Bismarck* represented the very latest in battleship design, although he had no real information about her fighting capability. Her speed was probably comparable to that of his two ships, and in theory her guns were no more powerful than those of *Hood*. The German battleship had spent a long time training her crew, while *Hood* was fresh from a gruelling series of Atlantic patrols. As for *Prince of Wales*, Holland had grave doubts about her fighting efficiency, both in terms of her largely inexperienced crew, or the new battleship's technical reliability. After all, she still had civilian technicians on board, tinkering with her guns.

Then there was the question of protection. Again, while Holland had no intelligence reports to draw upon, he expected *Bismarck* to be superbly well armoured. By contrast, while *Prince of Wales* was brand new, and relatively well protected, *Hood* was a mere battlecruiser, and more than a quarter of a century old. Holland knew her armour wasn't really up to the job. That was especially true of her deck armour. As a gunnery expert, he understood perfectly well that at long ranges, due to the necessarily high elevation of the guns, shells flew in a curve, almost like a mortar shell, before plunging down on their target, dropping at a steep angle. That meant that at extreme ranges, shells were more likely to hit the deck of a target ship than its sides. At closer ranges, the trajectory was much flatter and the shells were far more likely to strike the hull or superstructure of the target. Therefore, to avoid exposing *Hood* to plunging fire, he had to close the range as quickly as possible.

At the moment, however, he had one major advantage. The Germans were to the north of Holland's ships and were heading almost due south. By contrast, the British were steaming towards the south-west, so when the Germans appeared they would probably do so off *Hood*'s starboard beam. That meant that despite all their night-time manoeuvring, the chances were that Holland might be able to cross the enemy's T after all. That gave him a significant tactical edge, but it still didn't solve the problem of *Hood*'s vulnerability at long range. Visibility that morning was expected to be pretty good, and dawn was now breaking. So, he could expect to spot the enemy when they were a little under 20 miles away. While in theory *Hood*'s 15in. guns could hit a target 15 miles away, her maximum effective range was around 25,000 yards (12.5 miles). Then, the closer they got, the more chance there was of hitting the target.

Another factor was penetration. The closer the target was, the more likely the shells were to penetrate its armour. Also, given Holland's estimation of *Bismarck*'s protective armoured belt, he expected that for his shells to be truly effective, he needed to close the range to around 18,000 yards (9 miles). As for *Prince of Wales*, her 14in. guns were a new design, and unlike the 15in. guns of the kind mounted in *Hood*, their effectiveness hadn't been tested in battle. Still, he expected a roughly similar level of effectiveness from them, albeit with slightly less penetrative power. That meant the *Prince of Wales* might need to close to within 16,000 yards (8 miles) before her shells could smash their way through *Bismarck*'s armoured belt. Also, to be fully invulnerable to plunging fire, *Hood* needed to be within 12,000 yards (6 miles) of the enemy.

Unfortunately, all this meant that even though he might enjoy a superior position at the moment, when the enemy finally appeared he would have to close the range with both ships as quickly as possible, and so surrender this slim tactical advantage. Each of his two ships had slightly different advantages and disadvantages, and the British Admiralty needed to weigh these up before they opened fire. Then, he had the problem of coordinating the fire of his two capital ships, carrying guns of different calibres. By firing on the same target this would lead to problems when it came to observing the fall of shot, when his gunnery director teams watched the salvo land and corrected their aim until their shells were hitting the target. With two ships firing at the same enemy ship, this job would be a little harder. However, as a ballistics expert he was certain that closing the range was the thing to do. So, as dawn broke, and the lookouts and radar scanned the northern horizon, Holland had a lot to think about.

Two dozen miles to the north, just after 05.25, the *Prinz Eugen*'s hydrophone operator detected the sound of fast-moving propellers somewhere off the port bow.[12] The report reached Captain Brinkmann on the cruiser's bridge, by which time the sound of not one but two ships had been identified. Something was out there in the pre-dawn darkness, to the east-south-east. That made sense. If the enemy did appear at dawn, then it would probably be in the south-east quadrant, which was where the lookouts on the two German ships were concentrating their gaze as the ships raced on towards the south-west, with *Prinz Eugen* steaming ahead of the battleship. The report was signalled to *Bismarck*, and the two ships continued on their way. By now, though, it was pretty clear to both sides that action was imminent.

Two minutes later, at 05.27, a lookout on board the *Prinz Eugen* spotted two smudges on the southern horizon.[13] The officer of the watch that morning was Kapitänleutnant Paul Schmalenbach, the cruiser's second gunnery officer. Everyone with binoculars peered at the southern horizon, lighting up now with the rising sun. Then, two minutes later, just as Captain Brinkmann came on to the bridge, Schmalenbach saw them for himself – two distinct columns of smoke. He immediately sounded Action Stations, and signalled news of the sighting to *Bismarck*, following a half-mile astern of the cruiser. Two minutes later and 15 miles to the south, a teenage seaman, 'Knocker' White, was perched in the mast of *Prince of Wales* when he spotted something on the starboard beam. Again, it was a plume of smoke. He yelled the news down to the deck, and on the battleship's bridge everyone peered in the direction the youth's arm was pointing. At first nobody saw anything. Then, gradually, the watchers on the bridge saw the smoke too. By then, White could clearly see the masts of a ship, and the smoke of a second vessel astern of her. At 05.35 he repeated his first cry – 'Enemy in Sight!'[14]

OPENING SALVOS

So, both pairs of ships had spotted each other. As they were still 15 miles apart, neither side could make out what the enemy ships were, but at least the British knew they were facing *Bismarck* and *Prinz Eugen*. By contrast, the appearance of these two ships came as a complete surprise to the Germans. On *Prinz Eugen*, 1.4 miles ahead of the *Bismarck*, they had a better view of them than they did on the battleship, and Captain Brinkmann thought the approaching ships were enemy light cruisers. In fact, at 05.32 he signalled Lütjens, suggesting exactly that. Lt Jasper, his first gunnery officer, was less certain. He thought at least one of the approaching ships might be a battleship. All four ships were at Action Stations now, the crews tense, alert and waiting for orders. Another 15 miles astern of *Bismarck*, Wake-Walker's two cruisers were still following the Germans from a safe distance. They would play no part in the coming battle, but if called on, they could

Even her British enemies described *Bismarck* as a very elegant warship. Her sleek lines are shown to perfection in this photograph, taken while she was anchored off Kiel in September 1940. (Photo by ullstein bild/ullstein bild via Getty Images)

When *Bismarck* was launched in Hamburg on 14 February 1939, the event was attended by the German Führer and many of the Nazi elite. After she was launched into the River Elbe, she was towed to the nearby equipping pier to be completed. (Bettmann/Getty Images)

Once she was commissioned, *Bismarck* and her crew underwent an extensive period of trials and training exercises in the Baltic Sea. This photograph was taken from the *Prinz Eugen*, while the two warships were conducting joint exercises off Gotenhafen in April 1941. (Photo by Apic/Getty Images)

Kapitän Ernst Lindemann (1894–1941) was an experienced officer and gunnery expert who first saw action during World War I. However, he never held a seagoing command before the *Bismarck*. (The Stratford Archive)

On 5 May 1941, the German Führer Adolf Hitler visited *Bismarck* while she was lying off Gotenhafen. He spent four hours on board, and seemed particularly interested in examining her gunnery fire control systems. (Photo by Apic/Getty Images)

Another view of *Bismarck*, seen from the *Prinz Eugen* in April 1941, as the two warships were preparing for Operation *Rheinübung*. The battleship carries a 'Baltic scheme' of disruptive camouflage. These chevrons were painted over before the two warships left Norwegian waters. (Photo by ullstein bild/ullstein bild via Getty Images)

This is the aerial photo taken by Fg Off. Suckling at 13.15 on 21 May as he flew over the Grimstadfjord at a height of 27,000ft. It revealed the presence of the *Bismarck*, accompanied by two supply ships. (Photo by The Print Collector/Getty Images)

The modern battleship *King George,* flagship of the Home Fleet. Early on 27 May, in company with the older battleship *Rodney*, she was finally able to bring *Bismarck* to battle. (The Stratford Archive)

As commander of the Home Fleet's Battlecruiser Squadron, V. Adm. Lancelot Holland (1887–1941) flew his flag in the *Hood* when she encountered the *Bismarck* in the Denmark Strait. While his battle plan was sound, he was thwarted by a combination of bad luck and the poor armoured protection of his flagship. (The Stratford Archive)

Earlier in 1941, Admiral Günther Lütjens (1889–1941) had led a successful sortie into the North Atlantic using the battlecruisers *Scharnhorst* and *Gneisenau*. He now hoped to repeat this success using *Bismarck* and *Prinz Eugen*. (Photo by ullstein bild/ullstein bild via Getty Images)

Out to stop Admiral Lütjens was Admiral John Tovey (1885–1971), commander of the Home Fleet, who flew his flag in the battleship *King George V*. He more than anyone was responsible for hunting down and destroying the *Bismarck*. (Photo by Popperfoto/Getty Images)

The battlecruiser *Hood* in Scapa Flow, pictured in early 1941 from the deck of another battlecruiser, the *Repulse*. While *Hood* was the most prestigious capital ship in the fleet, her design was flawed, and she lacked the armoured protection she needed to take on an adversary as formidable as the *Bismarck*. (Photo by Lt. R G G Coote/ IWM via Getty Images)

In May 1941, R. Adm. Frederic Wake-Walker (1888–1945) commanded the heavy cruisers *Norfolk* and *Suffolk* as they shadowed the *Bismarck* in the Denmark Strait, and in the run south into the North Atlantic. (The Stratford Archive)

This photograph of *Hood* from the *Prince of Wales*, taken in the early evening on 23 May 1941, is the last known photograph of the famous battlecruiser. The following morning *Hood* would be torn apart by a shell from the *Bismarck*. (Photo by Keystone/Getty Images)

H.M.S. Prince of Wales

In May 1941 the *Prince of Wales*, pictured here off Iceland, was the most modern battleship in the Home Fleet. Despite the technical problems she encountered with her main guns, the hits they scored on *Bismarck* in the Denmark Strait had a dramatic influence on the course of the campaign. (Photo by Arkivi/Getty Images)

The heavy cruiser *Norfolk*, pictured in Scapa Flow shortly before the *Bismarck* made her sortie. Not only did she shadow the *Bismarck* during her breakout into the Atlantic, *Norfolk* was also there at the end, playing her part in the destruction of the German battleship. (Photo by Popperfoto/Getty Images)

Bismarck firing at the *Hood* during the Battle of the Denmark Strait, 24 May 1941. Although this photograph, taken from the *Prinz Eugen*, looks as though it was shot at night, the darkness is due to underexposure caused by the flash of the battleship's guns. (Photo by Apic/Getty Images)

This historically fascinating but slightly hazy photograph was taken from the *Prinz Eugen* just before 06.00. The smoke on the horizon comes from the two British warships – *Prince of Wale*s to the left, and *Hood* to the right, which is also surrounded by shell splashes from the *Bismarck*'s salvos. A minute or so later the *Hood* was blown up. (The Stratford Archive)

The fleet aircraft carrier *Victorious* pictured off Scapa Flow, 1941. Captain Bovell was determined that his carrier would play a part in the drama, despite the inexperience of his embarked air crews. (Photo by Lt. R G G Coote/ IWM via Getty Images)

Fg Off. Dennis Briggs of 206 Squadron, RAF Coastal Command, speaking to mine workers during a goodwill tour of the North of England in 1941. It was Briggs, piloting a Catalina flying boat, who finally spotted the *Bismarck* at 10.30 on 26 May. (Photo © Hulton-Deutsch Collection/CORBIS/Corbis via Getty Images)

The aircraft carrier *Ark Royal*, viewed from an escorting destroyer early in 1941 while operating off Gibraltar. On 26 May, she was the only warship available to the Admiralty that had any chance of stopping the *Bismarck*. (Photo by Keystone/Getty Images)

While the Fairey Swordfish TSR (torpedo-spotting reconnaissance) was obsolete – and painfully slow compared to more modern naval torpedo bombers – on the evening of 26 May, it and the 18in. aerial torpedo it carried were all that stood between the *Bismarck* and safety. (Photo by Popperfoto/Getty Images)

The light cruiser *Sheffield* off Scapa Flow in 1941. When *Ark Royal's* Swordfish attacked her by accident on 26 May, her commander, Captain Larcom, was described as being 'purple with rage'. (Photo by Lt. R G G Coote/ IWM via Getty Images)

While the *Rodney* was over 20 years old when she took on the *Bismarck*, her powerful armament of nine 16in. guns made her and her sister-ship *Nelson* the most powerful battleships in the Royal Navy. On 27 May, her gunnery would prove utterly devastating. (The Stratford Archive)

The *Bismarck,* seen on the left of this dramatic photograph, is seen being pounded by salvos from the battleship *Rodney.* (The Stratford Archive)

The final moments of the *Bismarck*, as seen from beside the deck of a British warship, probably the heavy cruiser *Norfolk*. Moments later the German battleship began listing to port, before capsizing and sinking from view. (Photo by Keystone-France/Gamma-Keystone via Getty Images)

Survivors from *Bismarck* being rescued by the crew of *Dorsetshire*. Many of the German sailors were either too injured or too exhausted to climb to safety. Just 86 of them were rescued before the cruiser had to leave the area. (The Stratford Archive)

Survivors from *Bismarck* being landed in Leith Docks near Edinburgh from the destroyer *Maori*. Her crew rescued a total of 25 sailors from the German battleship. They were subsequently interred in a POW camp in Canada. (Photo by Popperfoto/Getty Images)

Kapitänleutnant Burkhard von Müllenheim-Rechberg was the Fourth Artillery Officer on board the *Bismarck*, whose post was in the After Fire Direction Tower. He was the most senior of the battleship's officers to survive. (The Stratford Archive)

An artist's reconstruction of the wreck of the *Bismarck*, lying 15,700ft below the surface of the Atlantic. The battleship lost her turrets during her descent to the seabed, and her hull still bears the scars of her final battle. (Photo by Richard Schlecht/National Geographic/Getty Images)

at least take on the *Prinz Eugen*. The German cruiser might be more modern, but they each matched her in firepower, and they outnumbered her two to one.

At 05.32, Admiral Lütjens ordered his squadron to turn 50 degrees to starboard, on to a new course of 220°.[15] He now had plenty of room between his ships and the outer edge of the pack ice, so by turning away it not only allowed his aftermost guns to bear, but it also reduced the rate at which both sides were closing with each other. Whoever these enemy ships were to the south, they would now take longer to reach the Germans. This change of course was soon picked up on *Suffolk*'s radar and the news passed to V. Adm. Holland on the *Hood*. By now, the lookouts on the battlecruiser could make out the Germans, too – their masts were just appearing over the horizon. This change of course ruined Holland's well-laid plans. At that angle, the two sides would close too slowly, and *Hood* would remain vulnerable to plunging fire for longer than he wanted. It also meant that any chance of crossing the enemy's T had now gone. He thus had to alter course to close the range more rapidly. So, at 05.37 Holland ordered *Hood* to alter 40 degrees to starboard, on to a new course of 280°, or just a little north of due west. *Prince of Wales* duly followed her, keeping her position 800 yards (0.4 miles) astern of the flagship.

Until that turn, Lütjens had seen that the approaching ships were on an almost parallel course to his own – they were steering 240° while the Germans were on a course of 220°. This implied that they didn't pose much of an immediate threat – something that encouraged the idea that they were cruisers, sent to reinforce the two already patrolling the Denmark Strait. This change of course, however, set alarm bells ringing:[16] the two ships were heading almost directly towards him. This was far more confrontational, and suggested the enemy actually wanted to engage him – not something a pair of light cruisers would do. Two minutes later, at 05.39, the German commander ordered his own ships to turn to starboard, on to a new course of 265°. That meant the enemy weren't closing with him quite so quickly and it gave him more time to evaluate the threat they posed. After all, he still didn't know what kind of ships they were.

It took a minute before the two British ships steadied on their new course. At that angle, the rear turrets of both British ships could still bear on the enemy, but only if they were pointed as far forwards as possible. Holland was closing the range now – something he considered vital if he were to avoid undue risk to his flagship. Still, after pondering the situation for a few minutes he decided the range wasn't dropping fast enough. So, at 05.49 the British commander ordered *Hood* and *Prince of Wales* behind her to turn another 20 degrees to starboard, on to a new course of 300°. At the same time, he sent a signal to Captain Leach of the *Prince of Wales*, ordering him to stay close to *Hood* and to follow the flagship's lead.

Holland was determined to concentrate his force's fire on *Bismarck*, which he and the bridge staff on *Hood* still identified as the leading enemy ship. The *Prince of Wales*, however, had better rangefinder optics than the *Hood*, and her crew had already identified that the leading ship was a cruiser, and the *Bismarck* was behind her. From their perspective, she was the ship on the right. So, Captain Leach ignored his admiral's orders and instead ordered the battleship to prepare to shoot at the right-hand ship.

Part of the problem was that at such a long range, and at that particular angle, the silhouettes of both German warships looked remarkably similar. Holland was also seeing them against a still-dark sky, while the dawn light made his own ships stand out clearly to the Germans. It was only after *Hood* fired her first few salvos at the enemy cruiser that V. Adm. Holland and Captain Kerr realised their mistake. The cruiser was no real threat to them. Their real target was the German battleship. So, eventually, *Holland* ordered *Hood* to switch her fire to *Bismarck* – the right-hand target. For some reason, though, this all-important order took several minutes to be passed on to the gunnery teams. By the time they'd produced a new firing solution for this fresh target it was too late.

As the British ships turned, the gun direction teams on all four ships prepared for action, feeding in all those vital pieces of information – course speed and bearing of target and firer – as analogue computers mechanically calculated the right firing solution. This information was duly relayed to the guns, which were subsequently trained and elevated. Only then could the respective captains give the order to open fire. In the end, Captain Kerr was the first of the four captains to give the order. With his admiral's blessing he passed on the command to his gunnery officer, and the directive 'Shoot' was given. Then, at 05.52, *Hood's* two forward turrets erupted in simultaneous orange flashes, and the 15in. shells began screaming their way towards their target.[17] The range was now 25,000 yards (12.5 miles), and so the shells would take roughly 44 seconds to reach their target. Eventually, they saw four huge shell splashes erupt in front of their target. They were 1,000 yards (0.5 mile) short.

The flashes were seen from the German ships. The enemy ships were almost bow on to the Germans, making it hard to identify them. The fact they'd opened fire though suggested they weren't cruisers, since their guns wouldn't have the range. Any lingering doubts about just what the Germans were facing were dispelled when the enemy salvo landed in the water in front of the *Prinz Eugen*. Before they even landed the *Prince of Wales* opened fire too, at 05.53. She was a little astern of *Hood*, and so the range for her six forward 14in. guns was 26,500 yards (13 miles). Some 49 seconds later the salvo landed, nicely grouped, but almost 2,000 yards (1 mile) to the right of *Bismarck*. That was pretty poor shooting, probably the result of an inexperienced rangefinding team.

Worse, the left-hand gun of 'A' turret malfunctioned after firing, which meant that when *Prince of Wales* fired again, about 30 seconds after unleashing her first salvo, she was down to just five guns. The direction team also hadn't adjusted their fall of shot yet, as the first salvo was in flight, so that went wide too. Meanwhile, *Hood's* second salvo also fell short again. On both ships, the gunners now adjusted their aim, based on the fall of shot of their first salvo, so in theory their accuracy was bound to improve. For some reason, however, the gun director team on board *Hood* never really got their eye in before catastrophe overtook them. They also kept shooting at the *Prinz Eugen*, firing a total of ten salvos at her, and missing every time. By contrast, the less experienced gunnery teams on board *Prince of Wales* proved much more effective at ranging in on their target.

On the *Bismarck*, Admiral Lütjens still refused to give the order to open fire.[18] He was biding his time, and allowing the gunnery teams on both ships to complete all their calculations. He also wanted to properly identify his two adversaries. When *Hood's* shells landed he immediately learned two things. First, the enemy ships were no mere cruisers. These were capital ships, and the huge columns of water erupting in front of the *Prinz Eugen* were clearly made by heavy-calibre shells. The same was true of the next salvo, falling a mile away on *Bismarck's* quarter. The second point was that the right-hand British ship was firing at the *Prinz Eugen*, rather than the *Bismarck*. This made no sense – the cruiser represented no serious threat to an enemy battleship. So, that suggested that at least one British captain hadn't properly identified his target. Uncomfortable as that might be for the relatively poorly armoured cruiser, it gave *Bismarck* breathing space.

By now it was 05.54. *Hood* fired her third salvo at the *Prinz Eugen*, and while the shells had crept closer to the enemy cruiser, the battlecruiser's forward guns still hadn't scored a hit. The faster-loading turrets of the *Prince of Wales* fired three more salvos in the same time, but again, while their aiming improved, none of them came close to hitting the *Bismarck*. These were five-gun salvos, too – the crew of the faulty left-hand gun in 'A' turret were still trying to get it back into action. At that point both commanders decided to change course. Lütjens did it first, turning 45 degrees to port this time, on to a new heading of 200°. This meant that if the British ships stayed on course, the Germans would cross their T. Holland, however, was too wily for that.

A minute later, at 05.55, Holland ordered his ships to turn 20 degrees to port, to steer a heading of 280°.[19] This was probably a reaction to the enemy's move, but there was also another reason: the after turrets of both of his ships were still masked by their own superstructure. So, to 'clear the arcs' of these rear guns he had to turn to starboard. Now, both groups of ships were still closing the range with each other, and all of them were making 28 knots. At that moment, the two German warships were roughly 50 degrees off the starboard bow of the British flagship. The range from *Hood* to *Prinz Eugen* was now down to just over 11 miles, while at just under 12 miles, *Bismarck* was a mile further away from the battlecruiser. It was still too far away to guarantee a penetrating hit on the German battleship, but at 11 miles *Hood*'s 15in. shells could rip the enemy cruiser apart.

It was at that moment that Admiral Lütjens finally gave the order to open fire. A flag signal soared up *Bismarck*'s foremast, the signal the yeoman on *Prinz Eugen*'s bridge had been waiting for. Seconds later, Captain Brinkmann gave the order. The German cruiser fired first, targeting her eight-gun salvo at the *Hood*. While *Prinz Eugen*'s 8in. shells couldn't penetrate her armoured belt, Brinkmann hoped that plunging fire would have some effect. She missed with her first salvo, but the next one, fired 30 seconds later at 05.56, was perfectly aimed and after 45 seconds in the air, the shells straddled their target.[20] One struck *Hood* between her aftermost funnel and her mainmast, where it exploded beside an ammunition locker serving the battlecruiser's 4in. anti-aircraft guns, and these started a fire. It was fairly small though, and it wasn't a serious hit.

At 05.55 and 30 seconds, a few moments after the cruiser opened fire, *Bismarck* unleashed her first salvo.[21] Her eight-shell salvo took 32 seconds to reach its target, but the shells landed a little ahead of the battlecruiser, and 400 yards (0.2 mile) short. On *Prince of Wales*, Captain Leach noted how well grouped they were. The *Bismarck*'s gunners now had just enough time to adjust their aim before the second salvo was fired 90 seconds later, at 05.57. By now, the range had dropped by 1,000 yards (0.5 mile). It went wide and short too, landing 500 yards (0.25 mile) in front of *Hood*'s bows. At this point, gunnery direction teams on all four ships were making constant adjustments, trying to achieve a perfect straddle. The battle had been raging for less than four minutes, and the only hit scored was by *Prinz Eugen* on the *Hood*. However, things were about to change dramatically.

Chapter 10

Hood Has Blown Up

THE FATAL BLOW

At that moment, 05.57, Kapitän Lindemann altered five degrees to port, and increased speed to 30 knots.[1] He also ordered Brinkmann to slow down slightly. The idea was that the battleship would pull in front of the cruiser, and so shield her from *Hood*'s fire. *Hood*'s turn to port also made her a more visible target. So, for the first time the German commander was able to identify his adversaries – the *Hood* and a King George V class battleship. Lütjens thought the *Prince of Wales* was still conducting her sea trials, so throughout the battle he and his staff incorrectly identified the second British ship. Still, he felt *Hood* had the more experienced crew, and so he saw her as the greater threat.

In fact, the first ship to open fire was the *Prince of Wales*. Her first salvo had missed by more than 1,000 yards (0.5 mile), and No. 1 gun in 'A' turret had malfunctioned.[2] The next three salvos drew a little closer, but all of them missed their target. Still, the gun directors were getting their eye in. By then No. 1 gun had been fixed and so just after 05.55, the

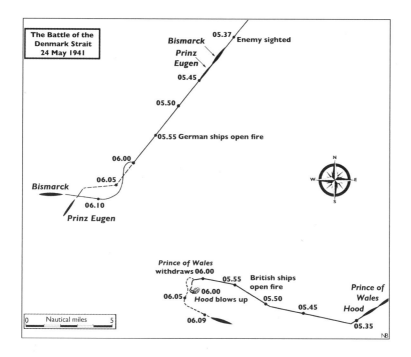

battleship fired her fifth salvo using all six of her forward guns.
It landed 40 seconds later, but it was still a miss, the shells
flying over their target. Worse, No. 1 gun malfunctioned
again, and remained out of action for the rest of the battle.
Meanwhile, *Hood* fired another four-shell salvo at the *Prinz
Eugen*, but it missed, as did her fifth and sixth salvos, fired
over the next 80 seconds. In terms of gunnery, *Hood* and her
crew weren't having a particularly good morning.

The gunners on board the *Prince of Wales* were having
more luck.[3] At 05.56, *Prince of Wales* fired two more salvos,
35 seconds apart. While the first one was over, the battleship's
sixth salvo straddled *Bismarck* and hit her on the port side
of her hull, near the bow. The shell penetrated the light bow
armour of the *Bismarck* and passed through her starboard side
without exploding. Nevertheless, the hit caused an oil leak

185

and some minor flooding. *Prince of Wales'* next salvo – her seventh – missed again, as did her eighth. By now, the range had dropped down to 20,000 yards (10 miles).[4] All four ships were firing steadily, two aiming at *Hood*, one at *Prinz Eugen* and one at *Bismarck*. At 05.57, *Prinz Eugen* fired two more salvos at *Hood*, some 30 seconds apart. Both of them missed, probably because the battlecruiser had turned slightly to port.

Bismarck fired at the same time. This was her third salvo, fired at a range of just over 20,000 yards (10 miles). This time she achieved a perfect straddle of her target.[5] All of the shells but one landed around the ship, but *Bismarck's* gunners claimed that one struck the battlecruiser on her 15in. gunnery director tower and control top, at the top of the foremast, above *Hood's* bridge. British survivors deny this happened, and it may just have been shrapnel damage. In any case, the director tower was put out of action, and her gunnery team there were presumably killed or wounded. As a result, at this crucial moment of the fight *Hood* lost her all-important fire control. Now her guns would have to fire without the outside help of high-quality rangefinders. The *Hood's* control tower and director on top of the bridge were still functioning, but it would take time to recover from the blow. Time that *Hood's* crew didn't have.

While *Bismarck's* shell was still in flight, *Hood* fired her seventh salvo at the *Prinz Eugen*. Any order to switch targets hadn't been received by that stage, and the imminent loss of her director tower wasn't going to help matters. It was another miss, but a close one this time. In fact, it was the best *Hood's* gunnery came to scoring a hit during the whole engagement. At the same moment, a five-shell salvo from *Prince of Wales* scored a hit on *Bismarck*.[6] The 14in. shell struck the port side of the battleship's hull near the waterline, below the forward port 6in. gun turret. Although the shell didn't hit the main armoured belt, which was 12.6in. thick at that point, it hit just below it, where the belt was just 6.7in. thick. The shell penetrated this weaker armour, and while the blast was dissipated in the void space behind it, the hit punctured a fuel tank and caused some flooding in the electrical plant room. So, *Prince of Wales* had now scored her second hit on *Bismarck*.

At this point in the battle a Short Sunderland flying boat operating from Iceland happened to fly over the Denmark Strait.[7] As a result, Fg Off. Vaughn of Coastal Command had a ringside view of the battle. The German ships opened up on him with their anti-aircraft guns, and the lumbering search plane was forced to turn away and hide in the clouds. Before he did, though, Vaughn saw the *Hood* below him. Two fires were burning on her, one at the base of her mainmast and the other below her bridge superstructure. The first had been caused by the hit from *Prinz Eugen* at 05.56, which ignited the 4in. gun ammunition, while the second was probably caused by burning debris from the hit on the director tower on top of the foremast. The flying boat turned away, with flak bursting all around, and moments later the panorama below was hidden from view by the clouds. It was now 05.58, and the battle had been raging for six minutes. Already, *Hood* and *Bismarck* had taken hits, and with the exception of *Hood*, all of the warships that morning had played their part.

Over the next minute *Hood* fired two more salvos, her eight and ninth, both of four shells, and both aimed at the *Prinz Eugen*.[8] With her gun director tower out of action there was little chance of achieving a hit, and sure enough both salvos fell short. The German cruiser fired back with an eight-gun salvo – her sixth and last at the battlecruiser. The range was now a little below 17,500 yards (8.25 miles), and so the flight time was 24 seconds. The salvo straddled *Hood* a little forward of amidships, and one of the shells struck her at the base of the foremast, just forward of the front funnel. This area was already littered with fallen debris from the director tower and foremast, and some of it was already burning.

This fresh hit from an 8in. shell caused the fire to intensify, its flames licking around the single 4in. gun mounting there. At that moment, Captain Brinkmann received a signal from Lütjens, ordering him to switch targets from the *Hood* to the 'King George V', which is what he called the British battleship throughout the battle.[9] Now that *Bismarck* had the range of the battlecruiser, he wanted Brinkmann's 8in. guns to do what they could to distract the enemy battleship's gunners.

Meanwhile, *Bismarck* opened up with her fourth salvo at *Hood*. The range was 18,600 yards (9.2 miles), but this time the eight German shells fell short, sending up huge columns of water off the battlecruiser's starboard bow. This was largely because of the battlecruiser's most recent turn to port. So, the German gunnery direction teams compensated for this and readied their next salvo. Meanwhile the *Prince of Wales* was firing rapidly, letting loose her tenth salvo at 05.58, and her 11th one 30 seconds later.[10] Both of these were with five guns – the forward armament, less the broken-down gun from 'A' turret. Both missed, and landed short. The range was 17,100 yards (9.2 miles), so the shells were taking around 26 seconds to reach their target. This gave no time to correct the aim between salvos; the gun direction teams were correcting aim every two salvos.

Meanwhile, on board *Hood*, V. Adm. Holland and Captain Kerr largely disregarded the fires burning behind them. Kerr's only visible response to the loss of his foretop director tower came when it rained scrap metal and body parts down on the compass platform and the teak deck of the platform surrounding it, whereupon he sent a midshipman out to identify a body that had landed outside the compass platform door. The ashen-faced youngster returned, saying there wasn't enough to identify, save that he had been a lieutenant. As for Holland, he was concentrating on the battle. In a few moments *Hood* would pass through her 'zone of vulnerability' – the outer range band where she was at risk from plunging shells hitting her deck, and so after evaluating the rapidly closing range he had to make a decision.

At 05.59, he ordered another small course change of 20 degrees to port.[11] This would put *Hood* on a course of 260°, and would finally clear the arcs of her two rear turrets. This meant she would be firing full eight-shell salvos at her target, which by now should have been *Bismarck*. However, for some inexplicable reason her forward 15in. guns were still trained on the *Prinz Eugen*, a little over 17,000 yards (8.4 miles) away. The order was passed to the helmsman, and the battlecruiser slowly began to turn. Astern of her, the *Prince of Wales* had drifted slightly to starboard of the flagship, thanks to the battlecruiser turning first, and the battleship was now lying about 750 yards (0.3 mile) off *Hood's* starboard quarter. Meanwhile, both sides continued to fire at each other. By now, *Prinz Eugen* had switched her fire to the *Prince of Wales,* and she fired three salvos at her in two minutes. These, her seventh, eighth and ninth salvos of the battle, all missed. Her gunnery direction teams were still trying to acquire the new target.

At 05.59, *Hood* fired her tenth salvo at the German cruiser, but once again all four of her shells fell short.[12] Soon, her turn would allow 'X' and 'Y' turrets to bear, and their gun teams were loaded and ready. Her 11th salvo would thus be her first full broadside of the battle. Behind her, the turn to port had already done the trick for the *Prince of Wales*. 'Y' turret with its four barrels now had a clear arc of fire, and so the battleship fired two salvos at *Bismarck* – her first with all three turrets. Instead of ten 14in. shells, however, only eight of them were fired towards the *Bismarck*. One of the four barrels of 'Y' turret malfunctioned before it could even fire, and so with the permanent loss of another barrel in 'A' turret, that brought her broadside down to eight shells. The British battleship's 12th salvo was fired at 05.59, at a range of just over 16,200 yards (8 miles), while the 13th salvo followed some 30 seconds later.

The first of the two salvos fell short, but the second one straddled the *Bismarck*, and one of them struck her after superstructure, on her after boat deck just below the mainmast. It exploded on the deck but did no real damage, apart from wrecking one of the battleship's wooden 37.8ft picket boats, and damaging another. She carried four of them on the deck, and the shell landed next to the pair mounted on the port side of the small, cluttered deck. A small fire started, but it was soon extinguished by a damage control party that was based a little further aft below the after gunnery director, where Müllenheim-Rechberg was stationed. He was ordered to keep an eye on *Norfolk* and *Suffolk*, shadowing the battleship 12 miles away to the north. As he put it: 'I found it very difficult to deny myself glimpses of the morning's main event.'[13] *Suffolk* fired the occasional salvo, but it fell far short, and *Bismarck* never replied – her gunners were too busy duelling with the *Hood*.

Apart from these brief glances forward, Müllenheim-Rechberg was only able to listen to the commentary supplied by Korvettenkapitän Schneider, the battleship's first gunnery officer. As the minutes ticked by and the duel continued, Müllenheim-Rechberg could hear Schneider order gunnery corrections after watching the previous salvo's fall of shot, and offered a brief commentary on the action. At 06.00 *Bismarck* fired her fifth salvo at the *Hood*. The range was 17,200 yards (8.5 miles), and the flight time was roughly 23 seconds. The salvo was a perfect straddle. Müllenheim-Rechberg heard Schneider exclaim: 'Wow, was that a misfire? That really ate into him!' He stepped over to the port director, which was trained on the *Hood* rather than the *Suffolk* and was rewarded with a sight he would never forget.

The *Hood* was still turning to port when the salvo landed, but the battlecruiser was 860ft 7in. long, so it took time for the water pressure on the rudder to push that long, slim hull around to its new course.[14] *Prince of Wales* was only 745ft 1in. long, and if *Hood* had been 115.5ft shorter things might have worked out very differently. *Bismarck*'s fifth salvo had landed a little short, and without the course change it would have landed just off the battlecruiser's starboard quarter. Instead, thanks to the turn and the ship's length, it straddled her. One of the *Bismarck*'s eight shells struck *Hood* behind her mainmast, just in front of the squat tower that was topped by her searchlight control position. What happened next is still a matter of some conjecture. The basics, though, were quite straightforward. The 15in. shell carved its way through the 2in.-thick upper deck armour and then travelled through it to explode in a compartment on the deck below.

Almost certainly, that main deck compartment was the working space for the battlecruiser's 4in. ammunition.[15] This set off charges stored there, and the resulting explosion triggered more ammunition in the small arms magazine beneath it, on the lower deck. In an instant, the fireball continued down to the 4in. main ammunition magazine below it. Just beyond it, through this magazine's after bulkhead, was the magazine for the propelling charges for 'X' turret. While the exact sequence of events may never be known, the most likely theory is that the explosion in the 4in. magazine went on to ignite these propelling charges, and in turn the rest of 'X' turret's magazine. Within a second, the resulting explosion blew the huge turret into the air, amid an enormous pillar of orange flame. The blast ripped the stern clear off the ship.

On the *Prince of Wales*, Captain Leach was on the battleship's compass platform, and while concentrating on his fight with the *Bismarck*, he also kept glancing over at the *Hood*, just 750 yards (0.3 mile) off his port bow.[16] He'd seen the fire erupt amidships and was hoping it was being brought under control. He was looking at the battlecruiser when *Bismarck*'s fifth salvo landed. He recalled the moment:

There were, I think, two shots short and one over, but it may have been the other way round. But, I formed the impression at the time that something had arrived on board *Hood* in a position just before the mainmast, and slightly to starboard. It was not a very definite impression that I had, but it was sufficiently definite to make me look at *Hood* for a further period. I, in fact, wondered what the result was going to be, and between one and two seconds after I formed that impression an explosion took place in the *Hood* which appeared to me to come from very much the same position on the ship. There was a very fierce upward rush of flame the shape of a funnel, rather a thin funnel, and almost instantaneously the ship was enveloped in smoke from one end to the other.

On the *Hood*, the full extent of the catastrophe wasn't readily apparent. Midshipman (Mid.) William Dundas recalled: 'It was the fifth salvo that really did for us. Wreckage began raining down again, and I saw a mass of brown smoke drifting to leeward on the port side.'[17] The whole ship seemed to shake, and then she began listing to starboard. On the bridge, the first indication that something was seriously wrong came with that huge judder. Then, the helmsman reported that the steering had gone. Captain Kerr ordered the ship switch to emergency steering – at that moment nobody on the bridge had any idea the stern of the ship had just been blown away. *Hood* righted herself for a few seconds, and then began listing rapidly to port. It soon became clear that the battlecruiser had suffered some kind of mortal blow. Without any order to abandon ship, the bridge crew began filing out of the starboard door, on to the surrounding platform. Ted Briggs recalled how orderly this was. He even remembered one officer stopping to let him through first.

As Briggs glanced back, he saw V. Adm. Holland sitting calmly in his chair in the middle of the bridge, with Captain Kerr standing beside him, struggling to remain upright as the ship kept heeling over.[18] In the old tradition of the service, both officers were going to go down with their ship. Mid. Dundas found himself unable to reach the door, thanks to the sharply sloping deck. So, he kicked out a window on the starboard side of the bridge, until there was enough space to squeeze through. Briggs found the angle was now so steep that he was actually walking down the side of the bridge, towards the water. As he went he stripped off everything that might encumber him. Further aft, Able Seaman Robert Tilburn was sheltering on the boat deck, and he felt the huge shaking too. Then, bits of debris and body parts began falling around him.

Two of his shipmates were ripped apart by shrapnel as he watched. He thought he was going to be sick, so he moved over to the starboard rail, where he narrowly missed being hit by the falling debris as he slid down on to the focsle, and then into the water.

On the *Bismarck*, Müllenheim-Rechberg heard someone yell out 'She's blowing up!'[19] He peered through the port gun director, where the magnification gave him a perfect view of the spectacle:

> At first the *Hood* was nowhere to be seen; in her place was a colossal pillar of black smoke reaching into the sky. Gradually, at the foot of the pillar, I made out the bow of the battlecruiser projecting upwards at an angle, a sure sign that she had broken in two. Then I saw something I could hardly believe: a flash of orange, coming from her forward guns. Although her fighting days had ended, the *Hood* was firing a last salvo. I felt great respect for these men over there.

On *Bismarck*'s bridge, the navigating officer Korvettenkapitän (Lt Commander) Neuendorff saw it too. 'Suddenly, the *Hood* split in two, and thousands of tons of steel were hurled into the air. More than a thousand men died. The fireball that developed where the *Hood* still was seemed near enough to touch... Every nerve of my body felt the pressure of the explosions.'[20]

On the *Prince of Wales*, a stunned Captain Leach ordered an immediate turn to starboard, to avoid colliding with the remains of the battlecruiser.[21] He watched as the *Hood*'s severed stern rose up out of the water and hung there for a few seconds. At that moment, the *Bismarck*'s sixth salvo landed just astern of the wreckage. Then Leach looked forwards and saw that the front two-thirds of the *Hood* was still moving forwards through the water, propelled by sheer momentum. Then, as water flooded into her broken hull the bows began rising out of the water, until both ends of the dying ship formed a giant 'V' shape. Next, they slipped under the oil-covered waves and disappeared, leaving nothing but a scattering of wreckage to mark the spot. Bobbing in the water were Briggs, Dundas and Tilburn. All three of them found themselves being pulled under, but somehow had managed to wrench themselves free, and so lived to tell the tale. Some 1,415 of their shipmates weren't so lucky. Everyone else went down with their ship.

Tilburn looked back and caught a final glimpse of the *Hood*: 'Just the bows were stuck out of the water, practically vertical, and then she slid under. The sea was bubbling and hissing as pockets of air broke the surface, and patches of oil were burning.'[22] Beneath them, the lucky ones had been incinerated in an instant, as the great fireball ripped through their ship, or were torn apart by the explosion. Others were crushed by tumbling machinery or shells, while hundreds more found themselves trapped in the blackness of a compartment or turret or magazine, as the icy water slowly poured in. On the *Prince of Wales*, Sick Berth Attendant Sam Woods summed up the feeling of his own shipmates as he watched *Hood* go down: 'All that remained was a huge pall of smoke, where just a few moments earlier had sailed the pride of the Royal Navy.' Many of them were utterly stunned, and couldn't believe what had just happened.

THE FINAL ACT

On board the *Norfolk*, Wake-Walker ordered that news of the tragedy be immediately sent to the Admiralty in London, and to Tovey on board the *King George V*.[23] Word also reached Holland's four destroyers, sent off on a fruitless search for the enemy earlier that morning. Three hours later they would be combing the spot, looking for survivors. The only ones they found there were Briggs, Dundas and Tilburn. Meanwhile, as the *Prince of Wales* raced past the scene of the calamity, she found herself under fire from both German ships. The battle, it seemed, was far from over. At 06.01, the *Prinz Eugen* fired two salvos at the British battleship – her tenth and 11th of the battle – but no hits were scored. The gunnery team on the *Bismarck* switched targets to the *Prince of Wales* – a fairly simple matter as she was now passing the place where the *Hood* was going down.[24] She fired her seventh salvo at 06.01, at a range of 16,400 yards (8.1 miles). None of her shells hit the *Prince of Wales*, nor did the next two salvos fired from the *Prinz Eugen*. Meanwhile, the British ship was fighting back as best she could.

The turn to starboard to avoid the wreckage meant that 'Y' turret could no longer bear on the *Bismarck*. Still, *Prince of Wales* fired three salvos in quick succession – her 14th, 15th and 16th – but all three fell short. It was almost as if the gun directors were still reeling from the shock of what they'd just witnessed and it was affecting their aim. Then, at 06.02, *Bismarck* fired her eighth salvo. The range was now down to 15,300 yards (7.5 miles). The 15in. shells were in the air for 23 seconds before they fell around the *Prince of Wales* – a perfect straddle. At that range, the shells fell at an angle of about 9 degrees, and one of them struck the compass platform of the British ship. It passed through it without exploding and continued on to splash into the sea off the battleship's port beam. However, the sheer impact of the hit killed or wounded virtually everyone on the crowded bridge.

Sick Berth Attendant Woods was just climbing up the ladder into the compass platform when the shell struck:

Suddenly there was a blinding flash in front of my eyes, and I felt enveloped in a pocket of searing heat. I was sucked up that ladder and seemed to float across the bridge area. After floating for what seemed an age, I finally came to rest on the deck amidst a shambles of torn steel fixtures, collapsed searchlights and human bodies. As I regained my senses the sweet smell of burnt flesh mingled with the acrid stench of high explosives.[25]

The compass platform resembled a charnel house, or rather it did when the acrid grey smoke cleared. With the exception of Captain Leach, the chief yeoman and Woods, everybody was either killed or wounded. In the compartment below, a lieutenant recording the ship's course changes during the battle saw blood dripping out of the bridge voice pipe to the bridge, and splattering on his plotting table.

Woods set to work, doing what he could for his injured shipmates. Some were past help, but others needed his skills. In all, some 13 officers and men were killed, and another nine wounded. Meanwhile, Captain Leach had been momentarily stunned, but he pulled himself together and got on with the job of assessing the damage to his ship. During that time the *Prinz Eugen* had been firing rapidly – six salvos in three minutes, her tenth to 15th, at ranges of between 16,000 and 15,000 yards (7.9 and 7.4 miles). None of them hit. Up above the compass platform, the *Prince of Wales'* gunnery direction officer Lt Cdr Colin McMullen had been unaware of the carnage below, although while peering through his binoculars he saw white smoke rising across the lens.[26] So, he kept on firing, using his five workable forward guns, and at 06.02 he fired two more salvos – his 17th and 18th – both aimed at the *Bismarck*. Both fell short. However, it showed that *Prince of Wales* was still in the fight.

This was about to change. Having recovered from his close brush with death, Captain Leach quickly realised that if the duel continued, and at the current range of a little over 14,175 yards (7 miles), *Bismarck* and *Prince Eugen* would pound the *Prince of Wales* mercilessly, and with his malfunctioning guns and inexperienced crew he had little chance of winning the fight. Instead, he would be placing his ship and her crew in danger. He could break off the action on his own accord, but this ran contrary to the spirit of the service. With V. Adm. Holland dead, the next most senior commander in the area was R. Adm. Wake-Walker. Leach therefore sent an urgent signal to *Norfolk*, asking permission to disengage. The cruiser commander had watched *Hood* explode and realised that the odds against Leach had now shortened dramatically, so he immediately agreed. All Leach had to do now was to extricate his battleship from the fight.

At 06.03 he ordered the *Prince of Wales* to turn hard to port, and to come round on to a new course of 160°.[27] The battleship also made smoke, in an attempt to hide herself from the enemy gunners. Just before *Prince of Wales* began her turn, the *Bismarck* fired her ninth salvo, and once more it straddled the British ship. One 15in. shell struck her on her starboard side amidships, below the waterline. The shell didn't explode and bounced off the battleship's armoured belt. However, it sprung her armour and caused some flooding. Another shell landed at the top of her forward superstructure, again on the starboard side, and put the director for the secondary guns out of action. It also silenced the battleship's search radar. At the same time, *Prinz Eugen* fired two salvos, her 16th and 17th, and the second of these scored a hit – her first on the *Prince of Wales*. The shell struck the battleship's starboard quarter, just above the rudder, but below the waterline. Again, the shell didn't do any real damage.

Then, as *Prince of Wales* was turning, a lookout on *Prinz Eugen* yelled out that he'd spotted torpedoes in the water, heading towards them. Captain Brinkmann passed the report to Kapitän Lindemann and then turned away to starboard. A few seconds later, *Bismarck* did the same, until both ships were steering 270°. It was later claimed that these torpedoes might have been fired off by the *Hood* moments before she blew up.[28] She carried two pairs of submerged 21in. torpedo tubes, located on each beam beneath the focsle. These Mark IV torpedoes had a maximum range of 13,500 yards (6.7 miles), running at 25 knots. That meant that just before the *Hood* sank, the closest enemy ship, the *Prinz Eugen*, was roughly 16,000 yards (7.9 miles) away, and therefore out of range. If they were launched, the command would have come from the torpedo control position on the battlecruiser's bridge. It seems highly unlikely this order was ever given. Perhaps the German lookout was imagining things. Whatever the case, that turn away, however, probably saved the *Prince of Wales*.

As this little drama was being played out the two German ships fired again, and despite their own course change and that of the enemy, both ships scored hits. The *Bismarck*'s tenth salvo was fired at a range of just under 17,000 yards (8.5 miles). It was another straddle, but this time only one shell struck her target, landing amidships, just astern of the after funnel.[29] Although this in itself wasn't serious, shrapnel riddled the funnel as well as the Supermarine Walrus seaplane that was perched in front of it on its catapult. This was now seen as a major fire risk, and so the floatplane was ditched over the port side before its fuel tanks could catch fire. The blast also wrecked a crane serving the battleship's boat deck. At the same time, 06.03, *Prinz Eugen* managed to straddle the *Prince of Wales* with her 18th salvo, and scored two hits, one on her port side, below 'Y' turret, but the shell didn't penetrate the armoured belt.

The second one could have been devastating since it hit a ready-use ammunition storage bin serving one of the battleship's secondary guns. Fortunately for the battleship's crew it failed to explode, and the live shell was eventually rolled over the ship's side. Meanwhile, *Prince of Wales* was firing back. By now the arc of fire of the forward guns was masked by the ship's superstructure, and so only 'Y' turret could bear. The salvo was aimed at *Bismarck*, but it fell short. Immediately, the ammunition hoists for three of the turret's four barrels broke down, leaving the turret with only one working gun. So, the 20th and 21st salvos, fired over the next minute, both consisted of just a single 14in. shell. Both of these fell short, too.

By now, the range was increasing, thanks to *Prince of Wales'* turn away and the starboard turn by the two Germans ships to avoid the imagined torpedo spread; by 06.05, when *Bismarck* fired her 11th salvo, the range had increased to 18,300 yards (9 miles). All eight shells missed the British ship, as too did the *Prinz Eugen's* 19th salvo. By that stage, the smoke generated by the *Prince of Wales* had made her hard to target. After firing these last salvos, Lütjens therefore ordered another course change for both ships, a 50-degree alteration to port to come round to the force's old bearing of 220°. Then, at 06.09, the German fleet commander ordered both ships to cease fire, as the chances of scoring more hits on the *Prince of Wales* were diminishing rapidly.[30] From its opening shots, this dramatic sea battle had lasted just 17 minutes. In that time, it cost the lives of almost 1,500 men. The Royal Navy had lost its most prestigious capital ship, and its latest battleship had also been outfought by its German rival.

Admiral Lütjens had every right to feel pleased with the outcome. After all, he'd won a spectacular victory. More importantly, *Bismarck* and *Prinz Eugen* were now at large in the North Atlantic. The *Bismarck* had been hit, though, and while none of the three 14in. shells from the enemy battleship had appeared to cause any serious damage, the fleet commander had to wait until the ship was fully inspected. Meanwhile, he continued on to the south, followed a mile astern by the *Prinz Eugen*. Some 13 miles away, Wake-Walker's two cruisers were still following the German ships. However, despite *Norfolk* firing a single salvo at *Bismarck* at 06.02, at a range of 21,800 yards (10.8 miles), she had taken no active part in the battle. Even this salvo was fired in an attempt to distract the German gunners, who were busy pounding the *Prince of Wales*. The four-shell salvo fell short, and the two British cruisers took no further part in the battle.

Wake-Walker was, nevertheless, still the senior naval officer, and as the minutes ticked by it became clear that he'd made the right decision in allowing Captain Leach to break off the action. As the *Prince of Wales* had limped out of range of the Germans, Leach sent Wake-Walker an assessment of the battleship's fighting potential. The report was grim: of her ten main guns, only three were still in operation. All the others had broken down in one way or another. Also, 'Y' turret could no longer rotate, due to an electrical fault. She had taken almost 400 tons of sea water in her stern compartments, and while this had been contained, it still had to be pumped out. Her bridge was a shambles, her gunnery director and search radar disabled, and her aircraft had been lost. Finally, her speed was now reduced to just 27 knots. Wake-Walker passed a summary of the report on to the Admiralty.[31] They, however, were still reeling from Wake-Walker's earlier brief signal, sent at 06.02. It had simply read: '*Hood* has blown up.'

Chapter 11

Breakout into the Atlantic

A CHANGE OF PLAN

The terse signal '*Hood* has blown up' came as a body blow.[1] Prime Minister Winston Churchill was told the news when he woke that morning, and he later said that for him, it was one of the most traumatic moments of the war. The rest of the British public agreed. While Wake-Walker had marked the news 'Secret', an event like that couldn't be kept quiet, and that afternoon the loss was reported by the BBC radio. The whole nation was shocked. Just as a generation later people remembered where they were when President Kennedy was shot, when the news broke that May afternoon almost everyone in Britain paused in shock. The same was true when news reached the ships at sea, many of whose crews had friends or relatives on board the 'Mighty *Hood*', or had served in her. For two decades she had been the very symbol of British naval pride. Now she was gone – ripped apart in a matter of moments. Soon the news travelled around the globe, picked up by news agencies, and it was the turn of the rest of the world to feel stunned – or jubilant.

Meanwhile, Wake-Walker ordered the *Prince of Wales* to head south, towards the rest of Tovey's Home Fleet.[2] His cruisers, however, still had a job to do. He had to continue shadowing the *Bismarck*, so that Admiral Tovey had a chance to intercept her. Perhaps *King George V* and *Repulse* would have more luck than *Hood* and *Prince of Wales*. He wasn't able to stop to search for survivors, but the *Norfolk*'s navigator sent the destroyers to the position where *Hood* went down, while the two British cruisers raced on past, keeping the *Bismarck* and *Prinz Eugen* in range of their radar. Also, the Short Sunderland was still in the area, as was a Hudson search plane, and both aircraft helped the destroyers reach the right spot.

The destroyer *Electra* was first on the scene, finding patches of oil and debris on the water.[3] There were also a handful of Carley floats, and three of them had survivors on them – Briggs, Dundas and Tilburn. They had tried to hold their floats together before the cold got to them and they gave up the attempt. They were taken on board *Electra* and given blankets and tea while the destroyers continued their fruitless search for other survivors. Briggs said he couldn't explain why he and his two companions had survived and more than 1,400 of their shipmates had not. Shortly after 09.00, the destroyers gave up the search and headed towards Hvalfjord. Meanwhile, almost 100 miles to the south, *Bismarck* and *Prinz Eugen* were heading south into the Atlantic.

Afterwards, Admiral Lütjens was criticised for not finishing off the damaged *Prince of Wales*. Given her faulty guns, she would have been hard-pressed to inflict much more damage on the German battleship. However, Lütjens himself had drawn up the rules of engagement for the operation, and they clearly laid out what his priorities were: he was to avoid all unnecessary fighting, particularly with British capital ships.

Instead, *Bismarck* and *Prinz Eugen* were there to disrupt British merchant shipping. So, his mission was clear. Yes, he might have doubled the glory by sinking Britain's newest battleship, as well as the *Hood*. However, he would be placing his two ships at risk, and more British battleships might be lurking just over the horizon. That wasn't why he was in the Denmark Strait. So, the two German ships continued on their way.

By then, Lütjens had been handed his damage report.[4] *Prinz Eugen* had come through the battle without a scratch, but *Bismarck* had received three hits, all from 14in. shells fired from the British battleship, which they still thought was the *King George V*. One had struck the boat deck, damaging a picket boat and temporarily jamming the aircraft catapult. Another struck the waterline amidships, just below the armoured belt. The shell had penetrated the hull and caused flooding in No. 2 boiler room, temporarily putting two boilers out of action. Five engineers had been wounded by scalding steam when a high-pressure pipe had been severed. The men were now being treated, the sea water pumped out, and the engineers were hoping they could repair the boilers. At that point of her hull the *Bismarck* had a void space, designed to absorb most of a shell's explosive force. It had done its job, and so the ship was spared more extensive damage.

The third hit was more of a problem.[5] The 14in. shell had struck the port bow near the waterline, immediately below the focsle. It had penetrated the lightly protected ship's side, passed through the hull and then the starboard side of the hull, all without exploding. On the way it had punctured two oil tanks and damaged their suction valves, which were used to move oil from the tanks to the engine room. This oil was now seeping out, and sea water was contaminating the oil that remained. As a result, *Bismarck* had lost upwards of a thousand tons of her fuel oil. When Operation *Rheinübung* had been organised, Lütjens had stationed two tankers off the southern tip of Greenland. However, with *Norfolk* and *Suffolk* shadowing him, he couldn't rendezvous with them without placing the tankers at risk.

Thanks to the flooding, the battleship's bows were also riding rather low in the water and she had a slight list to port. As a result, the starboard propeller was riding high and breaking the surface. So, Kapitän Lindemann ordered the ship to be counter-flooded to restore his ship's trim. In theory this would all be sorted out once the holes were plugged and the sea water pumped out. Meanwhile, with two of her boilers out of commission, *Bismarck* was limited to a top speed of 28 knots. Over the next hour or so Lütjens would find out how the repair teams were faring. The reports from them weren't encouraging. No. 2 boiler had been completely flooded and, next to it, electrical generator No. 4 had been damaged. This reduced the ship's electrical output slightly. All of this was, however, largely immaterial compared to the loss of the fuel.

It was all a matter of capacity and consumption. When *Bismarck* sailed from Gotenhafen she had 8,100 tons of fuel oil in her tanks. A little over 1,200 tons of this was consumed during the voyage to Bergen, and she hadn't refuelled there when she had the chance. Another 1,600 tons of fuel had been burned up during the voyage from Norway to the Denmark Strait, and she had used up another 440 tons that morning. By 07.00, when Lütjens requested an updated fuel report, *Bismarck* had used approximately 3,240 tons of her fuel oil, leaving her with roughly 4,860 tons in her tanks. Of these, about 1,000 tons was now either contaminated or had leaked out through the shell holes in her hull. That left around 3,860 tons of fuel available to her. As such, the lucky hit from *Prince of Wales* had deprived *Bismarck* of some 20 per cent of her remaining fuel.

Lütjens was well aware that *Bismarck* used up 1,000 tons or so of fuel every day while she was at sea, as long as she kept at something close to her top speed. The hit had therefore not only deprived him of fuel, but it had also reduced the battleship's radius of operations by a little over 1,000 miles. That meant that unless she managed to rendezvous with one of her tankers, she needed to put in to a friendly port within the next four days. With Wake-Walker shadowing him and the Home Fleet probably just over the horizon, refuelling at sea wasn't really a viable option. So, Lütjens could either attempt to break contact with them, with no guarantee of success, or he could put in to a friendly port. These meant either returning to the Norwegian coast or even the Baltic, or pressing on into the Atlantic and heading towards Brest or another of the French ports. The first option was unappealing, as the Home Fleet was well placed to intercept him. So, that left the French coast.

Shortly after the battle ended, a signal had been sent to Group North in Wilhelmshaven.[6] It said simply: 'Battlecruiser, probably *Hood* sunk. Another battleship, *King George V* or *Renown*, turned away damaged. Two heavy cruisers maintain contact.' Interestingly, this suggested their second adversary hadn't been properly identified. However, both Lütjens and Lindemann were fairly certain she was the *King George V*. Due to atmospheric problems, the signal wasn't received or acknowledged for seven hours, despite being sent repeatedly. Thirty minutes later he expanded on it, giving the position of the engagement, although he now referred to the vessel he'd sunk as a 'battleship'.

Shortly after 07.00, Lütjens sent another signal. This time it was directed to Group West, based in Paris. The dividing line between the sea area controlled by Group North and Group West ran westwards from the northern line of the Outer Hebrides. So, as he intended to cross this line later that day, he had to keep Generaladmiral Alfred Saalwächter in Paris informed of his intentions. This signal read: '*Hood* destroyed within five minutes in gunnery duel at 06.00 this morning. *King George V* turned away after hits. My speed reduced. Stem down due to hit in foreship.' This time there was no mention of the *Renown*. Then he waited for more news from *Bismarck*'s damage control parties, and discussed the situation with both chief-of-staff Harald Netzband and with Kapitän Lindemann. By 08.00, the admiral had reached a decision.

At 08.01, Lütjens sent the following signal directly to Grossadmiral Raeder in Berlin.[7] It declared: 'Intention: To proceed to St Nazaire. *Prinz Eugen* cruiser warfare.' In essence, this meant that he intended to detach the heavy cruiser if the opportunity presented itself, so it could continue to prey on British shipping in the Atlantic. Then, after shaking off her pursuers, *Bismarck* would head to St Nazaire on her own. Raeder would have quickly worked out that *Bismarck* could make the journey to the French coast in about 60 hours, which meant that if all went well, she would arrive there by the evening of 26 May. More likely, given the need to evade the Home Fleet, she would reach St Nazaire the following morning. While Raeder would have preferred *Bismarck* to return to German waters, the important thing now was her safe return to a friendly port.

At 08.30, a celebration was being held in *Bismarck*'s wardroom, where everyone was congratulating Schneider, the first gunnery officer. Kapitän Lindemann was there too, but he didn't take the opportunity to brief his officers on this change of plan. Instead, according to Müllenheim-Rechberg, all his fellow officers thought that Operation *Rheinübung* was still going ahead as planned. It was only at noon, when the two ships changed course and headed due south, that he realised something was up. Later, he wrote: 'The only thing clear to me at the moment was that our operation had not gone at all according to our hopes: Our breakthrough was anything but undetected. In fact, we had been in a battle.'[8] He added, though, that while he would have preferred that the operation would continue, he wasn't privy to the information available to his fleet commander.

Lütjens was well aware that he was being shadowed, and that Tovey would be steaming to intercept him. So, his first priority was to steam away from Tovey by continuing on to the Atlantic. Next, he needed to shake off his pursuers. Only then could he safely detach the *Prinz Eugen* and head for the French coast. Still, both Lütjens and Lindemann were fairly confident they could find a way to evade the British cruisers during the night. They spent the afternoon considering that problem, while *Bismarck's* crew continued to try to repair their ship. Captain Brinkmann of the *Prinz Eugen* was also informed of the plan via a series of visual signals.

Meanwhile, at Lütjen's request in another signal, Admiral Dönitz, commanding the U-boat fleet, had ordered the seven U-boats in the vicinity to form a patrol line to the south-east of Cape Farewell in Greenland.[9] There they would lay an ambush for the Home Fleet. The problem, however, was that neither Lütjens nor Dönitz knew exactly where Tovey was. By contrast, thanks to Wake-Walker's signals, Tovey knew exactly where the *Bismarck* was, as well as her course and speed.

THE SHADOWERS

Throughout the forenoon Wake-Walker kept shadowing the Germans, sending a regular stream of contact reports to both Tovey and the Admiralty. The *Prince of Wales* had now joined the two cruisers, as her gunners and the civilian technicians struggled to overcome the many problems with the battleship's main guns. This force kept 15 miles astern of the Germans, who were now sailing in line ahead, with *Bismarck* in front and *Prinz Eugen* a mile behind her.[10] At one point the Germans slowed down, so *Bismarck*'s crew could slip shot mats over the side, to cover the waterline shell holes. This allowed divers to pump out the water from the flooded compartments, so that the damage control teams could make temporary repairs. The British detected this change of speed, and kept their distance. The Germans were still on a course of 220°, heading towards the south-west, and keeping close to the western edge of the Greenland pack ice. However, that morning the fog returned, and they could only follow the German ships using their radar.

Meanwhile, on board the *King George V*, Tovey was around 330 miles to the south-east of the *Bismarck*, steaming at high speed, accompanied by *Repulse*, *Victorious*, four cruisers and nine destroyers. The initial shock caused by the news that *Hood* had been lost was gradually being replaced by a new feeling. Now, the sailors of the Home Fleet were out for revenge.

The same was true in the Admiralty. The job of the First Sea Lord, Admiral Sir Dudley Pound, was to control the operations of the fleet. It was a task his predecessors had done so superbly against Napoleon's admirals, and again during the last war, against the Kaiser's man, Admiral Scheer. Now

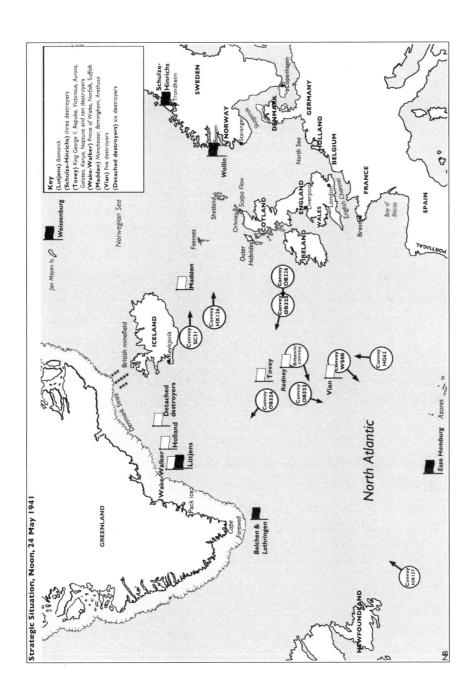

Strategic Situation, Noon, 24 May 1941

Key

(Lütjens) Bismarck

(Schulze-Hinrichs) three destroyers

(Tovey) King George V, Repulse, Victorious, Aurora, Galatea, Kenya, Neptune and ten destroyers

(Wake-Walker) Prince of Wales, Norfolk, Suffolk

(Madden) Manchester, Birmingham, Arethusa

(Vian) five destroyers

(Detached destroyers) six destroyers

Pound was flexing the might of Britain's naval power to bring the weight of seapower to bear. First, the three light cruisers east of Iceland were moved to the Denmark Strait, in case the German ships doubled back and headed home the way they had come.[11] Next, the powerful battleship *Rodney*, which was in the mid-Atlantic escorting the troopship *Britannic*, was ordered along with three destroyers to head north to join Tovey, leaving the troopship with a much-reduced escort. Similarly, two old battleships, *Revenge* and *Ramillies*, were peeled off from convoy escort duties and ordered west to lend their limited support to the Home Fleet. Like a giant chess game, the pieces were moving across the board.

Meanwhile, Wake-Walker's cruisers were still shadowing *Bismarck*. So important was this that the Admiralty even signalled him, ordering him to continue until his cruisers ran out of fuel. All the while his contact reports kept on being sent in. At 12.40, he reported that the Germans had changed course, and were now heading almost due south at 24 knots. This was inevitable, in order to clear the pack ice around Greenland's Cape Farewell, but unknown to the Admiralty, it also placed the German ships further from their waiting tankers. It also meant that they were on a course that gave Tovey a chance of intercepting them. When the report came in, Tovey and Cdre Brind went into the admiral's Plotting Room, where Cdr Wilfred Cameron, Tovey's staff operations officer, had just marked the new course on his chart.

At 08.00, when the force was 120 miles south of Reykjavik, Tovey had altered course to the west-south-west. At 11.00, he turned south-west, when it seemed *Bismarck* was less likely to double back through the Denmark Strait. *Bismarck* was about 330 miles away to the west. Glancing at the chart,

Tovey realised that on their present course, and by sailing at their maximum speed, the Home Fleet might possibly make contact with the *Bismarck* that evening.[12] Tovey began considering splitting off the *Victorious*, with a suitable escort, so she wouldn't get in the way during a surface action. It also raised the possibility of launching an air strike against *Bismarck* when the two forces came within range. With luck, that might slow down *Bismarck* enough to allow *King George V* and *Repulse* to overhaul the German battleship.

Meanwhile, back in the Admiralty, the first sea lord decided to intervene. He ordered a signal to be sent to Wake-Walker asking him what his intentions were regarding the *Prince of Wales* re-engaging the enemy. Clearly, Pound was desperate to stop *Bismarck*, and was considering risking the loss of his old battleship in the area, and a faulty and damaged one at that.[13] Wake-Walker replied that he considered *Prince of Wales* should not re-engage until she had been reinforced by other battleships. It was the prudent course of action, and one that Tovey heartily agreed with. So, the first sea lord gave up the attempt to intervene and instead sent Wake-Walker a signal, congratulating him on his good work in shadowing the enemy. However, in order to cover himself against any charge of lacking zeal, Wake-Walker decided he would move *Prince of Wales* up ahead of his cruisers during the early evening, just in case *Bismarck* tried to escape during the night.

OPERATION *HOOD*

Meanwhile, on board the *Bismarck* the B-Dienst radio intercepts confirmed that the shadowers were sending regular contact reports to the Admiralty, and that other

British warships were at sea. They were not within the area controlled by Group West in Paris, and Saalwächter's staff kept Lütjens informed of all new pieces of intelligence that he might find useful. Late that morning, the weather to the east of Greenland deteriorated, and a mixture of intermittent rain and fog meant that visibility became patchy – conditions that would only help the Germans when it came to breaking contact. That afternoon, Lütjens worked on his plan, which he code named Operation *Hood*.[14] A series of visual signals explained the scheme to Captain Brinkmann. Once contact was broken, the *Prinz Eugen* would refuel from the waiting German tankers to the north-west and then continue the mission on her own. He also explained his intentions for driving off his shadowers and sending the cruiser off on her own. He then dropped astern of her again.

Just before 14.00, *Bismarck* and *Prinz Eugen* were 240 miles east of Cape Farewell, the southernmost tip of Greenland. At that point, Lütjens sent a fresh signal to both Paris and Berlin explaining that he intended to evade his pursuers after dark. In fact, his chance came sooner than he thought. At around 15.00 he noticed that the visibility had dropped even further, and his two ships were sailing through a rain squall. So, at 15.40 he signalled the *Prinz Eugen*, ordering Operation *Hood* to be implemented right away.[15] He was seizing his moment. *Bismarck* increased speed to 28 knots, turned in a circle and then headed off to the west. The hope was that by forcing the British to turn away they would lose radar contact with the *Bismarck*. The British, however, saw the move and reacted accordingly. As Müllenheim-Rechberg put it: 'We were out of sight for a few minutes, then ran out of the squall, right back into the sight of one of our pursuers.'

To the British, the action seemed like that of a hunted wild animal turning to savage her weaker pursuers. Nevertheless, Wake-Walker had immediately ordered his ships to drop back, then follow the battleship as she turned. When the squall passed, Lütjens saw *Suffolk* was now heading west too, shadowing her at a range of 8 miles. In response, the German fleet commander gave up the attempt, and by 16.00 he was back on his old course, in company with the *Prinz Eugen*.

That afternoon they were also intermittently shadowed by a Catalina flying boat, which merely added to the Germans' growing sense of frustration. Lütjens, however, was convinced his plan would work, given the right circumstances. That afternoon he had merely been unlucky with the squall ending so quickly. Next time, he would have more luck.

By 18.00, the fog had returned, and visibility had dropped to less than 4 miles. So, 14 minutes later Lütjens repeated his earlier signal to *Prinz Eugen*: 'Execute Hood.'[16] *Bismarck* increased speed again, and turned through 180 degrees to starboard. This took the pursuing British cruisers completely by surprise. Meanwhile, the *Prinz Eugen* also increased speed and sped away towards the south, hidden by the fog. Looking northwards, her crew saw *Bismarck* open fire on the enemy, as great orange flashes lit up her turrets. Then the battleship was lost from view in the swirling fog. As the cruiser's gunnery officer put it: 'There goes our big brother. We're going to miss him very, very much.' Nobody at the time realised it then, but it was the last time any of them would see the *Bismarck*. On board the battleship, Müllenheim-Rechberg watched her go: 'We in the *Bismarck* also had heavy hearts as we parted with the faithful *Prinz*. Only reluctantly did we leave her to her own destiny.'[17]

The manoeuvre came as a shock to the British. *Suffolk* had to routinely power down her radar every few hours, and it was at one of these moments that *Bismarck* made her move. The cruisers were 13 miles astern of *Bismarck* at the time of the manoeuvre. Now the range was dropping rapidly. Captain Ellis was 10 miles away when the fog and rain squalls parted and he could see *Bismarck*. As Lt Cdr Charles Collet put it: 'Suddenly she appeared out of the mist, a huge terrifying monster, and much too close for our liking.'[18] *Suffolk* turned away and made smoke, and the shells missed, landing well astern. *Suffolk* fired back, but her aim was wide. Several more German salvos followed, creeping closer to *Suffolk* before she lost herself in the fog.

Wake-Walker ordered *Norfolk* and *Prince of Wales* to do what they could to distract the German gunners. Both ships were about 15 miles to the north of *Bismarck* at the time. *Prince of Wales* opened fire with her forward guns, even though her gunnery direction teams didn't have a clear view of the enemy. Having driven off the enemy cruisers, *Bismarck* then turned back on to her southerly course and replied with her four after guns. This gunnery duel, carried out at extreme range and in patchy visibility, was little more than a show of force by both sides. *Bismarck* fired four salvos, and *Prince of Wales* 12, before both sides ceased fire at 18.56, as the *Bismarck* drew out of range.[19]

By then, two of the four guns in *Prince of Wales'* 'A' turret had malfunctioned, and Captain Leach considered himself lucky that *Bismarck* had turned away. However, despite the continuing problems with his guns, *Prince of Wales* had acquitted herself well, and one of her salvos had come very close to straddling the *Bismarck*. Even *Norfolk* had joined in, firing three salvos at *Bismarck*, despite being at the very limits of her range. Later, Wake-Walker said he thought the brief action had a good effect on Leach and his crew. He also hoped it would help to placate the first sea lord.

At this point, the two British cruisers were back on station, shadowing the *Bismarck* from a safe distance astern. However, something had changed. This time, the *Bismarck* was on her own. The *Prinz Eugen* was nowhere to be seen.

Operation *Hood* had worked. Captain Brinkmann sped away to the south before turning west and then north, working his way around the back of the British shadowers. Thus, at 19.14, Lütjens was able to signal Paris: 'Short action with *King George V* without result. *Prinz Eugen* released to refuel. Enemy maintains contact.'[20] However, while Lütjens had successfully detached the *Prinz Eugen*, the *Bismarck* was still being shadowed as she continued on to the south-south-west, and Admiral Tovey's Home Fleet were still closing in. Now, everything depended on shaking off the British pursuers during the night.

VICTORIOUS INTERVENES

Earlier that afternoon, Admiral Tovey had realised that it was now unlikely that he was going to intercept *Bismarck* before dark. So, at 16.00, he detached Captain Bovell in the *Victorious*, accompanied by R. Adm. Alban Curteis' 2nd Cruiser Squadron: *Galatea* (flagship), *Aurora*, *Kenya* and *Hermione*.[21] The new fleet carrier was faster than the rest of his capital ships and so Tovey hoped that by continuing on towards the south-west, she might just be in position to launch an air strike against *Bismarck* before it got dark. In fact, Bovell hoped to be within strike range of the enemy by 22.00. Given the limited range and performance of the Fairey Swordfish, that meant reaching a point 120 miles from the target. Meanwhile *King George V, Repulse* and another screen of destroyers would alter slightly to port and head towards the south-south-west. That way, they might be in a position to intercept the *Bismarck* at dawn the following morning – 25 May.

Meanwhile, *Bismarck* held her course, although by now she was heading due south. Just before 21.00, Lütjens signalled Group West, informing them: 'Shaking off contact impossible due to enemy radar. Due to fuel, steering direct for St Nazaire.' This suggested that he was becoming increasingly frustrated by his shadowers, but that he felt he now had a chance of avoiding the Home Fleet. As a result of this signal, Dönitz abandoned his U-boat screen south of Greenland and instead began marshalling his boats to cover the approaches to the French coast. However, Lütjens had by this stage learned from radio intercepts that an aircraft carrier was somewhere at sea, and looking for him.

Unknown to the Germans, at that moment *Victorious* was a little over 130 miles away to the west and steering a converging course. That meant she was almost within range of an air strike. An air attack at sea was a dangerous undertaking at the best of times. Many things could go wrong, such as failing to locate the enemy, attacking friendly ships by accident, or the aircraft failing to make it back to their carrier. This was particularly true for *Victorious* that evening, as she headed towards her flying-off point in difficult weather conditions. Her aircraft and their crews had only been embarked four days beforehand and she only carried a fraction of her normal aircraft complement, as she'd also embarked crated-up fighters, bound for Malta. Now, these inexperienced pilots and handful of aircraft were being sent out to attack the most powerful battleship in the world.

At 22.15, Bovell turned *Victorious* into the wind and the nine Swordfish torpedo bombers of 825 Squadron took off, each laden with a single 18in. Mark XII torpedo. The flying conditions were hardly ideal – there was low cloud at 1,500ft, rain squalls, and the north-westerly wind was becoming stronger, blowing into the faces of the pilots.[22] The squadron was divided into three flights, each of three aircraft. While most of the pilots were green, the strike was headed by a veteran, Lt Cdr Eugene Esmonde. He led one flight, while the others were commanded by two other experienced pilots, Acting Lt Cdr Philip 'Percy' Gick, and Henry 'Speed' Pollard.

At the time, *Bismarck* was 120 miles away – the utmost limit the aircraft could reach. That meant that not only would they be attacking in the dark, but there would also be barely enough fuel left to get back to the carrier. So, after launching off, *Victorious* would steam on, trying to close the distance, despite the increasingly rough seas. Within seconds of the Swordfish taking off, the carrier was lost from sight in a rain squall. They managed to form up, though, and Esmonde led them off to the south-west, and the enemy. Meanwhile, a flight of three Fulmars was also launched. The job of these fighters was to observe the attack and to help guide the slower biplanes home.

Overall, the chances of success were slim. Several of the pilots had never trained for a torpedo attack and some had only made their first carrier landing a week before. Sending them was a real gamble, but Tovey felt he had no other choice. The plan was to head towards Wake-Walker's cruisers, who could guide them in using radar, then continue on to the south until they found the *Bismarck*. The Swordfish had their own radar, and just before 11.30

they made radar contact. It was *Norfolk*. She then directed Esmonde on to the south. At 23.50 they made radar contact again, but it proved to be a neutral ship – the US coastguard cutter *Medoc*.[23] Then, just a few miles beyond her, was the *Bismarck*. This meant that the crew of the *Medoc* had a ringside seat for what followed.

At midnight, Esmonde began his attack, as each of the three flights split up to simultaneously attack the battleship from both port and starboard.[24] *Bismarck*'s anti-aircraft guns opened fire as soon as the lumbering aircraft came within range. There were eight of them now, since one had got lost in the clouds. As Müllenheim-Rechberg said of the attacking aircraft: 'They were moving so slowly that they seemed to be standing still in the air, and they looked so antiquated. Incredible how the pilots pressed their attack with suicidal courage, as if they did not expect ever again to see a carrier.'[25] Gick attacked from the port bow, Esmonde from the port beam, and the rest from starboard. Esmonde noticed *Bismarck* was nicely silhouetted against the setting sun. Amazingly, only one of the biplanes was hit and they all reached their attacking positions. The three Swordfish of Esmonde's flight dropped their torpedoes at a height of 100ft, then turned away, pursued by a hail of flak.

Despite this, Kapitän Lindemann was able to turn *Bismarck* and comb the torpedo tracks (steering the ship so the torpedoes passed harmlessly by her like hair running through a comb). He did the same when Gick led his attack, but he couldn't evade all of the eight torpedoes. Sub Lt Lawson, attacking from the starboard beam, released his torpedo and turned away, while *Bismarck*'s helmsman was busy evading the torpedoes coming in from the port side. One of the Fulmars saw a huge column of water erupt on

Bismarck's starboard beam. On the *Bismarck*, Müllenheim-Rechberg recalled feeling a slight shudder, but the explosion was absorbed by the armoured belt and did little damage. However, one crewman was killed – the battleship's first casualty – and six injured. Despite this, not only did *Bismarck* survive the attack, but the crew were also heartened since it seemed that her armour was impervious to aerial torpedoes.

Now came the problem of landing back on their carrier. She was roughly 100 miles away to the north-east, and Esmonde led his planes towards her estimated position. Unfortunately, her homing beacon had broken down and so they had to reach her by dead reckoning – no easy feat in the dark, wind and rain. Captain Bovell expected them back by 01.00 and had signal lamps and searchlights switched on to guide them in, but the rain reduced visibility to almost nothing. The minutes ticked by, and now he worried they would run out of fuel. This possibility was going through Esmonde's mind too, until at 01.55 he spotted the red signal lamp on one of the cruisers. Dropping down, he and his pilots found the carrier, and one after the other the Swordfish landed safely.

Three of them had never made a night landing before. One plane ran out of fuel as it was landing, but made it down safely and was snagged by the carrier's arrester wires.[26] Eventually, all nine Swordfish and their crews were accounted for. Two of the three Fulmars weren't so lucky: they had to ditch in the sea, but their crews were rescued. So ended *Victorious*' first air strike. Given the conditions and the lack of experience of most of the air crews, it was lucky that they'd scored a hit at all. It was even more surprising that everyone had made it back, or at least was still alive. Unfortunately for Admiral Tovey, however, that one torpedo hit hadn't been enough to slow down the *Bismarck*. Now he had to hope Wake-Walker could maintain contact through the night so his capital ships could intercept the German battleship in the morning. He now estimated that would take place at around 09.00.

It wasn't to be. During the air strike, and while passing the *Medoc*, Wake-Walker's force had temporarily lost contact with the *Bismarck*. Radar contact was regained by *Suffolk* at 01.10, and 20 minutes later lookouts on the *Prince of Wales* spotted her, some 16,400 yards (8 miles) away to the south. She fired two salvos with her working forward guns and *Bismarck* replied with her four after guns, but neither side came close to straddling the enemy. However, by then it was clear that the high-speed manoeuvring to avoid the torpedoes had dislodged the collision mats covering the shell holes from the morning's battle. Because of this, *Bismarck* had to slow to 16 knots to allow divers to replace them over the holes in the hull. This was completed by 02.00, by which time Lütjens had reported his 'immaterial' torpedo hit to Group West, as well as his skirmish with '*King George V*'. Now, with his speed back, it was time to try to evade his pursuers.

The Germans had noticed that for the past hour or so the British cruisers had been steering a zigzag course. This was because the Admiralty had intercepted German signals that suggested a screen of U-boats was being assembled to block their path, causing Wake-Walker to order his ships to steam in an evasive pattern. This presented Lütjens with a heaven-sent opportunity. The *Bismarck*'s hydrophones and after radar allowed Lütjens to track these manoeuvres, and he soon saw that the British zigzag pattern took the enemy ships to the port side of *Bismarck*'s wake, but not over to the starboard

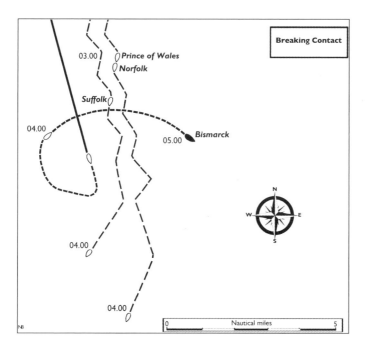

side. So, at the height of the 'zig', the three British ships were roughly 13 miles off *Bismarck*'s port quarter, to the north-east. He also judged that *Suffolk* would be at the extreme range of her radar.

Armed with this information, at 03.06, when the British ships neared the end of their eastward 'zig', Lütjens made his move, ordering an increase of speed to 27 knots and turning hard to starboard, heading directly away from the British ships.[27] Sure enough, the British had temporarily lost radar contact. When they turned on their inward leg or 'zag', heading towards the south-west, there was no sign of *Bismarck*. This wasn't alarming at first – everyone was dog-tired and this had happened before, only for the signal to be reacquired. By 03.30, though, Captain Ellis of the *Suffolk* was becoming worried. His radar was the best in Wake-Walker's force, and she was the westernmost ship. So, if anyone would locate

Bismarck again it would be her. By 04.00 there was still no contact, and Ellis was forced to tell Wake-Walker the bad news. The British commander ordered his ships to spread out, *Norfolk* heading west, *Suffolk* south-west and *Prince of Wales* south. They searched in vain.

In fact, Kapitän Lindemann had headed west, then at 03.40 turned to starboard and steamed north, about 8 miles west of his original course.[28] Now the British ships were due east of him, heading south. This meant that *Bismarck* was working her way astern of them. At 04.00 he turned towards the north-east, and at around 04.15 he bisected his original course, 11 miles north of where he'd begun his evasive manoeuvre. By then, the nearest British ship was 16 miles away to the south, and steaming in the wrong direction. Lütjens had pulled it off. After more than 33 hours of being shadowed, he had broken contact with Wake-Walker and his cruisers.

By 04.30 *Bismarck* had turned on to a new heading of 130°, and was heading towards the French coast.[29] Meanwhile, the British kept searching in vain for their elusive prey.

Chapter 12

Hunting for the *Bismarck*

TOVEY'S OPTIONS

On board the *King George V*, Admiral Tovey was roused from his cot by the bad news. He dressed and stepped into his Plotting Office next door, where Cdre Brind was waiting for him. Together, they considered the problem. Captain Ellis of the *Suffolk* lost contact with *Bismarck* at around 03.20 on 25 May. After fruitlessly attempting to reacquire *Bismarck* on radar, he told R. Adm. Wake-Walker in *Norfolk*.[1] Then the two cruisers and the battleship *Prince of Wales* spread out and searched to the south and west, but found no trace of the enemy ship. Wake-Walker also didn't tell Tovey about this until well after 05.30. So, at roughly 06.00, Brind inscribed a circle on the chart, centred on *Bismarck*'s last known position. Depressingly, at 28 knots, its diameter was over a hundred miles across. The German battleship could be anywhere in that circle, which was expanding by the minute.

So, as Tovey didn't have the ships and aircraft to search everywhere, he had to make some hard choices. First, Wake-Walker informed him that his ships had spread out in a quadrant, to the south and west of *Bismarck*'s last known position.[2] Dawn was approaching, and while no contact had yet been made, at least the improved visibility meant that Wake-Walker's cruisers could launch their floatplanes. *Prince of Wales* had lost hers in the Denmark Strait. During the night, *Repulse* and Tovey's flagship *King George V* continued on their original course towards the south-west, as Tovey had hoped to intercept the *Bismarck* at around 09.00 the following morning. Now, though, it was clear that wasn't going to happen. At 06.00, he therefore ordered Wake-Walker to release the *Prince of Wales* to him, hoping that if *Bismarck* were found he'd have the firepower to deal with her. This was necessary as *Repulse* was running low on fuel, and would soon have to break off to replenish.

That left Wake-Walker's two cruisers, which continued their search to the south and west of *Bismarck*'s last position. Meanwhile, to the north, R. Adm. Alban Curteis, who had command of the 2nd Cruiser Squadron, had also fanned out his light cruisers *Aurora*, *Neptune* and his own flagship *Galatea*, as they searched to the north of Wake-Walker's ships. *Kenya* stayed with *Victorious*, which as the news broke was preparing to launch her own search aircraft. Captain Bovell was disappointed that the three Fulmars he had sent up at 04.00 hadn't managed to maintain contact during the night.[3] Still, he was hopeful that his newly blooded Swordfish crews would find the enemy battleship, despite the murky visibility. In fact, at 07.00 he was preparing to launch seven Swordfish, led by Lt Cdr Esmonde, to probe the waters to the east of the carrier. He sensibly thought that if *Bismarck* were heading to the French coast, that's where his airmen could find her.

Then, at 07.16, as the aircraft were preparing to take off, a signal arrived from Admiral Tovey.[4] It ordered Bovell to send his aircraft out to the north and west, fanning out in a quadrant. So, Bovell had to change Esmonde's orders. The Swordfish then took off and began their search – one that would prove fruitless. The reason for Tovey's decision was simple: he had limited resources and he had to consider all the likely options. *Bismarck's* course during the previous evening suggested she was probably heading towards the French coast, but she might also be doubling back and heading home through the Denmark Strait. This was the more dangerous of the two options, as the *Bismarck* in Brest or St Nazaire could be more easily neutralised by the RAF.

For Tovey, though, the most dangerous option was if *Bismarck* was planning to refuel from a German tanker in the mid-Atlantic and then rendezvous with the *Prinz Eugen*. The point where contact was lost with her lay astride the main transatlantic convoy lanes, and several British convoys were to the east and west of her last known position. Therefore, she might be planning to attack them, so they had to be protected or moved out of the way. Of the three possible options, the French port one was the least threatening. Had he known it, by simply reversing course he could have intercepted *Bismarck* in a few hours; she was only 100 miles away at the time. The admiral, of course, lacked the gift of hindsight and instead had to make his plans based on his own professional assessment of the situation.

Meanwhile, he began marshalling his resources.[5] He had three groups of warships concentrated in the area. First, there was his own force: *King George V* and *Repulse*. Heading towards them from the north-west was Captain Leach in the *Prince of Wales*, whose crew were still battling to overcome their gun's technical problems. Further to the north-west was Wake-Walker with *Norfolk* and *Suffolk*, both searching for the elusive *Bismarck*. To the north was Curteis, with *Victorious* and the 2nd Cruiser Squadron. All three groups of ships were now engaged in fruitlessly searching to the north and west of *Bismarck*'s last position.

To the east of Tovey was Captain Dalrymple-Hamilton, commanding the battleship *Rodney*. Having been detached from escort duties and accompanied by the destroyers *Somali*, *Mashona* and *Tartar*, she was now en route to join Tovey. Far to the west, between him and Newfoundland, the old battleship *Ramillies* was steaming east to help protect the now-exposed convoys. Her sister ship *Revenge* was in Canadian waters. Still, *Rodney* would more than make up for the loss of *Repulse*, which was about to steam off to refuel.

Best of all, though, were the reinforcements approaching him from the south. On the evening of 23 May, the Admiralty ordered Force H to sea, to protect a convoy, WS8B.[6] It had left the Forth of Clyde two days before and was heading to Gibraltar. Force H had been set up to fill the vacuum in the Western Mediterranean left by the collapse of France. Under V. Adm. James Somerville it had shelled the French fleet at Mers-el-Kébir and the Italian port of Genoa, it had fought the Italians at sea off Sardinia, and it had helped run convoys through to Malta. Occasionally, though, it ventured west into the Atlantic, and this was one of these occasions. Sailors were bundled out of the fleshpots of Gibraltar, and by 02.00 the next morning, while *Bismarck* was heading south through the Denmark Strait, Force H put to sea.

Somerville flew his flag in the battlecruiser *Renown*, and while the rest of Force H varied depending on what was available, that night it consisted of the light cruiser *Sheffield* and the aircraft carrier *Ark Royal*.[7] Unlike *Victorious*, the *Ark Royal* had been in service since late 1938, and she carried over

50 aircraft – a mixture of Swordfish and Fulmars. Better still, for the most part their crews were experienced and battle-hardened. So, while *Renown* might be too vulnerable to take on *Bismarck* and survive, the presence of *Ark Royal* meant that Force H had some real teeth. When it left Gibraltar, the force also included six destroyers, but these were detached the following day and returned to Gibraltar. The plan was for the rest of Force H to rendezvous with the convoy off the south of Ireland, so Somerville led his ships north.

Somerville was off the Gulf of Cadiz when news of *Hood*'s demise reached him. He felt the blow keenly as the battlecruiser had served as his flagship during the Mers-el-Kébir operation. Soon, however, he would have the chance to avenge her loss. Force H spent the rest of 24 May steaming north up the Iberian coast, and by 06.00 on the 25th they had reached the latitude of Cape Ortegal, the north-west corner of Spain. They had been battered by a gale and were making heavy weather of it. Still, that meant that two hours later when the Admiralty ordered Force H to join in the hunt, it was actually heading north on a course that would bisect *Bismarck*'s track if her commander decided to make for the French coast. While Force H remained under the control of the first sea lord, Somerville was asked to assist Tovey in the hunt for the *Bismarck*.

Somerville soon realised that if the *Bismarck* headed west or north, Force H would play no part in her pursuit. If, however, *Bismarck* headed towards the French coast, then only Force H would be in a position to intercept her. In addition, as Force H drove north towards St Nazaire and Brest, there was a danger that the battlecruisers *Scharnhorst* and *Gneisenau* might put to sea, join *Bismarck* and then crush Somerviille's smaller force before it could escape. Little wonder, then, that

25 May was a tense day for everyone in Force H as it battled its way northwards.

The same, of course, could be said for *Rodney* and her escort of three destroyers. Since *Bismarck* had first been sighted off Bergen, Captain Dalrymple-Hamilton had assembled a 'committee' of his senior officers, to discuss the latest reports concerning the battleship. This meant that he and his crew were ready to play their part. The only drawback was that *Rodney* could barely make 23 knots, and so she had little chance of catching *Bismarck*.

The remaining pieces on Tovey's chessboard that morning were cruisers and destroyers.[8] Heading up from the south was the light cruiser *Edinburgh* and the heavy cruiser *Dorsetshire*, which was accompanying the northbound Convoy SL74. Both were available if he needed them. Also, westbound Convoy WS8B was well to the east of Tovey, halfway between him and the south-western coast of Ireland. Of the convoy's escort, while the aged light cruiser *Cairo* was of little use, she was accompanied by five destroyers: *Cossack*, *Maori*, *Piorun*, *Sikh* and *Zulu*. These were commanded by the veteran destroyer commander Philip Vian, who the year before had won fame when as the commander of *Cossack* he had boarded and captured the German supply ship *Altmark* and freed the British merchant seamen held prisoner aboard her. Tovey hoped he might show the same degree of élan if it came to carrying out a torpedo attack against *Bismarck*.

The trouble was, Tovey was well aware that until he located the *Bismarck* he could do little to bring her to battle. Instead, he could just continue the search. Unwittingly, however, most of his ships were not only looking in the wrong place, but they were also heading in the wrong direction – a fact that meant that when *Bismarck* was eventually found, much of the Home Fleet would be too far away to intercept her. He had other issues, too.[9] He had already had to detach *Renown* that morning, which was now steaming to Halifax to refuel, and soon he would lose *Prince of Wales* too, which would head north to Hvalfjord, also to refuel. He seriously doubted *King George V* had the firepower to subdue *Bismarck* on her own. Of his two other capital ships to the east and south, *Rodney* was too slow and *Repulse* too lightly protected to do much good. So, that meant pinning his hopes on using either *Ark Royal* or *Victorious* to slow the *Bismarck* down to enable his ships to catch up with her. After the failure of the last air strike, that must have seemed like little more than wishful thinking.

LÜTJENS MAKES A MISTAKE

By 09.00 that morning, 25 May, *Bismarck* was far to the east of Tovey, Wake-Walker and Curteis, and well out of radar range of the British ships. As Lt von Müllenheim-Rechberg put it: 'If the *Suffolk's* radar, with its range of 24,000m, could not regain contact with *Bismarck* at 0330, what chance did it have of doing so at 0700, by which time the *Bismarck* had been steaming for hours in a south-easterly direction?'[10] Strangely, though, Admiral Lütjens seemed less convinced he had shaken off Wake-Walker and his cruisers – which explained his rather bizarre next move. Normally, in the situation in which *Bismarck* found herself, signals were kept brief. That way, if the enemy had direction-finding equipment, there wouldn't be enough time for them to work out which direction the signal was coming from. If, however, two or more listeners did manage to identify a direction, then they could work out the enemy's location, based on the place where the bearing lines crossed. Lütjens was all too aware of this.

Nevertheless, at 09.00 that morning, he ordered a long and detailed radio signal to be sent to Group West in Paris.[11] It began by complaining that the enemy had radar sets with a range of at least 19 miles – a third more than was actually the case. So, he explained his plan: 'Refuelling in general no longer possible, unless high speed enables me to disengage.' He went on to give more details of the battle in the Denmark Strait, and the damage received by *Bismarck*. The crux, however, was the suggestion that despite successfully breaking away and losing contact with the enemy, he still thought he was being shadowed. This explained his comment about still having to disengage. Possibly, *Bismarck*'s passive radar detectors were still receiving traces of radar pulses from the Home Fleet, even though they were well beyond radar range. The key point is that this long and unnecessary message gave away *Bismarck*'s position.

Strangely, on board the *Prinz Eugen* the cruiser's B-Dienst unit, having listened in on the Home Fleet's radio traffic, had reached the correct conclusion that *Bismarck* had successfully evaded her pursuers.[12] The steady stream of contact reports had stopped. The same assessment had also been reached by Group North in Paris, which made Lütjens' fresh signal all the more perplexing. Perhaps the B-Dienst team on board *Bismarck* had accidentally given the admiral misleading information. In fact, Lütjens almost got away with it. His signal was picked up by two receivers in the UK, but they were close together, so the bearings they gave were fairly similar – too much so for an accurate location fix. Better-placed receivers in Iceland or Newfoundland didn't pick up the signal due to range and atmospheric interference. Nor were they picked up by the Home Fleet, as of the two destroyers designed to monitor just such signals, one was in Hvalfjord and the other was experiencing an equipment malfunction. The result was that while it was clear *Bismarck* was west of Tovey, her exact whereabouts was still in some doubt. In fact, when he was given the same bearing information, Tovey placed her over a hundred miles further south than did the Admiralty.

However, it was now clear that *Bismarck* was heading towards the French coast. A quick glance at the chart showed Tovey that neither *King George V* nor *Rodney* could intercept her – she was just too far to the west. Now, his only chance to catch her lay with Force H, and a successful air strike from *Ark Royal*. That morning, it was clear that the British Admiralty had run out of all other options.

According to Müllenheim-Rechberg, Lütjens' next action was to give an equally inexplicable address to the battleship's crew. He began by praising the crew for sinking the *Hood*,[13] then he added a darker note:

Henceforth, the enemy will try to concentrate his forces, and bring them into action against us. I therefore released the *Prinz Eugen* at noon yesterday, so that she could conduct commerce warfare on her own. We, on the other hand, because of the hits we have received, have been ordered to proceed to a French port. On our way there, the enemy will gather and give us battle. The German people are with you, and we will fight until our barrels glow red hot and our last shell has left our barrels. For us seamen, the question is now victory or death!

Müllenheim-Rechberg remembered: 'I can still see the leading petty officer who operated one of my directors returning dejectedly from the loudspeaker, and still hear him remarking that it was really all over.'[14] Before Lütjens' spoke, most of the crew were well aware that they'd sunk the *Hood* – the news had been broadcast on German radio, which the battleship had picked up. They also realised they were now heading towards France, and had evaded their pursuers. Almost to a man they imagined they were safely out of danger and heading to a friendly port. Now, thanks to their admiral, their morale was shattered by his talk of an imminent fight to the finish. Dejection spread throughout the ship, and, as Müllenheim-Rechberg put it: 'The high morale that permeated the ship in the preceding days was irretrievably lost.' Many of *Bismarck*'s crew were young sailors, and if their veteran admiral was talking of impending death then their situation must be very bleak indeed.

As the day wore on, fresh signals came in. Some passed on German naval intelligence reports that Force H was at sea, that the battleship they'd damaged was the *Prince of Wales* rather than the *King George V*, and that Tovey's flagship had now been joined by the battleship *Rodney*. Others were congratulatory. 25 May was Admiral Lütjens' birthday, and the German Führer sent him a personal message of congratulations.[15] Another was from Raeder, repeating these birthday wishes, and congratulating him on his recent victory. Meanwhile, *Bismarck* maintained her steady course, while Tovey's ships were falling ever further behind her. Had the battleship's crew realised the strategic situation, they would have been a lot less pessimistic. Apart from Force H, nobody else could catch them.

That afternoon, the officers of *Bismarck* had an idea. They would build a dummy after funnel, made out of wood, canvas and metal sheet. The idea was that if they were spotted by land-based search planes then they might pass themselves off as a British or an American warship. It wasn't really a particularly convincing form of disguise, but it gave the crew something to do and served as a much-needed morale-boosting project. Also, it might deter an inexperienced RAF Coastal Command observer. When it was finished, someone came up with the problem that no smoke was coming out of the dummy funnel. This, according to Müllenheim-Rechberg, resulted in an announcement over the ship's tannoy: 'Off-duty watch report to the First Officer's cabin to draw cigars, to smoke in our second funnel!'[16] In the end, though, the dummy funnel was left lying on the deck, waiting for Kapitän Lindemann's order to erect it.

Meanwhile, the oil tanks were running low. It was calculated that *Bismarck* had enough fuel to make it to Brest or St Nazaire, but only if she reduced speed to a more economical 20 knots. In fact, during the afternoon she slowed down even more, to just 12 knots. This allowed divers to enter the flooded forward compartments and open the oil tank valves there. This enabled a small amount of oil to be pumped aft, giving the ship another few hundred tons of fuel – enough to let *Bismarck* increase speed a little if she had to. However, once the repairs had been completed, Lütjens ordered that *Bismarck* continue at 20 knots. While this would give the British a better chance of catching her up, it meant she wasn't depleting her fuel stocks quite so rapidly. And so *Bismarck* continued on her course, heading west-south-west. This wasn't a direct course to the French ports – it was a little south of that – but it meant she stayed further from British air bases and thereby reduced the chances of being spotted.

CHASING THE FOX

Away to the south-east, V. Adm. Somerville's Force H was steaming north-north-west, and would reach a position some 350 miles west of Brest by the following morning, 26 May. If *Bismarck* was indeed steaming towards the French ports, then this put Somerville's three ships in the best possible place to intercept her. Admiral Tovey in *King George V* was far to the west, and was now on her own, as *Repulse* and *Prince of Wales* had both broken off to refuel.[17] So too had *Suffolk*, although *Norfolk* with R. Adm. Wake-Walker on board was able to continue the pursuit for a little longer. Further to the north, while *Victorious* had enough fuel to stay at sea, R. Adm. Curteis' cruisers were now running dangerously low on fuel. However, *Victorious* was too valuable a ship to stay at sea on her own without an escort screen. So, after one last evening air search towards the south-east produced no contact, Curteis headed back to Scapa Flow, accompanied by the carrier. That meant that Tovey was running short of ships.

There was still *Rodney*, of course. In fact, that afternoon Captain Hamilton-Dalrymple disregarded Tovey's signal ordering him to steam towards the north-west.[18] He knew *Rodney* was too slow to catch *Bismarck* if she chased after Tovey. However, if the German battleship was steaming towards France, then he was actually well placed to intercept her. However, if she actually did make contact, then if *Bismarck* turned away, the British battleship, with a top speed of 23 knots, would be unable to catch her. Even if she did, in a straightforward gun duel *Rodney* might have nine 16in. guns to *Bismarck*'s eight 15in. ones, but she lacked her German rival's modern fire control systems and

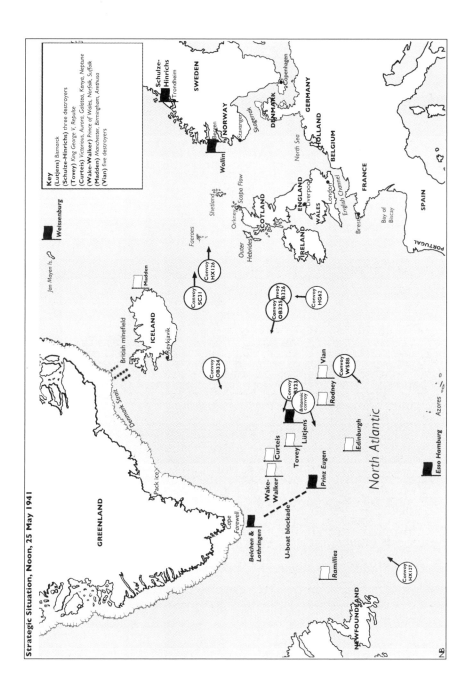

Strategic Situation, Noon, 25 May 1941

Key
(Lutjens) *Bismarck*
(Schulze-Hinrichs) three destroyers
(Tovey) *King George V, Repulse*
(Curteis) *Victorious, Aurora, Galatea, Kenya, Neptune*
(Wake-Walker) *Prince of Wales, Norfolk, Suffolk*
(Madden) *Manchester, Birmingham, Arethusa*
(Vian) five destroyers

first-class rangefinders. Thus, Hamilton-Dalrymple was not particularly confident he could stop *Bismarck*, or even slow her down.

Now the long and nerve-wracking day was drawing to a close. Despite the radio signal sent that morning, *Bismarck*'s exact location was unclear. While both the Admiralty and Tovey were now convinced she was heading towards France, for much of the day Tovey had been trying to cover two eventualities: *Bismarck* heading south-east to France, or northwards to the Iceland–Faeroes gap. So, for part of the afternoon *King George V* had sailed towards the north-east, then the east. What clinched it, though, was the decoding of a signal sent from a senior Luftwaffe commander – who was in Greece supervising air attacks on Crete – to Group West, asking for an update on *Bismarck*, probably because his nephew was serving on board.[19] The reply, forwarded through Luftwaffe channels, revealed that *Bismarck* was heading towards Brest. This left both Tovey and the Admiralty in no doubt about *Bismarck*'s destination.

Still, it was only in the early evening that Tovey's flagship turned towards the south-west, on a course that was roughly parallel to that of *Bismarck*, but a little to the north of the German ship's track. However, *Bismarck* was roughly 150 miles ahead of *King George V*. As darkness fell, *Rodney* also turned on to a similar course. By then, Tovey had another problem. The closer he and his ships got to St Nazaire, the more exposed they would be to attacks from U-boats; signal intercepts had revealed that the Germans were sending these to sea in an attempt to support *Bismarck*, and the Luftwaffe were also marshalling bombers to attack British ships, and fighters to provide air cover for the lone battleship. In fact, that evening, at 19.30, Group West signalled Lütjens, saying that Luftwaffe bombers would be providing cover for him as far as 14° West, some 360 miles west of Brest.[20] With their range of 1,900 miles, Focke-Wulf Condor reconnaissance planes would be ranging even further west.

However, these weren't the only search aircraft in the skies. In order to help Tovey as much as they could, the Coastal Command had stepped up their reconnaissance flights over the Western Approaches, their planes ranging as far south as the Bay of Biscay. Their Short Sunderland and Consolidated PBY Catalina flying boats had a range of 1,780 and 2,520 miles respectively, and so could stay in the air for hours on end. They kept patrolling until darkness fell on the evening of 25 May, but still *Bismarck* hadn't been spotted. While this was reassuring for Lütjens, it did little for Tovey's peace of mind that night. His only consolation was that at least now he knew which direction he should be looking in. *King George V* and *Rodney*, Force H, the cruisers *Norfolk* and *Dorsetshire*, and Cdr Vian's five destroyers were now in pursuit of the fox. This, though, was all irrelevant if *Bismarck* couldn't be found.

At 04.30 on 26 May, an announcement was made on board the *Bismarck*.[21] Over the ship's tannoy the crew were told: 'We have now passed three-quarters of Ireland, on our way to St Nazaire. Around noon we will be in the U-boats' operational area, and within range of German aircraft. We can count on the appearance of Condor planes after 1200.' This was a great boost to morale, and helped counter the admiral's fatalistic announcement of the day before. Now, for the first time, the young German sailors began thinking of what France might be like – a country most of them had never visited – and dreaming of the delights offered by a foreign port. Other signals from Group West had assured Lütjens that preparations were underway to escort *Bismarck* in – destroyers and U-boats were putting to sea, and the port's defences were being strengthened. All he had to do now was to get within air range of the French coast.

That morning, though, the Luftwaffe wasn't the only air force sending out search planes. The lumbering maritime reconnaissance planes of Coastal Command were preparing for another sweep of the Western Approaches, and in bases from Northern Ireland to Hampshire air crews were boarding their aircraft. One of these was a Catalina flying boat of 209 Squadron, RAF, piloted by Fg Off. Dennis Briggs.[22] This craft was unusual in that it had a US Navy co-pilot on board. When Catalinas were sent to Britain as part of the Lend-Lease programme, Ensign Leonard 'Tuck' Smith had volunteered to accompany them to help train the British pilots to fly them. Before dawn, the Catalina raced down Lough Erne, then climbed aloft, banking over the green-brown hills of County Fermanagh in Northern Ireland before heading out towards the Atlantic coast. She was one of two Catalinas flying from the Lough that morning, but they soon split up as each had its own designated search area to cover.

In theory, the Catalina could stay airborne for up to 28 hours, so the crew worked a watch system: three hours on and one off. When off watch, the crew cooked meals on a small camping stove, or else read or played cards. Four bunks were fitted for those who were able to catnap amid the incessant noise and vibration. Those on watch either piloted the plane or kept their eyes peeled for the *Bismarck*. Ensign Smith had only been with 209 Squadron for two weeks and he was still getting used to British ways. Now, at 09.45, after three hours in the air, they were flying over the Celtic Sea, 480 miles from Lough Erne, and almost 3,600 miles south-west of the Irish coast. That was the start of their designated search area. Visibility was poor – no more than 8 miles or so – and the low cloud meant they had to fly at 500ft. Below them, the sea looked rough. All eyes were scanning it for the telltale sign of a vessel's wake.

At the start of their search, Smith took over the controls and Briggs moved into the co-pilot seat for a break. Then, after just over 30 minutes of searching, Smith sat up and pointed.[23] 'What's that?' he asked. Briggs, a far more experienced pair of eyes, saw a dark shape at the limit of visibility. It appeared to be a warship. Smith banked a little to starboard and flew up into the clouds, hoping to approach the mystery ship without being seen. He was now flying at just under 2,000ft. He was about to dive down again when a gap in the clouds appeared. The warship was just 500 yards in front of them. She was a large warship, and as soon as she saw the plane she began turning hard to starboard. Then her port side erupted in orange flame.

She was firing her flak guns, and seconds later shells started bursting around them. To Briggs, the ship looked like she was one great winking flame. One close blast made the Catalina buck, and a crewman was thrown from his bunk. Smith, who later claimed he'd 'never been so scared in [his] life', reacted at once. He began evasive manoeuvres – not easy in such a lumbering seaplane – and banked and climbed back towards the cover of the clouds. At the same time, he ditched the four depth charges the plane carried, to give the Catalina a little extra lift. Meanwhile, Briggs was hastily scribbling out a message on a signal pad, which he handed to the radio operator. The haste was to get the message sent off quickly, in case they were shot down. The signal, sent just before 10.30, read: 'One battleship bearing 240°, five miles, course 150°, my position 49° 33' North, 21° 47' West. Time of origin 1030/26.'[24] Now, after 31 hours and 10 minutes without any contact, *Bismarck* had finally been sighted.

Chapter 13

Air Strike

FORCE H

When Fg Off. Briggs sent off his sighting report, it wasn't just picked up by RAF Coastal Command: as it was uncoded, it was also received by Admiral Tovey on board the *King George V*, by the Admiralty in London, and by Group West in Paris. It was also received by the B-Dienst team on board the *Bismarck*. This placed the German battleship 690 miles from Brest, or 34 hours of steaming at her economical speed of 20 knots. Tovey saw that *King George V* was 135 miles to the north of *Bismarck*, and *Rodney* was 125 miles to the north-east of Briggs' position.[1] That meant that they had absolutely no chance of catching her during the following day. For Lütjens, it meant that his flagship was 320 miles from the longitude line of 14° West, where he could expect Luftwaffe air cover. He was even closer to the line of U-boats Dönitz was assembling. So, even at 20 knots, she would be underneath a friendly air umbrella in 16 hours – or rather by dawn the following morning.

Clearly, the only way the British could catch *Bismarck* was to find a way to slow her down. Only two formations were in a position to do it. Cdr Vian's five destroyers were fairly close to the enemy battleship, and so without waiting for orders Vian altered course and headed off to intercept her.[2] So too did Captain Benjamin Martin of the heavy cruiser *Dorsetshire*. She had been escorting a convoy far to the south, but had been sent north to lend a hand. Now, using his own initiative, Martin headed off to cut *Bismarck* off from the French coast.[3] That left V. Adm. Somerville, and Force H. When Fg Off. Briggs' report came through, Somerville was to the south-east of *Bismarck's* position. He was an unorthodox commander, a lively man, with a ribald sense of humour and a zest for life. Now it looked like he would have his chance to bring *Bismarck* to battle.

During the voyage north from Gibraltar, Somerville had detached his destroyers, which left him with the battlecruiser *Renown*, which served as his flagship, the light cruiser *Sheffield*, and the fleet aircraft carrier *Ark Royal*. The other two ships could be easily brushed aside by *Bismarck*, but the *Ark Royal*, with her embarked squadrons of Swordfish torpedo bombers, stood a chance of damaging the German battleship. It was a slim chance, though; as the air strike from *Victorious* showed, *Bismarck* appeared virtually immune from attacks by aerial torpedoes. Nevertheless, that morning, Somerville had ordered Captain Loben Maund of *Ark Royal* to carry out a search of the waters to the north and west.[4] The previous day, the carrier had suspended flying because Force H was sailing through a south-easterly gale. By dawn, while the seas were still rough, the gale had eased a little, and Cdr Henry Traill, in charge of flying operations on the carrier, deemed it safe to fly.

However, it was still very hazardous. The carrier's flight deck was 62ft above the waterline, and it was pitching over 50ft between the huge wave crests. It was rolling, too – so much so that the flight deck crew were worried the planes would slip off the deck. Spray was still breaking over the bow, and any launch in those conditions was fraught with danger. Yet desperate times called for equally desperate measures. Only *Ark Royal's* Swordfish could stop *Bismarck* now, and first they had to find her. So, the search aircraft had to be launched. Originally, it had been intended to launch the aircraft at 07.00, but this was delayed by two hours in the hope that conditions would improve. They did a little, but not enough to make the undertaking anything short of reckless. Thus, at 08.45 Maund turned *Ark Royal* into the wind, reduced speed and signalled Traill to begin the launch.[5]

It was all in the timing. This turn into the wind stopped the carrier from rolling but it didn't stop the pitching. So, Traill had to judge his moment, launching each plane as the flight deck began to rise to meet another wave. With a 50-knot wind facing them, the Swordfish only needed to reach a speed of 35mph before they could take off. All eyes were riveted to each biplane as it rolled forwards, picked up speed and lurched into the air. Some timed it better than others, and a few planes skimmed the water as the flight deck dropped towards a trough. Nevertheless, they all made it. Then, after circling over the carrier the Swordfish fanned out and began their search. All of them were fitted with long-range fuel tanks and carried experienced observers on board. If anyone stood a chance of finding *Bismarck* it was them.

The ten search planes were still airborne at 10.30 when Fg Off. Briggs' signal was transmitted. Somerville could see from the chart that *Bismarck's* position was 112 miles to the north-west, and that her projected course took her straight into the quadrant covered by his Swordfish. Sure enough, at 11.14

Sub Lt 'Jock' Hartley flying aircraft 2A sighted *Bismarck*, but he thought she was a cruiser.[6] Minutes later, at 11.21, Lt John Callander in 2F spotted her and correctly identified the ship. Upon hearing this, Somerville ordered two more Swordfish aloft, equipped with radar, to take over from Callander's and Hartley's planes, which were now shadowing their contact. The other eight Swordfish were recalled, in order to refuel and be armed with 18in. torpedoes. By this time Force H had turned to steer a parallel course to *Bismarck*, 50 miles north of her.

Now came the next tricky problem – landing the aircraft again in such treacherous conditions. Again, timing was crucial, and all but one of the planes landed safely; misjudging it, one pilot brought his Swordfish in too late, as the carrier's stern rose and crushed his plane to pieces. The three-man crew were bruised and battered but survived the experience. The Swordfish lining up astern of the carrier then had to wait until the wreckage was swept from the deck. That tricky job done, the flight deck crews brought the aircraft back down into the hangar, where they were better protected, and set about refuelling and arming the biplanes. Throughout the day, the two Swordfish shadowing *Bismarck* were replaced, which ensured that the battleship was kept under continual surveillance.

Meanwhile, during the course of the morning Somerville kept *Renown* well to the east of *Ark Royal*, but within visual contact, despite the fog patches that were drifting over the sea.[7] The idea was first to protect *Ark Royal*, in case *Bismarck* moved to attack her, and second to be ready to block the German ship's route to France, if the need arose. This, however, would be little more than a suicide mission. *Renown* was a battlecruiser, protected by a 9in. armoured

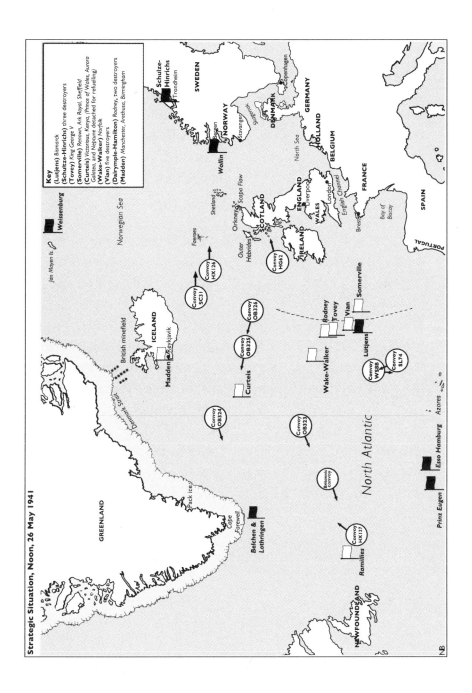

Strategic Situation, Noon, 26 May 1941

Key
(Lutjens) *Bismarck*
(Schulze-Hinrichs) three destroyers
(Tovey) *King George V*
(Somerville) *Renown, Ark Royal, Sheffield*
(Curteis) *Victorious, Kenya, (Prince of Wales, Aurora Galatea, and Neptune detached for refuelling)*
(Wake-Walker) *Norfolk*
(Vian) five destroyers
(Dalrymple-Hamilton) *Rodney,* two destroyers
(Madden) *Manchester, Arethusa, Birmingham*

belt, and up to 6in. of deck armour. So, although she had been first launched in 1916, at least her deck armour had been reinforced during the inter-war years. This, though, was still not proof against modern 15in. armour-piercing shells. She also carried six 15in. guns, in three twin turrets, which, though powerful, gave her just three-quarters of *Bismarck*'s firepower. She also lacked the German battleship's modern fire control equipment. All in all, she didn't stand much of chance in a fight.

That left Somerville with a problem. If *Ark Royal* was unable to delay *Bismarck*, then it would be up to *Renown*. The admiral talked it over with the ship's commanding officer, Captain Rhoderick McGrigor, and they both agreed that the situation demanded it: if there was no alternative, the *Renown* would sail into action, regardless of the odds. This meant placing her 1,200-man crew in serious danger, but there was no other option. If *Bismarck* were to be stopped, *Renown* would have to slow her down. However, Somerville planned to use what few advantages he could. For instance, he would attack upwind, from the north-west, so that if things started to go badly he could more readily disengage under cover of a smoke screen. With a top speed of 32 knots, *Renown* was also faster. So, he would also approach *Bismarck* from astern, forcing the German battleship to turn towards him, therefore helping to delay her progress towards France.

Later that morning, though, the Admiralty, with the *Hood* disaster fresh on their minds, ordered Somerville and McGrigor to avoid battle, unless *King George V* or *Rodney* were also engaging the enemy. This may well have spared the lives of 1,200 British sailors, but it also robbed the British of their one last-ditch chance to slow *Bismarck* down. That meant it was solely up to *Ark Royal*.

However, Somerville had one other ship at his disposal. The light cruiser *Sheffield* was doing nothing apart from escorting the *Ark Royal*. So, at 13.15, Somerville ordered Captain Arthur Larcom to detach from the rest of the force, head south and then shadow the enemy battleship from astern.[8] The limitation was that she only carried a Type 79Y Air Search radar, so unlike *Norfolk* or *Suffolk* she had to keep within the bounds of visibility and rely on her lookouts. Unfortunately, Somerville neglected to tell Captain Maund of the *Ark Royal* about the cruiser's redeployment.

'SORRY FOR THE KIPPER'

Meanwhile, on board *Ark Royal* the last two search planes, 2F and 2H, landed back on the carrier at 13.34. By now the gale had eased a bit, making carrier operations slightly less fraught, although the seas were still extremely rough and in normal circumstances flying operations would have been suspended. This, however, was no ordinary day. So, as these last two planes were refuelled and armed with torpedoes, the air crews trooped into the briefing room. There they learned that *Bismarck* was 40 miles away to the south, and steering a parallel course to the carrier. The mission was fairly straightforward. A total of 14 aircraft would be used in the attack, with another aircraft being held in reserve in case of problems taking off. Each of these Swordfish carried an 18in. torpedo, similar to the ones carried by *Victorious'* aircraft. Once more, the planes would be grouped into smaller groups of two or three aircraft, which would split up when sighting the target and approach her from both sides to make it harder to dodge the torpedoes. The strike would be led by Ulsterman Lt Cdr James Stewart-Moore, the commander of 820 Squadron.

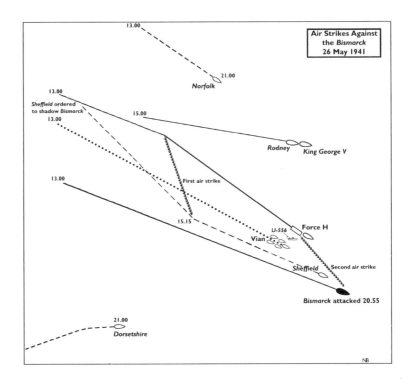

The crews boarded their Swordfish, and at 14.50 the first of them took off. After they assembled over the carrier, Stewart-Moore led them off to the south. The sea was hidden by the low cloud but some of the planes carried ASV radar, which in theory could detect a large surface target at a range of 26,330 yards (13 miles).[9] At 15.20, they picked up a contact, which could only be *Bismarck*. So, still keeping above the clouds, Stewart-Moore ordered his strike to split up into sub-flights and to move into their attacking positions to port and starboard of the contact. Strangely, though, the contact was some 20 miles closer than they'd expected. It was also heading towards the south-east, rather than due east, as the briefing had told him to expect. Still, at 15.45 all the aircraft were in place, and Stewart-Moore signalled them to launch their attack. The biplanes then began dropping through the clouds, and on towards the enemy battleship.

On board the *Sheffield*, the crew were delighted they had been given a real job to do: a £2 reward was offered to the first sailor to spot the *Bismarck*. Morale was high as they steamed south at 31 knots, the crew at Action Stations and everyone keyed up and ready. In the cruiser's gunnery direction platform at the top of her forward superstructure, Mid. David Repard's job was to look out for the Luftwaffe, who might well turn up to escort the *Bismarck* home.[10] So, he was there when he saw aircraft tumbling out of the low clouds like falling leaves. They were *Ark Royal*'s Swordfish. He raised the alarm, and remembered hearing someone say, 'My God, they're attacking us.' Sure enough, the biplanes were deploying on to either beam of the cruiser and starting their attack runs. On *Sheffield*'s bridge, Captain Larcom saw them too and realised the airmen were about to attack his ship.[11] He immediately rang the telegraph for full speed and began turning. At the same moment, he snapped an order to his gun crews: 'On no account fire!'

Stewart-Moore saw the target through a break in the clouds and realised they were attacking the wrong ship.[12] His pilot yelled the same over the intercom and pulled out of his approach dive, waggling his wings as a warning to others. By then, though, it was too late. Only three other crews realised the mistake and pulled away. The others must have been surprised at the lack of flak coming from the enemy ship, but released their torpedoes anyway. The first one struck the water from 80ft, and began heading towards *Sheffield*'s port beam. The second exploded on contact with the water. Larcom managed to comb the torpedo track, and it shot past the cruiser's port side. Another three torpedoes also exploded when they hit the water, but the remainder – five of them – were launched successfully, both from the cruiser's port and starboard sides. Amazingly, Larcom threaded through them, and they all missed.

Some of the pilots realised their mistake as they approached, but one got so close that they strafed the cruiser's decks with machine-gun fire. Fortunately, nobody was hit. Another sheepishly signalled the cruiser by Aldis lamp, saying, 'Sorry for the kipper' – Fleet Air Arm slang for a torpedo.[13] Captain Larcom, however, was not in a particularly forgiving mood that afternoon. In fact, he was described as being 'purple with rage'.[14] What had saved his ship was the fact that the torpedoes were fitted with a duplex, a new kind of magnetic detonator. These proved temperamental and their pistols all fired prematurely when the torpedoes landed in the water. So, rather shamefacedly, Stewart-Moore gathered his flock of aircraft together and headed back towards the carrier. As they flew home, the ASV radar picked up more contacts, 10 miles away. At first they thought these were German destroyers, but they flashed a British recognition signal. It was Vian, whose destroyers were steaming at top speed to make contact with Somerville.

By now, the seas had picked up again, and although *Ark Royal* turned into the wind for the landing it was still extremely hazardous. The three Swordfish still carrying torpedoes were therefore ordered to ditch them before attempting to land. It was a sensible precaution. Three of the Swordfish were damaged while landing, as the stern of the carrier rose up and buckled their undercarriage as they touched down. Nevertheless, they all made it back safely. As Stewart-Moore headed towards the island and the debrief, he was clutching a piece of paper. It was a signal telling him to 'Watch out for the *Sheffield*, which he'd received just minutes before. He and his air crews had messed up by attacking the wrong ship, but the fault also lay with Somerville and his staff, who duly apologised to Maund for net telling him about *Sheffield* sooner.[15] The debriefing was described as being 'animated'.

THE LAST ROLL OF THE DICE

The last of the returning air strike landed back on the carrier by 17.20. Immediately, the aircraft had their wings folded and were towed to the lifts, then taken down to the hangar for refuelling. Captain Maund and Cdr Traill decided there was still just enough time to launch one more strike before nightfall. This would be their last airstrike of the day. After that, a combination of darkness and the rough weather meant that a night attack was prohibitively dangerous. Like Tovey and Somerville, both men knew that by dawn the *Bismarck* would be under the aerial umbrella of Luftwaffe fighters, which, fitted with long-range fuel tanks, would be able to provide air cover for *Bismarck*. This meant that the chances of pulling off another Swordfish strike the following morning were non-existent. It would be suicide. So, this was effectively the last roll of the dice.

The near-disaster now proved to be something of a blessing since it had highlighted the problem with the new detonators.[16] These would now be replaced by old-fashioned but reliable contact ones. It took the hangar crews almost 90 minutes to prepare the aircraft, but by 18.45 they were ready. This time the strike would consist of 15 aircraft – the last of *Ark Royal's* operational Swordfish. Four each were 810 and 818 Squadrons, while 820 Squadron provided another seven aircraft. This strike would be led by Lt Cdr Treventen 'Tim'

Coode, commander of 818 Squadron. Stewart-Moore was flying too, leading the flight from his own squadron; he and the others saw it as a chance to redeem themselves. In the briefing, they were told that *Sheffield* would serve as a beacon. After making contact with her, they were to fly ahead of the cruiser, locate the *Bismarck* and carry out their attack. This time, there would be no room for error.

Since 17.40 *Sheffield* had been in visual contact with *Bismarck*, and despite the bad weather and poor visibility she was now shadowing her, from 10–12 miles astern.[17] To some, she still looked dangerously close, and everyone on board was well aware that her 15in. guns could rip *Sheffield* apart in a single salvo. Yet the German battleship didn't open fire.

At 19.00, some 35 miles to the north, *Ark Royal* turned into the wind and Maund gave Traill the signal to launch aircraft. A 50-knot wind was whistling over the flight deck, so Maund had reduced speed to 10 knots. The flight deck was still pitching alarmingly, and spray was breaking over the flight deck crews holding the planes in place. Despite this, everyone on board or in the planes was grimly determined. They knew it was all up to them. Finally, at 19.10, Traill lowered his green flag, the flight deck crew removed their chocks and the first Swordfish began rolling forwards.

Again, it was all in the timing. Traill and his team were watching the waves, so they timed each launch as the carrier's bows were rising out of a trough. One by one the biplanes moved along the deck, picking up speed, and then rose into the gale-tossed air. Eventually, all 15 Swordfish were airborne.[18] Coode had them form up over Somerville's flagship, and at 19.25 they set off, heading towards the south-west.

This time, despite the poor visibility and low cloud, the approach was uneventful, and shortly before 20.00 the *Sheffield* appeared on radar. Coode signalled for the strike to drop down below the clouds and they approached the cruiser from their port quarter. On this occasion, nobody launched a torpedo. Instead, they formed up again over the *Sheffield*, as Captain Larcom had a message flashed to them, saying that *Bismarck* lay 12 miles away, on a bearing of 110°. With that, the 15 Swordfish raced on into the gloom, and towards the waiting enemy.

The cloud was a little higher this time, at about 2,000ft, covering seven-tenths of the sky. Coode led his aircraft above the cloud layer to hide his approach, and after a false start when he lost the bearing, they set off towards the east while climbing to 6,000ft. At 20.30 they split up into sub-flights, each group of three planes following the one in front, with Coode's sub-flight in the lead. There were mist patches at sea level and the light was fading, so he hoped it would help screen their approach for a few vital seconds while the Swordfish made their attack runs. His plan called for half of the strike to attack the *Bismarck* simultaneously from each beam. Now, however, the poor flying conditions made this set-piece attack look unlikely. The low clouds meant there was a good chance that the sub-flights would lose contact with each other. For this reason, he signalled them to act independently and choose their own approach.

At 20.45, Coode reckoned they were getting close, so he ordered the planes to start their dive. Later, he recalled: 'Visibility was limited – a matter of yards. I watched the altimeter go back. When we reached 2,000ft I started to worry ... At 1,000ft I felt sure something was wrong, but still we were completely enclosed by cloud.'[19] The clouds were thicker over *Bismarck* – and lower. They finally broke through them at 700ft. As Coode had feared, the strike had been broken up by the cloud. It was just as well. They had overshot their target, and *Bismarck* lay 4 miles behind them. Turning and attacking upwind in such lumbering planes would have been suicidal, so Coode had the three planes accompanying him bank around, then climb back into the clouds. The rest of the strike were nowhere to be seen. A few minutes later, just before 21.00, Coode dropped down again, followed by his three companions. As they emerged from the clouds, they saw the *Bismarck* dead ahead of them.[20]

To Coode's slight annoyance, he saw they weren't the first planes to arrive. Over beyond *Bismarck*, two planes of Lt David 'Feather' Godfrey-Faussett's second sub-flight could be seen, approaching the battleship from starboard, but aiming slightly ahead of her. The textbook called for the torpedoes to be launched 900 yards (0.14 miles) from the target, at a height of 90ft above the water, and with the Swordfish travelling at 90mph. At that range it would take the 18in. Mark XII torpedo 40 seconds to reach its target. In that time, though, a battleship making 28 knots would travel 622 yards – and *Bismarck* was 274 yards long. Thus, the Swordfish had to 'lead' the target by around 500 yards (0.25 mile), aiming in front of her to make sure the torpedo hit her squarely. As the two planes levelled off and began their run, *Bismarck*'s side erupted in orange flame and lines of multi-coloured tracer began streaking towards them. Seconds later, flak bursts erupted, but mercifully for the air crews, they were in front of them.

Godfrey-Faussett's Swordfish 2B and Sub Lt Kenneth Pattison in 2A had climbed above the clouds, but were forced down due to ice forming on their wings.[21] However,

Godfrey-Faussett had ASV radar and they emerged well placed off the battleship's starboard beam. It looked like every gun on board was aiming at them as they made their run. Tracer and shells ripped through their wings, but they held their nerve long enough to drop their torpedoes before banking away to starboard, trying to climb away from the flak. Kapitän Lindemann was already turning to starboard though, but not fast enough to avoid one of the torpedoes, which struck the battleship near her stern. This may well have been the crucial rudder hit that crippled the *Bismarck*.

This turn also meant that Coode's four planes were now approaching the *Bismarck* from her port side, which erupted in flame as the battleship's flak batteries once more opened up on the four Swordfish. Three of them were from Coode's first sub-flight, made up from 818 Squadron.[22] Sub Lt Edward Child's aircraft 5B had been hit by shrapnel, but somehow it stayed in the air. Amazingly, none of them was knocked out of the skies before they released their torpedoes. Coode loosed his moments after Child, and just before Sub Lt John 'Jock' Moffat, the youngest member of the sub-flight. Born in the Scottish borders, he had only joined the Fleet Air Arm the year before, and *Ark Royal* was his first operational assignment. As he flew closer to *Bismarck* he was awestruck by her size: 'If you're facing a ship that size, twice as big as your own ship, and they're firing everything they have at you, it is simply unbelievable. The stuff was coming in at such a rate I don't mind admitting that I was petrified.' Still, Jock released his torpedo and banked away, the tracer following him as he went.

Moffat released his torpedo at a signal from his observer, Sub Lt John 'Dusty' Miller, who'd been watching the wave tops.[23] If the torpedo landed in a trough, it was likely to run deep and strike below the battleship's armoured belt. Hitting a wave or its crest meant it would run shallow and was less likely to do any real damage. Jock and Dusty timed their drop to perfection, although they were still about 1,500 yards (0.75 mile) from the *Bismarck*. At this point, Kapitän Lindemann was turning *Bismarck* hard to port, and as the Swordfish turned away it looked like the four torpedoes would miss. Looking back, Lt Edmond Carver, who was Coode's observer in 5A, thought he saw a column of water erupt on the battleship's port side, just by her funnel. That may have been an illusion, however; the hit was actually further aft.

The fourth pilot in the group, Lt Keane of 818 Squadron, flying 5K, dropped his 'kipper' at a similar range. Later, both Keane and Moffat laid claim to scoring a hit, but the likelihood is that it was 5K's torpedo that struck the ship on her port side. Now, as the other three planes flew off, Coode hung around as he wanted to see if the rest of his strike aircraft would have better luck. The third sub-flight of two planes had been split up, one accompanying Coode and the other joining the fourth sub-flight, which was still nowhere to be seen. Clearly, the whole strike had been badly scattered in the clouds. At the next moment, Coode saw them drop through the clouds and head towards *Bismarck*'s port quarter.

There were four aircraft in this attack – three from the fourth sub-flight, and Sub Lt Charles Jewell's plane 2A, from the third sub-flight. Stewart-Moore commanded the attack, from the observer's seat of Swordfish 4A.[24] His planes had been in a tight formation as they entered the cloud layer, but by the time they emerged they were strung out, and so there wasn't any chance of a coordinated attack. Regardless, they pressed on. Sub Lt Alan Swanton's Swordfish 4C was one of these. To him, *Bismarck*, now less than half a mile away, 'looked black and menacing' – a sinister humpbacked ship whose flak guns seemed to be aiming directly at him. Indeed, some of them were. They approached the battleship from her port beam.

First, two other planes dropped their torpedoes – Swordfish 4A and 4B, both from 820 Squadron. Then it was Swanton's turn He released his torpedo, then turned away. As he banked, a flak shell erupted just beneath them and pieces of shrapnel ripped through the flimsy plane. The Swordfish staggered, but she stayed in the air. Both Swanton and his gunner were wounded, and afterwards they counted no fewer than 175 holes peppering 4C's airframe. The flak was terrifyingly thick and it seemed miraculous that none of the other planes was hit. Later, all the air crews agreed that the Germans seemed to be firing ahead of the aircraft – almost as if they couldn't imagine that a torpedo-carrying aircraft could be quite as slow as a lumbering Swordfish.

All three Swordfish of Stewart-Moore's sub-flight launched their torpedoes and made off, as did Lt Jewell in 2M of the third sub-flight, who had tagged along for the attack.[25] They attacked almost simultaneously with Godfrey-Faussett's sub-flight, coming in from the battleship's port side. That in theory should have made it harder for Kapitän Lindemann to avoid the torpedoes. Somehow he managed it, and all of the fourth sub-flight's 'kippers' missed the battleship. They were now heading away from the ship and so the flak eased as they drew out of range of the battleship's smaller anti-aircraft guns. They weren't home safe yet though – at that moment *Bismarck* fired her main 15in. guns, and the salvo landed right in front of Stewart-Moore's plane. The columns of water they threw up were even higher than the altitude of the planes. In fact, Swanton had to fly through one of these columns of collapsing spray.

So, Coode's four aircraft attacking from off the battleship's port bow, Stewart-Moore's four from the port beam and Godfrey-Faussett's two from the starboard beam had all launched their torpedoes. Of these, one had hit the battleship on her port side, but there was no visible sign of damage. Coode had watched the other two attacks go in, and was disappointed that *Bismarck* seemed virtually unscathed. Still, he had five more aircraft left, somewhere above him in the clouds. These were the four Swordfish making up the fifth and sixth sub-flights, and one missing plane, 2P, flown by Sub Lt Tony Beale of 810 Squadron. He had been part of the second sub-flight but had lost his way in the clouds.[26] So, he calmly returned to *Sheffield* and his observer flashed a signal lamp, asking for directions. With these, Beale set off again and spotted *Bismarck* ahead of him, 7 miles away. He skirted the clouds, working his way around to her port side, before turning in to start his attack.

His observer, Charlie Friend, thought *Bismarck* looked particularly wicked, with her huge humped back.[27] Beale kept the Swordfish low, just 50ft from the water, and he held his nerve, too, closing to within 800 yards (0.4 miles) before dropping his torpedo. The flak was intense. As Friend put it as they flew closer and closer to *Bismarck*: 'Her decks seemed to explode into crackling flame, the sea was lashed with shot and fragments.' As they released the torpedo and banked away, at the back of the Swordfish Leading Airman Ken Pimlott opened up on the battleship with his machine gun, just for the heck of it. Next, Friend saw a big plume of water erupt on the port side of the *Bismarck*, amidships, near the funnel.

Pimlott danced a little jig as they sped away, ignoring the tracer chasing after them.

Lt Alistair Owen-Smith, leading the two Swordfish of the fifth sub-flight, was behind the others, and as the first planes attacked he was still diving through the cloud. He saw shells bursting near him as he dived, and when he dropped through the cloud cover he found he was astern of *Bismarck*. He was working his way forwards towards the starboard beam of *Bismarck* when he saw a column of water erupt near the battleship's stern, on what he thought was her port side. He closed to within 1,000 yards (0.5 mile), 'flying through a wall of smoke and water', then launched his torpedo before turning away.[28] It missed, as the battleship turned hard to port. At the time he thought this was an unusual manoeuvre, as he expected her to be turning the other way. Still, he was more successful than the second Swordfish of the flight, which made two attempts to attack but was forced back by the wall of flak. After this, the pilot jettisoned his torpedo and headed home.

That left the two planes from the sixth sub-flight, both from 820 Squadron. They lost each other in the clouds, and while one gave up and headed home, the other, Swordfish 4G, approached *Bismarck* from her starboard side. By now the other planes had gone, so her pilot, Sub Lt Willcocks, felt horribly exposed, as all the flak now seemed to be directed at his solitary plane. As a result, he released early, at 2,000 yards (1 mile), but *Bismarck* continued to turn to port, and the long-range torpedo attack failed as it surged past the battleship, well off her starboard side. That was the last roll of the dice. From start to finish the attack had lasted roughly 25 minutes, from 21.00 onwards. Now, as the last plane departed, the *Bismarck*'s guns fell silent. Several of the Swordfish flew over

Sheffield on their way home, and the cruiser's crew cheered them, not from any expectation they'd achieved anything, but really in celebration that the airmen were still alive.

Lt Cdr Coode had watched it all. With the attack complete, it was with a heavy heart he ordered a signal to be sent off before turning for home. It simply read: 'Estimate no hits.'[29] With that, the last Swordfish departed, heading back towards *Ark Royal*, and the prospect of another dangerous landing in rough seas and the growing dark. The first Swordfish began landing on the carrier just after 22.00, and the last of them touched down just before 23.00. The landing itself was almost as dramatic as the attack had been. *Ark Royal* was still pitching violently, and five of the Swordfish had been hit by flak. The worst was 4C, piloted by the wounded Swanson. He landed her safely, but she turned out to be so badly damaged that she was deemed a write-off and was ditched over the side. Three of the others crash-landed on the carrier's deck, either through mistiming the pitching of the ship or from damage to their undercarriage. Nevertheless, everyone survived the experience.

When Coode sent his signal, he presumed that none of the torpedoes had hit their target. On the bridge of *King George V*, Admiral Tovey had been waiting for Coode's signal, and when it came he merely smiled, and said nothing.[30] At that moment he must have thought that he was beaten. He had come very close, but *Bismarck* seemed to lead a charmed life. The same signal was also received by V. Adm. Somerville in *Renown*, Captain Maund in *Ark Royal*, Captain Dalrymple-Hamilton in *Rodney*, Captain Larcom in *Sheffield* and Cdr Vian in *Cossack*.

Larcom, however, had his own problems, as *Bismarck* had opened fire on her. She even straddled the cruiser before

Sheffield made smoke and disappeared from view. By then, though, Larcom had noticed something strange.[31] *Bismarck* was no longer heading away from her, towards the French coast. Instead, she had turned to port. This may have been merely so that all her 15in. guns could bear on *Sheffield*, but somehow it seemed slightly more unusual. Accordingly, Larcom sent a signal to Tovey. It read 'Enemy's course 340°'. It meant that *Bismarck* was now heading north-north-west, almost straight towards the *King George V.* Tovey laughed it off, saying rather cuttingly, 'I fear Larcom has joined the reciprocal club.' He meant, of course, that he expected *Bismarck* was probably heading in the opposite direction.

While the attack had been taking place, Maund and Traill had launched two more aircraft from *Ark Royal,* to continue shadowing *Bismarck* for another hour or so. After all, there might still be a chance that the aircraft carrier might launch another strike at dawn, before the Luftwaffe arrived to escort *Bismarck* home. Then, one of these shadowing aircraft sent its own signal, which proved Captain Larcom wasn't getting his bearings mixed up. It read: 'Enemy steering due north'.[32] Everyone who heard it must have greeted the news with amazement. Larcom was correct: *Bismarck* was now heading north instead of east, and straight towards Tovey's flagship. Somehow, one of the air strike's torpedoes must have caused some serious damage to *Bismarck* after all. In that instant, the whole game had changed.

Chapter 14

Destroyers in the Night

ONE IN A HUNDRED THOUSAND

During the air attack, Lt von Müllenheim-Rechberg was at his post in *Bismarck's* after gun director tower. Later, he recalled the moment: 'The attack must have been almost over when it came, an explosion aft. My heart sank. I glanced at the rudder indicator. It showed "Left 12°". Did that just happen to be our correct heading at that moment? No. It did not change. It stayed at "Left 12°". Our increasing list to starboard soon told us that we were in a continuous turn.'[1] Then, Müllenheim-Rechberg was distracted, as the order came to fire on the light cruiser *Sheffield*. She was roughly 9 miles away, and the battleship fired six salvos at her. The first was a miss, but the second straddled the target.[2] The cruiser immediately turned away, making smoke, and the next four salvos all fell short. Although no serious damage was done, shrapnel thrown up as the 15in. shells exploded next to the ship killed one crewman and injured seven more. Later, one of these would die from his wounds. All the time, though, *Bismarck* kept turning to port.

Müllenheim-Rechberg looked back at the rudder indicator. It still said 'Left 12°'. As he put it: 'At one stroke, the world seemed to be irrevocably altered. Or was it? Perhaps the damage could be repaired? I broke the anxious silence that enveloped my station by remarking: "We'll just have to wait. The men below will do everything they can."'[3] In fact, *Bismarck* had been hit twice. The first was from a torpedo that ran shallow and struck the battleship amidships on her port side, where it exploded against her armoured belt just below the waterline, but did no real damage. The second though – the one launched by Sub Lt Moffat – hit the battleship's stern, on her port side. The blow shook the whole stern of the ship. At the time, *Bismarck*'s damage control teams thought the damage was done to her steering compartment, protected by a watertight bulkhead that was just 45mm thick. In fact, the damage was far more serious than that.

According to Müllenheim-Rechberg: 'The torpedo hit had shaken the ship so violently that the safety valve in the starboard engine room closed, and the engines shut down. Slowly the vibration of the ship ceased.'[4] Then: 'The control station re-opened the safety valve and we had steam again. The floor plates of the engine room buckled upwards about half a metre, and water rushed in through the port shaft well.' He added: 'It would not take long, however, to seal off the room and pump it out.' This proved to be over-optimistic. The damage control parties inspected the stern compartments and found that the steering rooms were flooded, and the men working there had been forced to evacuate them. Attempts to pump out the compartment were delayed due to an electrical fault, no doubt caused by shorting caused by flooding. Then they discovered that the pumps were damaged.

The plan now was to shore up the after bulkhead, to stop the flood spreading. Next, divers could enter the flooded compartments, seal them and pump out the water. All this took time, however, and meanwhile *Bismarck* was still steaming in a long, lazy circle to port. The rudders simply weren't responding. Kapitän Lindemann tried to counteract this by steering with his propellers, but this proved difficult, as for some reason, while *Bismarck* had three propellers, the centre one wasn't responding.[5] In consequence, he had to juggle the port and starboard propellers, with one running at full speed and the other at half speed. It wasn't really a workable solution. The only sensible course was to fix the steering gear if it was damaged, or the rudder. In the end, though, it became clear that nothing could be done in the steering compartment. So, the ship continued on her erratic course.

Lindemann tried everything he could – varying the speed, and trying to rig some form of emergency steering. However, as the night drew on it was clear that *Bismarck* had been irrevocably damaged. During the training period in the Baltic, one machinist remembered how he had played dead during a damage control exercise, to simulate a hit on the steering compartment. They had been told then that the odds of being damaged there were extremely low – one in a hundred thousand.[6] Now those words came back to him.

In fact, the steering gear was the least of *Bismarck*'s problems; the torpedo explosion had all but sheared off the port rudder, so it didn't respond at all. At the same time the starboard one had been blown forwards and had jammed against the central propeller, so that now both rudder and propeller were locked in place. It was the sort of damage that could only be repaired in a dry dock, like the one in St Nazaire. Now, the chances of *Bismarck* reaching it had become non-existent.

The torpedo hit took place at around 21.20. Just over two hours later, at 23.30, a rudimentary form of emergency steering was rigged, a hand-operated rudder, dropped over the side and attached to the port rudder yoke.[7] The crew of the 6in. gun turret were called on to operate it, but it proved unmanageable and the attempt was abandoned. So too was the notion of demolishing the aircraft hangar door and dropping it over the side as a makeshift rudder. All attempts by divers to uncouple the starboard rudder failed, too, as it was jammed too tightly and the coupling wouldn't budge. The bad weather made it an impossible task.

Thus, with all other options exhausted, Lindemann was forced to continue trying to steer some sort of eastward course using his engines alone, but even that proved too much and the ship's general direction that evening was towards the north-west – away from the safety of the French coast. Effectively, *Bismarck* was doomed.

While *Bismarck* was steering erratically, Admiral Tovey was gathering his forces. At 15.36 that afternoon, *Rodney* came within sight of Tovey's flagship, *King George V.*[8] This meant that the admiral now had the combined firepower to sink the *Bismarck,* if he could only catch her up during the night. At the time, the chances of doing so seemed very slim indeed, yet the Home Fleet were continuing the chase, more for form's sake than anything else. A little later, using signal lamps, Tovey and Captain Dalrymple-Hamilton discussed their fuel states. While *Rodney* still had enough fuel in her tanks for a few more days at sea, she was approaching the limit of what she'd need if she resumed her journey to the USA, where she was going to undergo a much-needed refit. The *King George V,* however, was now running perilously low, and Captain Patterson had already warned Tovey that if they were to make it back to Scapa Flow then they would have to break off pursuit by midnight.

This calculation was made on the basis that they continued to steam at full speed. However, now that the lumbering *Rodney* had joined her, both battleships were making just 22 knots – the fastest that Rodney's aged engines could manage. Patterson therefore recalculated his fuel stocks and extended the deadline to 09.00 the following morning. Still, Tovey insisted that the two battleships continue to head towards the south-east, on a course roughly parallel to that of *Bismarck*. He was pinning his last hopes on the air attack from *Ark Royal*. Then, later that evening came the news that the air attack had failed. *Bismarck* was now unstoppable. A sense of gloom hung over the bridge of the flagship, but this dissipated slightly with the news from *Sheffield* that *Bismarck* was heading towards the north-west. Only when this was confirmed by the shadowing aircraft did Tovey allow himself to believe he might still have a chance of bringing *Bismarck* to battle.

Now, after a slight change of course, the two British battleships and their German adversary were heading towards each other, and the distance between them was dropping fast. At 23.00, the last of the strike aircraft had returned to *Ark Royal*. Then, gradually, as the air crews were debriefed, it became apparent that instead of not being hit at all, as Coode had reported, the battleship had been struck by two torpedoes, possibly more. Only damage to her rudder or steering gear would cause her to circle to port and abandon her ruler-straight course towards France. Thus, Tovey now had reason to hope he could bring the *Bismarck* to battle the following morning. Besides, he now had one more small but deadly naval force at his disposal: Cdr Vian's destroyers could now harry the German battleship, while *King George V* and *Rodney* steamed on through the night.

ATTACK WITH TORPEDOES

That night, the conditions were grim. All of the warships in that part of the North Atlantic were steaming through very rough seas. The Sea States was 5, going on 6, which meant it was just short of being a full-blown gale. The waves were capped with angry white crests, and were between 10 and 15ft high, which meant that all of the ships were pitching and rolling through the sea, their decks slick with spray. The smaller ones, like Vian's destroyers, were 'shipping it green', with their focsles awash with the waves and spray as the small ships punched through the seas. The wind was blowing hard from the north-west, at 25 knots, but with gusts of more than 40mph. Streaks of white foam were splattering the decks of these smaller ships, too. All in all, especially for those standing on open bridges or upper decks, it was a dirty night. Vian's destroyers were taking a real pounding from the weather, but their crews hardly noticed.[9] They were steaming into action.

Shortly before 22.00, Captain Vian's destroyers had come upon *Sheffield*, which was still gamely trying to shadow the *Bismarck*. After nearly being hit by large German shells, Captain Larcom was keeping a respectful distance from the enemy battleship. The cruiser's radar had been put out of action by shell splinters, so it was the cruiser's lookouts that first spotted the lean black shapes. Larcom was certain they were friendly – they were still too far from the French coast for German destroyers to be at sea. In fact, these were the same ones spotted by *Ark Royal*'s returning first strike, after it had mistakenly targeted the *Sheffield*. Vian approached the cruiser from the north-west, and Larcom used lamp signals to tell him where the *Bismarck* lay.[10] Then the destroyers filed past and disappeared into the gloom.

There were five of them. Four – *Cossack, Maori, Sikh* and *Zulu* – were Tribal class destroyers of the 4th Destroyer Flotilla, all of which had been commissioned shortly before the start of the war. Captain Philip Vian had taken command of the flotilla in early 1940, with *Cossack* acting as the flotilla leader. These were powerful modern destroyers, armed with eight 4.7in. guns in four twin turrets, and carrying four 21in. torpedoes in a quadruple launcher mounted amidships.[11] In theory, they could reach 36 knots, but that night, given the rough seas, they were lucky to make half that. This didn't deter Vian though. As he knew the *Ark Royal* had recalled her shadowing aircraft for the night, and *Sheffield* had lost visual contact, he decided to press ahead, make contact with *Bismarck* and then see what he could do to slow her down even further.

The fifth destroyer was the *Piorun*. She began life as a new British J, K and N class destroyer, laid down in Clydeside, and launched in May 1940 as the *Nerissa*. However, that October she was transferred to the Polish Navy. She was duly commissioned as the ORP *Piorun*, a ship of the Polish Republic – a government in exile. *Piorun* (or 'Thunderbolt') was crewed by Polish volunteer sailors, and after a period of working up with other Polish warships she joined Vian's flotilla. Although she only carried six 4.7in. guns, in three twin turrets, she was usually armed with ten 21in. torpedoes, in two quadruple launchers. Unfortunately, that evening her tubes were empty. That meant that for what was about to follow, she was the worst-equipped destroyer for the job. So, the five destroyers pounded on, following the bearing given to them by

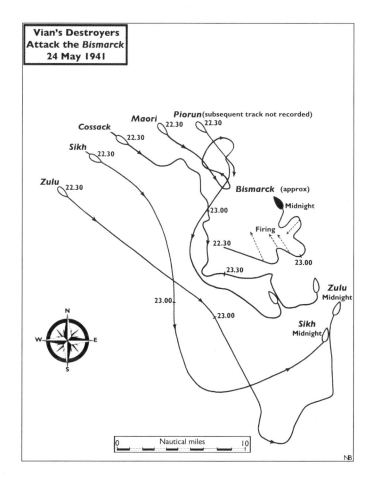

Captain Larcom. Meanwhile, as the light faded, on the open bridge of *Cossack*, Vian worked out his plan of attack.

He really had three objectives. The first was to sight *Bismarck*, so that he could send a series of contact reports to Tovey. This would help the British battleships make contact with the enemy at dawn the following morning. The second was, if the chance arose, to attack her with torpedoes, in the hope of crippling the battleship or at least slowing her down. While between them the Swordfish had carried 15 18in.

torpedoes, Vian's destroyers had a total of 16 of them, all 21in. torpedoes, with a greater range and a more powerful explosive warhead. Then, even if the torpedo attack didn't achieve anything, he could harry *Bismarck* and her crew and keep them at Action Stations. This should mean that when Tovey engaged her the following morning, the battleship's crew would be exhausted.

He had already strung his destroyers out into a line, 2,000 yards (1 mile) apart, to increase the chances of making contact in the dark.[12] They were making 15 knots through the rough cross-seas. The destroyers were heading on a south-easterly course, with *Cossack* in the centre, *Sikh* and then *Zulu* to port of her, and *Maori* and *Piorun* to port. Visibility was poor – little more than a couple of miles, as rain squalls lashed the little warships. It was 22.38 when the *Bismarck* first appeared out of the darkness, during a break in the rain.[13] She was 8 or 9 miles away, heading almost due north, and making about 12 knots. It was *Maori* and *Piorun* who spotted her first. Vian's plan was for the five destroyers to spread out, so that two destroyers were each side of the battleship, on her bow and stern quarters. *Cossack* would shadow her from dead astern. Then, as the destroyers moved in to take up their positions, *Bismarck* opened fire.

Müllenheim-Rechberg was one of the gunnery team that evening. Salvos of both 15in. and 6in. shells were fired at *Piorun*, although at the time the *Bismarck*'s crew didn't know which destroyer was which. He remembered the fight:

Our rangefinders worked to perfection. From 8,000m down to 3,000 we tracked the destroyers. Tension in my station rose as the incoming ranges went down, 7,000m … 6,500 … 4,000… In spite of the darkness I could see through my director the shadowy attackers come nearer and nearer, twisting to attack – each time I thought 'the torpedoes are hissing out of the tubes' – then drawing off. They dared not stay near us for long, because of the speed with which our gunnery found its targets.[14]

This was despite the continual turning of the battleship, as Lindemann struggled to maintain a steady course. In fact, she kept circling throughout the action. By now she had increased speed too, and was making between 15 and 20 knots.

Bismarck began firing at *Piorun* within a minute or so of the destroyer first spotting the German battleship. The range was just under 7 miles, but it was dropping fast. Although *Piorun* fired back with her puny 4.7in. guns, they wouldn't have been able to do much damage even if they'd been able to hit her. In those rough seas, accurate aiming was all but impossible. It was easier to take aim from the larger and more stable battleship, but what probably saved the Polish destroyer was the erratic course being steered by her adversary. This threw the German gunners off slightly, and while the third 15in. salvo landed dangerously close to the destroyer, she emerged unscathed. Sensibly, Komandor Eugeniusz Pławski decided he'd done enough for now, and turned away under cover of a smoke screen.[15] As a result, *Piorun* lost contact, not just with *Bismarck* but also with the other destroyers. Just before he broke contact, Pławski flashed a lamp signal to *Bismarck* that read, 'I am a Pole' – just so the Germans knew who they were dealing with.

By now, *Maori* was somewhere off *Bismarck*'s starboard bow, *Sikh* and *Zulu* off her port beam, and *Cossack* behind her. It was now up to these four Tribal class destroyers. So, at 23.24, Vian ordered them to launch a synchronised torpedo attack.

As she moved in, *Zulu* was spotted by *Bismarck* and a curtain of 15in. and 6in. shells fell in front of her.[16] The destroyer hurriedly turned away, her puny gun turrets barking in reply. On the gun director tower, Sub Lt James Galbraith thought *Bismarck* looked enormous.[17] Huge columns of water fell around *Zulu*, as two salvos landed dangerously close to her. Then a third salvo from the battleship's 6in. guns straddled the destroyer as she bore away. A shell splinter scythed through Galbraith's left wrist, and wounded two seamen working next to him. Still, Cdr Harry Graham, a charismatic Australian, managed to launch a spread of four torpedoes before he broke contact. However, *Bismarck* kept turning, and they all missed their target.

At 23.40, Vian in *Cossack* had a clear view of his prey, some 4 miles away, her hull lit up by the flashes of her guns. Unfortunately for him, the guns were firing at *Cossack*. While the larger guns missed, 6in. shell splashes surrounded the ship – a perfect straddle. Vian could actually see the 15in. shells heading towards him, as they were picked up by *Cossack*'s radar. It was, as he said later, a rather alarming image. *Bismarck* was also firing starshells now, and these lit up *Cossack* as she made her torpedo run, an almost impossible move in those tempestuous seas. Still, *Cossack* surged forwards into her attack, ignoring the heavy fire. Signalman Eric Farmer remembered the moment: 'The first salvo was 50 yards short. The next one burst over the bridge, causing everyone to duck. The range was less than a mile now.'[18] That was when Vian turned the destroyer about, and fired his torpedoes.

Some of *Cossack*'s crew thought they'd hit the battleship, since they saw a bright flash through the murk. In fact, it was a flare landing on *Bismarck*'s focsle, which her crew hurriedly extinguished. Gunner Ken Robinson described what happened next: 'After the attack we turned away, and with the sea up our stern, at what seemed to be the fastest we ever went, with the stern sea throwing us all over the place.'[19] Then, Vian discovered that one of her torpedoes hadn't launched. So, the destroyer went in again. They sped in, launched the torpedo and made off under the cover of a smoke screen. Again, they saw flashes on *Bismarck*, which might be a torpedo hit, or merely the battleship's guns firing. In any case, *Cossack*'s captain didn't hang around to find out.

By now, all of Vian's destroyers had lost touch with *Bismarck*. They almost lost contact with each other too, but after midnight *Cossack* came across *Piorun*, and then *Zulu*. Of *Sikh* and *Maori* there was no sign. Both had been ahead of the others, one on each bow of *Bismarck*, and both had made torpedo runs during the night. *Maori* was driven off by accurate gunfire, but a little after 01.00 she went in again. Cdr Harry Armstrong, known as 'Beaky' to his men, was wary enough to zigzag as he approached *Bismarck* from her port beam. However, the battleship was continually turning, so when she was 5,000 yards (2.5 miles) off her port quarter he fired off two torpedoes. At the time, *Bismarck* was heading towards the north-east, but at that range the chances of hitting were slim and the torpedo spread ran astern of her target. *Bismarck* fired at her, allowing Captain Graham of *Zulu* to see *Bismarck*, clearly lit up by her gun flashes. Again, *Maori* escaped into the darkness.

Finally, Cdr Gary Stokes of *Sikh* had lost touch with both her quarry and her own consorts, but when *Zulu* saw the battleship, Captain Graham gave a sighting report that allowed *Sikh* to intercept *Bismarck*, approaching her from her starboard beam.[20] She fired her torpedoes at 7,000 yards (3.5 miles), but again, all of them missed. So, apart from *Maori*, all of the destroyers had used up their torpedoes, without achieving a single hit. This was hardly surprising, given the mountainous seas and the pitch-black night. Then there were the actions of the *Bismarck*, continually turning and whose speed was fluctuating wildly. Then, however, there was something of a lull. *Bismarck* stopped for an hour, as one of her turbines had been shut down to allow repairs to be attempted to the shaft and rudder. When this failed, at around 02.20, *Bismarck* got under way again and resumed her erratic course.

By then, Vian was content with maintaining contact with the enemy battleship and sending up starshells to mark her position. This was actually done on the orders of Admiral Tovey.[21] Now that the admiral knew *Bismarck* wasn't getting away, he reduced the speed of his two battleships to 19 knots, to conserve fuel. He'd taken a gamble by not pressing on to attack *Bismarck* at the first opportunity. However, he knew that *Rodney* lacked the modern fire control radar that would allow her to fight effectively in the dark. So, he was content to wait until dawn. Of course, there was the risk that *Bismarck* might repair whatever damage she'd suffered and speed off towards France, but as the night wore on, this became increasingly unlikely.

Vian stopped firing starshells at around 15.30, as all it seemed to do was to draw German fire on to his ships.[22] His destroyers lost contact with *Bismarck* at 16.00, but she was boxed in by them, and unlikely to escape under cover of the filthy night. At 05.50, contact was regained as *Maori* sighted her, steering erratically towards the north-west – and straight towards Tovey's battleships. Cdr Armstrong signalled the other destroyers, and once again they took station all around the enemy battleship. Rain squalls were still lashing the ocean and the night's storm showed no real sign of wearing itself out. Just before 07.00, Maori fired off her last two torpedoes, at a range of 9,000 yards (4.4 miles), but they didn't hit their target. At 05.00, Vian ordered *Piorun* to return to Plymouth since she was running desperately low on fuel. The Poles were hugely disappointed not to be in at the finish, but they'd played their part. Now it was up to the capital ships to play theirs.

THE DARKEST HOURS

It was 23.40 when Admiral Lütjens was told that the rudder damage couldn't be repaired. Until then, he'd harboured the lingering hope that *Bismarck* could still escape. Now that last optimistic flame was snuffed out. It meant that, come the morning, *Bismarck* would have to fight. While her guns and fire control systems were still in full working order, the ship's inability to steer a proper course made it much harder for the gunnery teams to calculate their fall of shot. Instead, it would be the enemy who'd have the advantage, not just in terms of numbers of ships and guns, but also in their ability to hit their target. Thanks to radio signals intercepted by the B-Dienst unit on board, and through intelligence reports sent from France, both Lütjens and Lindemann knew *King George V* and *Rodney* were steaming to meet them, as were several smaller British ships.[23] The wolves were gathering out there in the dark.

On *Bismarck's* bridge the mood became dark and sombre. At 23.52, Lütjens sent a signal to both Paris and Berlin, which read: 'Ship incapable of manoeuvres. We will fight to the last shell. Long live the Führer.'[24] News of that gloomy signal slowly spread through the ship. The sense of finality was added to when Lindemann announced over the ship's tannoy that the crew could take what they liked from the ship's stores. So, the men dined on tinned ham, cheese, beer and sausages. At least nobody would go into battle hungry. Lütjens then addressed the crew, saying: 'The German people are with you, and we will fight until our barrels glow red-hot and the last shell has left the barrels. For us seamen, the question now is victory or death.'[25] It was a reprise of his address of a day-and-a-half before. This time it didn't just lower morale – it had a devastating effect on it, as the crew now realised they were unlikely to survive the coming battle.

Just before midnight, the fleet admiral sent another signal to Berlin. It said that *Bismarck* and her crew would fight to the last, adding that they remained steadfast, 'in our belief in you my Führer, and in the firm faith in Germany's victory'. Less pessimistically, Lindemann added his own signal: 'Armament and engines still intact. Ship, however, cannot be steered with engine.'[26] So now the German Naval High Command knew what the real problem was. It was almost as if Lindemann was still clutching at a straw – the slim hope that U-boats and the Luftwaffe could throw a screen around them at dawn and allow them to reach port. In fact, Dönitz had already ordered all available U-boats to head towards the stricken battleship. According to Müllenheim-Rechberg, a rumour was circulating, claiming that a large force of German bombers would attack the British the following morning. This, however, was little more than fantasy. The bombers were out of range.

At 01.53, a signal from Adolf Hitler arrived.[27] It read: 'All Germany is with you. What can be done, will be done. Your performance of duty will strengthen our people in the struggle of its destiny.' Several other signals were sent or received throughout the night, including one from Group West, promising the dispatch of 51 bombers. Nevertheless, as dawn approached it was clear to all but the most optimistic that the *Bismarck* and her crew were on their own. One by one, officers and men slipped away to write letters, gather their warm clothing or personal possessions, and put on their lifejackets. Then they returned to their posts and waited for the dawn. Müllenheim-Rechberg recalled: 'It didn't seem to want to pass, this sinister night of waiting, and waiting for nothing but the end. Enforced inactivity and the certainty of approaching defeat made it doubly depressing. The end must and indeed would come, but it was coming in agonising slow motion.'

Lütjens, though, was already occupying himself with another impossible task. He decided that whatever happened to *Bismarck*, the Fleet War Diary needed to survive. It contained information that might be useful to the German Naval High Command if they attempted another breakout, and it probably included Lütjens' own justifications for the various decisions he made during the operation. So, shortly before 05.00, Lindemann was ordered to prepare one of *Bismarck*'s Arado floatplanes, which would carry the diary to safety.[28] For an hour, the crew prepared the aircraft for take-off, and at 06.00 the order came to launch. Nothing happened. It turned out that the compressed air that powered the catapult wasn't reaching it. So, the launch was cancelled, and the floatplane was pushed over the side, as it was now full of highly combustible aviation fuel. Next, at 07.10, Lütjens demanded that Group West, 'Send a U-boat to save War Diary'.[29] It would be his last-ever signal.

Strangely enough, just over 50 minutes later, Paris replied, saying that *U-556* would retrieve the diary. That was Lt

Herbert Wohlfarth's boat – the man who swore he'd protect *Bismarck* from her foes. The previous evening, *U-556* had had a perfect opportunity to do just that, as *Ark Royal* and *Renown* swept in front of her. However, the U-boat was returning from a war patrol in the Atlantic and she'd already used up all of her torpedoes. Later, he sighted one of Vian's destroyers – too preoccupied with pursuing *Bismarck* to notice the lurking U-boat. Once again, though, Wohlfarth was unable to do anything to intervene. In his own War Diary, he wrote: 'What can I do for the *Bismarck*? I can see starshells being fired, and flashes from the *Bismarck*'s guns. It is a terrible feeling to be near, and unable to do anything.'[30] So, at the end, not even her protector Parsifal could save the doomed battleship, and Lütjens' Fleet War Diary would stay on board *Bismarck* until the end.

Chapter 15

The Final Battle

TOVEY'S REVENGE

Dawn that morning seemed to arrive with reluctance. While the seas had moderated slightly a few hours before, the north-westerly wind still blew at 30 knots. The sun could be seen trying to peek through the grey scudding clouds and visibility was fairly clear, apart from the numerous rain squalls that flitted over the sea, blown on by the strong wind. Conditions could be better, but they were certainly not as grim as they had been during the night. *Bismarck*, however, was large enough not to really care about the rough seas and 10ft waves. Though she was wounded, the graceful bows of the great steel beast still cut through the water with her customary style. Her guns were still fully operational, and with her broad beam they would fire as accurately as ever. Rather, they would if Kapitän Lindemann could keep his ship on a steady course, with all of her guns trained on the approaching enemy. Wounded and cornered though *Bismarck* was, she still had powerful teeth.

As dawn broke, Admiral Tovey was approaching the *Bismarck* from the west in his flagship *King George V*, with

Rodney following astern of her, off her port quarter.[1] The crew of the two battleships were at Action Stations, and captains Patterson and Dalrymple-Hamilton were on their compass platforms, where they had an unobstructed view ahead of them. Captain Vian had told Tovey where *Bismarck* was, so the admiral was able to choose the time and place of his arrival in the arena. Tovey's plan was simple: the two battleships would fan out into line abreast, six cables (or 1,200 yards/0.6 mile) apart.[2] As he later put it: 'I hoped that the sight of two battleships steering straight for them would shake the nerves of the range-takers and control officers, who already had four anxious days and nights.' This tactic was helped by the fact that six of *Rodney's* nine 16in. guns and six of the flagship's ten 14in. ones could fire directly ahead.

After closing to within 14,000 yards (6.9 miles), the battleships would turn and begin firing full broadsides. However, Tovey gave Dalrymple-Hamilton in *Rodney* complete discretion to manoeuvre on his own, if he saw the need. This gave *Rodney's* commander a lot more flexibility than V. Adm. Holland gave Captain Leach of the *Prince of Wales*. Also, by approaching from the west, *Bismarck* would be silhouetted against the rising sun. However, the battleship's lookouts weren't the first to spot *Bismarck* when dawn came. The previous evening, the heavy cruiser *Norfolk* had arrived in the area, having refuelled since her last encounter with *Bismarck*. So, at 07.53 that morning, R. Adm. Wake-Walker spotted his old adversary, 10 miles away to the north-north-east.[3] As he later put it: 'I felt it unwise to irritate her unnecessarily.'

Surprisingly, *Bismarck* didn't open fire, and the cruiser turned away and broke contact. A few minutes later she sighted Tovey's battleships. At 08.08 Wake-Walker signalled the flagship, reporting that: 'Enemy bears 130°, 16 miles'.[4] He then couldn't resist adding: 'On tin hats!' So, that meant that battle was imminent. He then took control of Vian's four remaining destroyers, *Piorun* having already turned for home. On the two battleships, the lookouts strained to be the first to spot her, while Tovey ordered Dalrymple-Hamilton to move forwards on his port side and deploy into line abreast. Then, everybody waited for their first glimpse of the *Hood's* nemesis. The crew in the two British ships were tense and keyed up, but morale was high and they were determined to finish the job.

At the time, Vian's four destroyers were stationed on the four quadrants of *Bismarck*, 7 or 8 miles from her. She wasn't shooting at them any more – it was almost as if she was conserving her strength for the coming fight. The German battleship was heading towards the north-west, making 10 knots. As well as Tovey's battleships, Wake-Walker's cruiser and Vian's destroyers, a second heavy cruiser was also approaching the battle arena from the south. The heavy cruiser *Dorsetshire* had been escorting a convoy heading north from Freetown in West Africa, but two days before she had been detached and sent to join the hunt.[5] Now, Captain Benjamin Martin's cruiser was about 10 miles to the east of *Bismarck* and steaming towards the north-west at 20 knots. Finally, Force H was 15 miles to the south of *Bismarck*, but after a dawn air strike from *Ark Royal* was cancelled due to rough seas, Somerville's force would take no further part in the unfolding drama.

At 08.43, through a gap in the rain squalls, lookouts on board the *King George V* finally spotted *Bismarck*, and as Lt Cdr Hugh Guernsey on the flagship's bridge remembered, she was 'a thick, squad ghost of a ship, very broad in the beam, coming straight towards us'.[6] *Bismarck* was 12.5 miles to the south-east and steering almost directly towards Tovey's two battleships. On Tovey's signal, *Rodney* altered slightly to port in order to widen the gap between the two British battleships. That way, they might split *Bismarck's* fire and make things slightly harder for the German gunners. At 08.47, *Rodney* opened fire with her two forward turrets.[7] The range was now 21,870 yards (10.8 miles). A minute later, *King George V* opened up too. At that range it took just 35 seconds for the shells to reach their target. These first salvos missed, but at 08.48 a near miss from *Rodney* threw up huge columns of water in front of *Bismarck*. The British were finding the range.

At 08.49, two minutes after *Rodney's* first salvo, *Bismarck* fired back using her two forward turrets. The after turrets couldn't bear. When he first saw the enemy, Kapitän Lindemann used his engines to try to turn *Bismarck* slightly to port, so all his four turrets could fire.[8] However, this proved extremely difficult and the battleship's course continued to be erratic; she maintained a roughly northern course throughout the battle, but she kept weaving first to port and then to starboard as Lindemann tried to stop her turning too far. It proved almost impossible to have all the guns bear all of the time. Müllenheim-Rechberg, in the after gun director, said: 'The swinging back and forth of the *Bismarck* allowed me only intermittent glimpses of the enemy.'[9] Still, given these circumstances, *Bismarck's* gunnery was impressive. She was aiming at *Rodney*, the more powerful of the two British ships, and while her first salvo fell short and the second overshot, the third straddled the target.

This was another four-shell salvo. The shells fell around *Rodney*, but none of them actually hit her. However, one

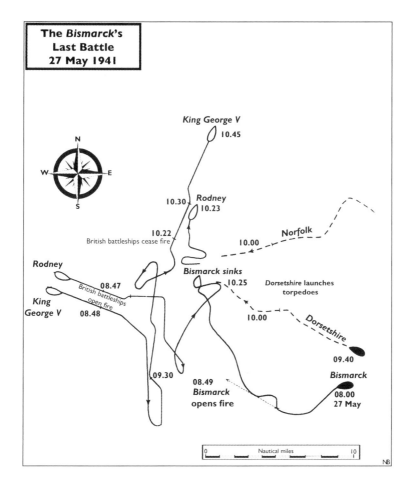

The *Bismarck's*
Last Battle
27 May 1941

King George V
10.45

N
W   E
S

10.30   *Rodney*
10.23

10.22
British battleships cease fire

Norfolk

10.00

Rodney

Bismarck sinks

08.47
*British battleships
open fire*

10.25   *Dorsetshire* launches
torpedoes

*King
George V*   08.48

10.00

Dorsetshire

09.40

09.30

Bismarck

08.49
*Bismarck
opens fire*

08.00
27 May

0   Nautical miles   10

landed just 66ft from her forward superstructure, and
shell splinters peppered the ship. Some struck the bridge
and others pierced the battleship's anti-aircraft director.[10]
Huge columns of water also drenched many of the men on
Rodney's upper deck. While nobody was seriously injured,
Dalrymple-Hamilton sensibly ordered the anti-aircraft gun
crews to take shelter below decks. Their small-calibre guns
wouldn't be needed in this fight. Meanwhile, the captain kept
giving the crew a running commentary of the fight through

the bridge tannoy, adding dryly that *Bismarck* had done *Rodney* the honour of choosing her as its first target. This was useful, as otherwise most of the men in the engine or boiler rooms or magazines would have had no idea what was going on 'topside'. All they could sense was the sound, noise and shaking as their own guns were fired.

The old battleship was almost tearing herself apart with the blast of her own guns. Steam and water pipes burst with the shock, rivets popped out, leaks started and the boiler furnaces flared up with the pressure caused by the blasts. The stokers had to dive out of the way to avoid being burned. Elsewhere, crockery smashed and sinks and toilets were ripped out of the bulkheads. Still, it was worth it. By now, Dalrymple-Hamilton had turned *Rodney* slightly to port, so her third triple 16in. turret could bear. Now *Rodney* was able to fire full salvos. Tovey had *King George V* turn slightly to starboard too, to allow 'X' turret to fire. So, both British battleships were now firing with everything they had. This heavy fire was starting to pay off. At 08.50, watchers on *Norfolk* saw *Rodney*'s shells straddle the German battleship, but none of the nine 16in. shells struck her. Instead, *Bismarck* was cloaked in huge fountains of water. It meant, though, that *Rodney* now had the range.

However, a problem with *Rodney*'s gun director led to her next salvos falling short. It took several minutes to get back on target, but at 08.59 *Rodney* achieved another straddle with her 18th salvo. This time she hit *Bismarck* twice – once on her focsle, and the other high in her forward superstructure.[11] On the *King George V*, all of the battleship's guns could now bear, and at 08.53 her shells straddled *Bismarck*, scoring a hit on the forward part of the ship. Tovey's flagship was using her fire control radar to register the fall of shot, and this proved highly effective. Her salvos began smashing into the enemy ship, one after the other. By this stage, *Norfolk* had joined in with her 8in. guns, firing at a range of 10 miles. *Bismarck* was now under fire from three enemy ships – with *Rodney* and *King George V* ahead of her, and *Norfolk* off her starboard beam – and she was being pounded relentlessly, with fires breaking out on her forward superstructure.

At 08.58, *Rodney*'s starboard battery of 6in. guns joined in, as they were finally within range. While unable to penetrate the battleship's armour, their shells might do some damage to *Bismarck*'s exposed upper decks. The German battleship was now half-hidden by shell splashes but the relentless pounding continued. A few minutes later, at 09.04, *Dorsetshire* appeared from the west, and at a range of 9 miles she began adding the weight of her own 8in. shells to the conflagration.[12] After leaving her convoy, she had steamed 600 miles and arrived just in time to join in the fight. *Rodney* and *King George V* were sailing away from each other, at divergent angles, the flagship heading towards the south-east and then the south, and the older battleship steering north-east. Both kept all their guns bearing on the *Bismarck*. The range was dropping rapidly – to just 8 miles – which of course made it easier to score hits.

On the *Rodney*, Dalrymple-Hamilton was coolly weaving around *Bismarck*'s shell splashes, none of which came close to hitting his battleship. Meanwhile, *Rodney* was straddling *Bismarck* with virtually every salvo. Her 16in. guns fired 1-ton shells, and at that range they had a velocity of 1,700ft per second. Their armour-piercing noses burrowed into *Bismarck*'s steel-clad superstructure or hull before exploding. At that range, they could inflict serious damage. At 09.02, a salvo from *Rodney* struck *Bismarck*, and at least one shell struck her forward superstructure.[13] This had a dramatic impact on *Bismarck*'s ability to fight. A sheet of fire was seen to shoot up around her bridge and conning tower. Almost certainly, it killed or seriously wounded everyone on *Bismarck*'s bridge, including Admiral Lütjens and Kapitän Lindemann. It also silenced her main gun director, where Korvettenkapitän Adalbert Schneider was controlling the battleship's gunfire.

That single salvo effectively prevented *Bismarck* from trying to steer and meant that no senior officer was able to control the battleship. So, her speed dropped and her rudder continued to force her in circles. Most of the fleet admiral's staff were probably killed at that moment, while Lindemann's second-in-command, Fregattenkapitän Hans Oels, was running the ship's damage control centre. So, at a stroke, the *Bismarck* was rendered leaderless. The loss of the main gunnery director also meant that the effectiveness of the battleship's fire was markedly reduced. Certainly, Lt Burkhard von Müllenheim-Rechberg had the ability to switch control over to the after gunnery director, but that took time. That was something *Bismarck* didn't have. Over the next few minutes the battleship would be stripped of most of her offensive muscle, and turned into little more than a floating charnel house.

Müllenheim-Rechberg himself said: 'Though I could not see what was going on around me from my completely enclosed, armoured control station, it was not hard to picture how the scene outside was changing. As the range decreased, the more frequent became the *harrumphs* of incoming shells and the louder grew the noise of battle.'[14] Then, at around 09.08, a salvo from one of the two British battleships struck the forward end of the *Bismarck*, and her two front turrets – 'Anton' and 'Bruno' – were put out of action. So, Müllenheim-Rechberg took over control of the two after turrets, 'Caesar' and 'Dora'. He wasn't given a target, so he ordered the guns to open fire on the only ship that was clearly visible – the *King George V*. By this time, she was 6 miles to the south of *Bismarck*. The lieutenant directed a salvo at her, and then fired three more, but while they landed close, the four shell salvos never straddled their target.

They were getting close, though; on Tovey's flagship, Guernsey involuntarily ducked as the fourth salvo screamed over his head.[15] *King George V* was firing back, however, and at 09.13 a 14in. shell struck Müllenheim-Rechberg's after gun director. Everyone was bounced around, but they survived. The rangefinders, however, were wrecked. So, *Bismarck*'s last two turrets now had to fire under local control, which meant the gun layers in each turret would have to direct the fall of shot of their own two guns. *Bismarck* was still turning, and *King George V* was lost from view, but *Rodney* could now be seen off *Bismarck*'s port beam. So, the turrets switched their fire to her. Without access to any centralised, computerised fire control, the chances of scoring a hit were slim. Still, both turrets kept up a steady fire until their own ship turned again, and their target was obscured once more. By now, though, it was clear that the end was drawing near.

THE DEATH OF A BATTLESHIP

It was now almost 09.15. On *Rodney*, *Bismarck*'s slow northerly progress had blocked the arc of fire of 'X' turret. Dalrymple-Hamilton therefore turned his battleship to starboard, until she headed south, on a course roughly parallel to that of *Bismarck*, at a range of 5 miles.[16] Just before she turned, *Rodney* fired off a spread of torpedoes from her submerged torpedo tubes, mounted in the battleship's bow. Three of them were launched from the starboard side of the bow, but they all missed, confounded by the constant turning of their target. She did the same from her port tubes, again without hitting her target. Chief Petty Officer (CPO) Frank Pollard began reloading the empty launchers, until a near miss from *Bismarck* jammed the external door of the starboard launcher and he gave up the attempt.[17]

Next, *Rodney* began slamming full salvos into the enemy battleship, achieving one or more hits every time. At 09.21, 'Dora' turret was put out of action when a shell exploded in the turret's right-hand barrel.[18] The blast ripped out the breech end of the gun, killing or maiming most of the turret crew. It might even have flashed down the magazine hoist, killing yet more. Soon after, the order was given to flood the turret's magazine, whether the men down there were alive or not. Anything else would have risked the very survival of the ship. *Bismarck* could have been ripped apart as *Hood* was. Instead, the seemingly callous order of Fregattenkapitän Oels might well have saved some of the battleship's crew. Nevertheless, the situation was deteriorating rapidly. Up near the bow, 'Bruno' turret was completely destroyed, with the back of the turret ripped open and one of its guns left pointing towards the sky.[19]

In 'Anton' turret, though, the crew had survived the blow that temporarily put them out of action.[20] It had severed the turret hydraulics, leaving the guns 'drooping like dead flowers', but after much effort the turret crew managed to get their guns working again, and at 09.27 'Anton' turret fired its final salvo. Seconds later, another hit by a heavy-calibre shell put it out of action for good. Now it looked as if *Bismarck* was on fire in several places and her superstructure had taken a real pounding. *Bismarck*'s armour was concentrated around her turrets, magazines and engines, but a lot of the compartments above her armoured citadel were only lightly protected; while they might be proof against shell fragments, they couldn't stop a 14in. or 16in. shell, fired at relatively short range. So, both above and below decks, *Bismarck* was being pounded into a scrap.

At 09.16, Tovey ordered *King George V* to make a turn to port, and reversed course.[21] Soon, she was heading north again, with *Bismarck* lying off her starboard beam. Unfortunately for Tovey and Captain Patterson, the flagship's guns had been taking turns to malfunction throughout the battle. It was the same problem faced by *Prince of Wales* three days before – the four-gun turret was a new design and it still had teething problems. As a result, the crew had barely repaired one gun when another would become defective, with the mechanism jamming or the hoist system refusing to work. At one point, *King George V* was reduced to just two operable 14in. gun barrels. At least by now, though, her secondary 5.25in. guns had joined in, and were peppering the upper works of the enemy battleship.

The German battleship was barely moving, and with all but 'Caesar' turret out of action her firing had become intermittent. Her secondary turrets were still firing if they could bear, but one by one they were being silenced too. Their armour wasn't able to protect the crews from such large shells, striking them at ranges of less than 4 miles. Then, at 09.26 one of the gun barrels in 'Caesar' turret was knocked out of action by a direct hit. With the turret optics shattered, the remaining gun couldn't even fire back with any chance of hitting. So, effectively, all of *Bismarck*'s main guns had now been silenced. Yet those British shells kept on pounding her, as *Bismarck* was still afloat, and this was a fight to the death.

So, in just under three-quarters of an hour, *Bismarck* had become a floating wreck. Surprisingly, while her superstructure was a tangled shambles of steel and her decks were on fire, her armoured belt still protected her from the worst of the enemy fire. She could no longer fight, but she was still afloat. It looked as if the British shells could batter *Bismarck*, but they couldn't sink her. Still the shells kept hitting her – several striking her every minute. So, the slaughter continued. On *Tartar*, just about to head for home due to lack of fuel, Sub Lt George Whalley saw *Bismarck* burning, and thought: 'What that ship was like inside did not bear thinking of ... her guns smashed, the ship full of fire, her people hurt.'[22] This sentiment was shared by many British sailors that morning. Hugh Guernsey on *King George V* felt the same. Afterwards, he wrote, 'Pray God I may never know what those shells did as they exploded in the hull.'[23]

The trouble was, the Admiralty's orders were clear. *Bismarck* had to be sunk. Prime Minister Churchill had been adamant. So, the salvos kept being fired, and the German battleship continued to burn. Afterwards, Captain Dalrymple-Hamilton of the *Rodney*, whose shells did most of the damage, wrote: 'I can't say I enjoyed that part of the business much, but didn't see what else I could do.'[24] Tovey was determined to finish the job. He knew that by 10.00 at the very latest, *King George V* and *Rodney* would have to break off the action, or run out of fuel on the way home. By then, though, it was becoming clear that shells alone wouldn't do the job. *Bismarck* would have to be finished off with torpedoes. In fact, at 09.56 *Rodney* tried to do just that, launching her last two torpedoes out of the submerged launcher on her port side.[25] The range was less than 3,000 yards (1.5 miles), and the battleship claimed one hit – perhaps the only torpedo hit ever on one battleship from another.

The destroyers had all fired their torpedoes, as had *Norfolk*, which had fired hers off and missed just before 10.00. That left *Devonshire*, which carried two quadruple 21in. torpedo launchers, one on each beam. The only other source was *Ark Royal*, and her Swordfish. In fact, that morning, V. Adm. Somerville had ordered *Ark Royal* to launch another air strike, and at 09.20, 12 Swordfish began taking off. After forming up they headed towards the *Bismarck*. When they arrived, though, the gun battle was in full spate. To make a torpedo attack in those circumstances would have been to invite being hit by friendly fire, so the attack was called off.[26] The aircraft kept their distance, circled, and waited. In fact, they *were* fired on from *King George V*, until someone identified them as British biplanes. Thus, the air crews merely enjoyed their grandstand view for a few minutes and then headed home.

Tovey, too, was heading home to Scapa Flow, with a desperately needed fuel stop on the way at Loch Ewe. He had left it longer than he should, but his two battleships now had to break off. There was no other option. So, at 10.16 the admiral ordered *King George V* and *Rodney* to cease fire and break off the action.[27] Until then, the guns had continued to pound the stricken battleship. In total, *King George V* fired 339 14in. shells that morning, and *Rodney* 380 16in. ones. Then there were the hundreds of 8in. shells fired by the cruisers, and the 6in. and 5.25in. ones from the battleship's secondary guns. *Bismarck* had been utterly pounded into submission. Her guns silent now, the German battleship was just wallowing there, her decks blazing fiercely, but with her German naval ensign still flying. By then, the order had been given to scuttle her, open her sea cocks, and then abandon ship.

Fregattenkapitän Oels gave the scuttling order, and charges were set.[28] Meanwhile, he passed through the ship, ordering men to head towards the upper deck and save themselves. However, he and hundreds of others were killed by the British shells before they made it. Meanwhile, as Tovey steamed away, he ordered Captain Martin of *Dorsetshire* to finish *Bismarck* off with torpedoes. She drew closer to the burning wreck and fired two torpedoes from a range of 3,300 yards (1.6 miles).[29] Both of them struck *Bismarck's* starboard side. By now, hundreds of men could be seen jumping into the water, mostly from the battleship's stern, as forward of the bridge she was a raging inferno of flame. Next, Martin circled round *Bismarck* and at 10.36 he fired a third torpedo, which struck the battleship's port side. Almost immediately, *Bismarck* began listing to port. Whether this was the torpedo hits or the scuttling charges was immaterial. *Bismarck* was now starting to sink.

Tovey looked back at *Bismarck* as the two battleships steamed off towards the northern horizon. He saw her list and, as he watched, the battleship leaned over even further, until her superstructure was parallel to the water. Pieces of her superstructure began to break away. Then she slowly rolled over and capsized.[30] Her gun turrets, held in place by gravity, preceded her on the long voyage towards the seabed. It was now 10.39. Men were still perched on her upturned hull as she went under. The stern sank next, and gradually the upturned battleship slipped from view, her passing marked by huge bubbles of escaping air. Her bows were the last to go, but by 10.40 these disappeared too, gurgling and hissing beneath the waters of the Atlantic. Now all that was left of the once-proud battleship was a scattering of floating debris, a large oil slick, and hundreds of men, left floating in the ice-cold water.

They were the lucky ones – the sailors who hadn't been trapped as the ship sank, or dragged under by the suction. Many of them were badly burned or injured. After almost an hour, *Dorsetshire* and the destroyer *Maori* inched towards the edge of the floating detritus of men and wreckage and began picking up survivors. The men in the water were no longer the enemy – they had become sailors in distress. So, ropes and rope ladders were thrown over the side and British sailors began pulling the survivors to safety. Müllenheim-Rechberg was one of these, having been hauled up on a rope and pulled on board.[31] Then, a lookout on *Dorsetshire* spotted a puff of exhaust smoke in the water, 2 miles off the cruiser's starboard beam. The Home Fleet had expected U-boats to be converging, and this could well have been one of them. So, Captain Martin reluctantly ordered his ship to get underway.[32]

It was now 11.40. Hundreds of survivors were still in the water, and most had been floating there for over an hour. A few lucky ones clung to ropes and were hauled aboard, but as the cruiser made off, followed by *Maori*, the remainder were left to fend for themselves. This, however, was a necessary and unavoidable decision by Captain Martin. He couldn't risk the lives of the 850 British sailors on the two ships. Between them, the two British ships had managed to rescue 111 survivors.[33] *Bismarck* carried a crew of just over 2,000 men. While most of these went down with their ship, hundreds of others had abandoned ship and were now in the water. Of these, only five were still alive the next day when they were rescued by *U-74* and the German weather ship *Sachsenwald*, which had arrived on the scene, along with a Spanish cruiser. The rest succumbed to the numbing cold, and quietly slipped away.

GÖTTERDÄMMERUNG

For many on board *Bismarck*, the end didn't come gradually. Instead, it involved a shattering explosion, a fireball, crushing from falling pieces of wreckage, dismemberment by shell splinters or simply entrapment, entombed by sealed hatches or blocked passageways, and having to wait for the water to claim them. The survivors – 86 on *Dorsetshire* and 25 on *Maori* – told a harrowing tale. The decks were littered with broken bodies, and slick with blood and gore. The dead sailors lay everywhere, while parts of the upper deck were an inferno of flame. Shells still exploded on the ship, several each minute, until the final order came to cease fire. *Bismarck* had become a floating charnel house of the dead and injured, while those still alive struggled to save themselves. Some had to clamber over badly injured shipmates, unable to help themselves, and doomed to go down with the ship.

Everywhere the noise of fires and explosions was punctuated by the cries of the wounded and the dying. Survivors recalled how many of the dead and wounded on the upper deck were washed into the sea when *Bismarck* started to list. Waves then threw their broken bodies back against the sinking ship, where most were sucked under. Hundreds of men were trapped inside the ship by jammed hatches, while others stayed at their posts, as if resigned to their fate. Some crewmen were driven mad, while some took their own lives.

Müllenheim-Rechberg was the only officer to escape from the sinking ship. When his after guns were silenced, he stepped out of his director tower and saw the real extent of the carnage: 'Everything up to the bridge bulwarks had been destroyed. The hatches leading to the main deck were jammed shut ... flames cut off the whole forward part of the ship. Hundreds of crewmen lay where they had been hit, in the foretop, on the bridge, in the control stations, at the guns, on the upper deck, and on the main and battery decks.'[34] He eventually jumped into the sea from the quarterdeck and swam away before the ship capsized.

By then, the shelling had stopped. Still, the dying continued. Men were seen blinded by the smoke, running along the upper deck, only to fall through a hole ripped in the deck by a shell and tumble into a fiery pit below. Others were seen trying to squeeze through jammed hatches, while yet others were overcome by the thick smoke that clung to the ship like a blanket. The ship had begun listing when, according to Müllenheim-Rechberg, 'Two powerful explosions rolled over the sea, as torpedoes from the *Dorsetshire* hit the doomed ship on the starboard side. They were followed by a third explosion on the port side a few minutes later.' Some of those who had jumped into the sea were knocked unconscious when the waves threw them against the hull, while others simply sank, too wounded or exhausted to swim. Those who made it faced the long ordeal of freezing to death in the Atlantic swell.

The crew of one of *Ark Royal*'s Swordfish flew over *Bismarck* as it sank, and they later spoke of seeing hundreds of heads bobbing in the water. One by one the cold or their injuries overtook them, and the heads disappeared. The lucky few made it to the *Dorsetshire* and *Maori*, but even then many were too cold, injured or inexperienced to climb the ropes to safety. Others simply gave up at the final hurdle. Then the British warships got underway, while hundreds of heads still bobbed in the water. By then, the *King George V* was over the horizon, and heading for home.

On board her, Admiral Tovey was framing the words of *Bismarck*'s epitaph. When finished, it read: 'The *Bismarck* had put up a most gallant fight against impossible odds, worthy of the old days of the Imperial German Navy, and she went down with her colours flying.'[35] As he wrote it, he must have recalled the day a quarter of a century before, when as a lieutenant commander, and the commander of the destroyer *Onslow*, he had seen the same scene – the capsizing of the German cruiser *Wiesbaden* at the Battle of Jutland. That time nobody stopped to rescue the survivors, and by the next morning only one of them was left alive. War at sea could be a heartbreakingly cruel business.

Epilogue

The sinking of *Bismarck* wasn't quite the end of the story. While Operation *Rheinübung* had ended in failure, the *Prinz Eugen* was still at large in the Atlantic. Since the evening of 24 May, the heavy cruiser had been cruising alone.[1] She was running low on fuel, though, so Captain Brinkmann set off to rendezvous with one of the German tankers. After some difficulty, she made contact with the tanker *Spichern* on 26 May. She then headed into the British convoy lanes in the middle of the Atlantic, and she was there when news of *Bismarck*'s sinking reached her. She lingered a little longer, but problems with her port turbine and propeller shaft resulted in Brinkmann cutting the cruise short. So, on 1 June the *Prinz Eugen* slipped into Brest, escorted by destroyers and fighter planes. That officially brought the ill-fated *Rheinübung* to a close. *Prinz Eugen* survived the war, only to be sacrificed in 1946 during an atomic bomb test in the Pacific.

As for the British warships in the drama, *Prince of Wales* was patched up and her guns fixed, but in December 1941 she was sunk by Japanese aircraft while operating in the South China Sea.[2] She was still less than a year old. The battlecruiser *Repulse* was sunk in the same air attack. *Dorsetshire* suffered a similar fate in April 1942, in the Indian Ocean. *Rodney* saw out the war, but after the *Bismarck* operation she was considered too mechanically unsound for operational duties. Instead, she served as the flagship of the Home Fleet, spending most of her time in Scapa Flow. *King George V* and *Victorious*, however, both had an active war, seeing service in the Mediterranean and the Far East. *Norfolk* and *Suffolk* survived the war, too, after serving with the Home Fleet. *Ark Royal*, though, was torpedoed by a U-boat in November 1941 and sank off Gibraltar; all but one of her crew survived her sinking. By then, though, new ships had entered service to make good these losses.

After Operation *Rheinübung*, the Kriegsmarine avoided further surface operations in the Atlantic, and instead relied on U-boats to disrupt Britain's convoys. However, despite the heavy losses in this campaign – known as the Battle of the Atlantic – this vital maritime lifeline was never severed. The entry of the USA into the war and the growing number of escorts and search aircraft helped turn the tide, and eventually the Kriegsmarine was forced to call off its offensive. *Bismarck*'s sister ship *Tirpitz* remained a latent threat, though, and her presence in Norwegian waters forced the Home Fleet to tie down capital ships to protect the Arctic convoys. Eventually, in November 1944, she was sunk off Tromsø by RAF Lancaster bombers.[3] By then, the Kriegsmarine was a spent force, lacking the surface ships, U-boats or even the fuel to present a serious threat to the Allied war effort. So, in some ways, Operation *Rheinübung* was its last great swansong.

In June 1989, the wreck of the *Bismarck* was discovered by an expedition led by Dr Robert Ballard.[4] He had achieved worldwide fame ten years before when he discovered the wreck of the RMS *Titanic*. Now he decided to look for the world's most famous battleship. The British claimed she sank in 48°10' North, 16°12' West, but thanks to the rough seas and overcast skies this was an approximate position, as it was impossible to obtain an accurate navigational fix using the sun or stars. So, when he found nothing there he widened the search area, and covered more than 200 square miles of seabed before he finally found her. She lay 15,719ft below the surface of the Atlantic, on the slope of an extinct underwater volcano, and her hull, though battered, was in remarkably good condition. Ballard discovered that the ship had glided some distance before she came to rest, although her four turrets, which dropped out of her as she capsized, fell directly down towards the seabed.

From this, Ballard was able to reconstruct her journey to the seabed.[5] When she capsized, *Bismarck* sank, but righted herself soon afterwards, and then the hull glided like a paper plane, until it struck the side of the volcano. It then careered down its slope another 1,000 yards before coming to rest, scattering debris as she went. By then, all of her remaining crew were dead. The hull was remarkably intact, which suggested that she was already full of water by the time she reached a depth at which an air-filled hull might be crushed by the water pressure. Ballard felt this supported the theory that she was scuttled, and her own crew sank the ship. Examination of her hull, however, uncovered torpedo and shell damage that showed she would have sunk anyway. So, the old argument over whether she was sunk by the British or scuttled by the Germans is largely irrelevant. Both fates befell her at the same time, and one merely hastened the other.

Using Remotely-Operated Vehicles (ROVs), the expedition was able to examine her hull, which revealed the pounding *Bismarck* suffered during her final battle. *Bismarck* is resting upright on the seabed, embedded in mud as far as her waterline. Her hull is remarkably intact, although the last 30ft of her stern appears to have broken off as she sank. This suggests some major structural failure took place, and may explain why she sank so quickly after she capsized. Debris fell off her as she glided towards the seabed, and Ballard followed this until he discovered the four turrets, lying upside down on the seabed. He could even identify 'Bruno' turret, which had had its back ripped off during the final battle. These, then, marked the actual spot where *Bismarck* sank.

The debris trail itself was littered with the mangled remains of the ship's superstructure, as well as her funnel and masts and gun directors. On the ship herself, the armoured conning tower was well preserved, but the bridge in front of it was completely destroyed. Most probably it was here that Lütjens and Lindemann were killed by a direct hit from a shell fired from *Rodney*. Further aft, the secondary turrets remain in place, some with their rear doors jammed shut, which trapped the gun crews inside them when the ship sank. Only the main turrets were missing, leaving enormous circular holes where their barbettes once sat, protecting the loading hoists that linked the turrets to their magazines. The aircraft catapult was still there, where the crew tried to launch a floatplane carrying Admiral Lütjens' Fleet War Diary. Some of her flak guns were swept away by British shells, but others still remain, where they fired at *Ark Royal*'s Swordfish on the evening of 26 May 1941.

Then, in July 2001, an expedition led by David L. Mearns discovered the last resting place of the battlecruiser *Hood*.[6] The expedition was sponsored by Channel 4, a British television company. Like *Bismarck*, the wreck was located using sidescan sonar, after a search lasting just two days. *Hood* lies in 9,200ft of water, but as the ship broke in two when she blew up, the wreck forms two distinct sites, some 300 yards apart. Other scattered debris, including a 15in. gun, lies further away from the two main wreck sites. Once the wreck was found, Mearns and the team set about investigating the remains. They soon found that a 200ft section of her hull was missing, forward of 'X' turret. This was the epicentre of the fatal explosion on 24 May 1941 that ripped the great battlecruiser in two.

What they did find was evidence of the immensity of the explosion. Turret plating was bent and bucked, as were parts of the armoured hull. To the team, and to the experts who examined the evidence, it all suggested that while the explosion might have been utterly catastrophic, structural faults in the old battlecruiser may have hastened her end, since the blast severed her so effectively into two parts while demolishing the section in between. Traces of this middle section were eventually found, but there wasn't enough to definitively pinpoint the location of the explosion, or explain the exact sequence of events that led to *Hood* breaking in two. However, it actually lies to the south of the two main wreck sites, and proves that *Hood* actually broke into three or more pieces, rather than two. This after part of the stern section was damaged, possibly suggesting a secondary explosion in one of the after magazines.

Her bow section was much less damaged, lying on the seabed on its port side. It showed fewer signs of damage, apart from the usual erosion expected after decades lying on the seabed. Incidentally, the 650-ton conning tower was found over 1,000 yards from the rest of the ship, having been blown clean off. However, even the bow section was broken in two, just forward of 'A' turret, which strengthens the notion that structural integrity of the hull failed, either as a result of the explosion or as the bow section dropped towards the seabed. So, this expedition confirmed all the eye-witness accounts – *Hood* was torn apart just forward of 'X' turret, and the two portions separated slightly as she sank. One other important discovery was the rudder, locked at an angle of 20 degrees. This confirms that V. Adm. Holland had ordered *Hood* to turn when she was hit by *Bismarck*'s fatal sixth salvo.

Interestingly, both expeditions treated the wreck sides they discovered and explored as war graves. After all, 1,415 British sailors went down with the *Hood*, and 2,086 German ones with the *Bismarck*. Both groups of undersea explorers went to great lengths to avoid disturbing the final resting places of these men. On *Hood*, though, the ship's bell was discovered and raised, and is now on display in the National Museum of the Royal Navy in Portsmouth – a tangible and very poignant reminder of a once mighty warship, and the men who lost their lives in her. Interestingly, one of *Hood*'s three survivors, Ted Briggs, was present on board Mearns' mother ship when *Hood* was rediscovered.[7] He was also there when an ROV laid a plaque on the deck of his old ship. A dozen years before, a similar plaque had been laid on the deck of the *Bismarck*. So, the two wrecks and war graves remain undisturbed, over a thousand miles apart, but linked by a common bond of history and sacrifice.

Notes

PROLOGUE

1 For the most part, this account of the engagement is drawn
   from Von Müllenheim-Rechberg, Burkard, *Battleship Bismarck:
   A Survivor's Story* (1990), pp135–152. Weapons and vessel data
   is drawn from Campbell, John, *Naval Weapons of World War
   Two* (1985) and Gardiner, *Conway's All the World's Fighting
   Ships* (1980), pp9, 15, 224–229.
2 Müllenheim-Rechberg, *op cit*, pp38–139. Also Gardiner, *op cit*,
   pp9–15.
3 This account is based on the testimony of a survivor, Ted
   Briggs, recounted in Coles, Alan & Briggs, Ted, *Flagship Hood:
   The Fate of Britain's Mightiest Warship* (1988), pp184–196.

TIME, SPEED, DISTANCE AND BEARING

1 For a full description of all of the maritime conventions
   described here, see Ministry of Defence (Navy), *Admiralty
   Manual of Seamanship* (1979), Vol. 1.

PREFACE

1 The depth of the *Bismarck* wreck site and its general description
   is drawn from Ballard, Robert D., *The Discovery of the Bismarck*
   (1990), pp163–179.
2 The official British version of the hunt for *Bismarck* is provided
   by Roskill, Stephen W., *The War at Sea* (1954), Vol. 1, pp395–
   416. Examples of the many others include Winklareth, Robert

J., *The Bismarck Chase: New Light on a Famous Engagement* (1998); Skwiot, Miroslaw Z. & Prusinowska, Elzbieta T., *Hunting the Bismarck* (2006); and Zetterling, Niklas & Tamelander, Michael, *Bismarck: The Final Days of Germany's Greatest Battleship* (2009). Several other accounts of this campaign are listed in the bibliography.
3 Kennedy, Paul, *The Rise and Fall of British Naval Mastery* (1983), p148 et passim.

CHAPTER 1: THE *BISMARCK*

1 Müllenheim-Rechberg, *op cit*, pp30–34.
2 The building of *Bismarck* and the design rationale behind her is described in more detail in Asmussen, *Bismarck: Pride of the German Navy* (2013); Konstam, *Battleship Bismarck 1936–41, Owners' Workshop Manual* (2015) and Zetterling & Tamelander, *op cit*.
3 Kennedy (1983), pp274–276. For a wider discussion of the topic, see Kaufmann, Robert G., *Arms Control During the Pre-Nuclear Era* (1993), pp180–215.
4 Gardiner, *op cit*, p227.
5 *Ibid*, p225. Also Gröner, Erich, *German Warships, 1815–1945, Vol. 1, Major Surface Vessels* (1983), pp31–32.
6 Broszat, Martin, *Hitler and the Collapse of Weimar Germany* (1987), pp9–10.
7 Maiolo, Joseph, *The Royal Navy and Nazi Germany, 1933–39* (1998), pp26–33.
8 Gardiner, *op cit*, p225.
9 *Ibid*, pp228–229. Also Gröner, *op cit*, pp65–67.
10 Konstam (2015), *op cit*, pp12–15.
11 *Ibid*, p15.
12 *Ibid*, pp16–19.
13 Asmussen, *op cit*, pp12–13.
14 Konstam (2015), *op cit*, pp19–21.
15 Gardiner, *op cit*, pp228–229.
16 Asmussen, *op cit*, pp213–214.

17 Konstam (2015), *op cit*, pp21–24.

18 Müllenheim-Rechberg, *op cit*, p27.

19 *Ibid*, p34.

20 *Ibid*, p35.

21 *Ibid*, p37.

22 See Konstam (2015), *op cit*, pp111–113; and Amussen, *op cit*, pp132–133. For a more detailed discussion of analogue gunnery direction systems see Brooks, John, *Dreadnought Gunnery and the Battle of Jutland: The Question of Fire Control* (2005). While this deals with an earlier conflict, it outlines the development of the system that was subsequently used on board *Bismarck*. Also see Friedman, Norman, *Naval Firepower* (2013), pp140–156.

23 Müllenheim-Rechberg, *op cit*, p42.

24 *Ibid*, p52.

25 *Ibid*, p52.

26 Konstam (2015), *op cit*, p31.

27 Müllenheim-Rechberg, *op cit*, pp64–66.

CHAPTER 2: GERMANY'S ATLANTIC STRATEGY

1 Mahan, Alfred Thayer, *The Influence of Sea Power on History* (1893), pp320–326. Also see Herwig, Holger H., 'The Failure of German Sea Power, 1914–1945: Mahan, Tirpitz, and Raeder Reconsidered', published in *The International History Review*, 10:1 (February 1988), pp72–73. Vego, Milan, *Maritime Strategy and Sea Denial: Theory and Practice* (2018) also discusses the concepts outlined by Mahan, and applied by the German navy in both world wars.

2 Herwig, Holger H., *"Luxury" Fleet: The Imperial German Navy, 1888–1918* (1987), pp17–20.

3 For a full discussion of the success of German naval strategy, see Sondhaus, Lawrence, *The Great War at Sea* (Cambridge, 2014), pp275–277.

4 Konstam (2015), *op cit*, pp34–35; Zetterling & Tamelander, *op cit*, pp18–23.

5 Whitley, M. J., *Battleships of World War Two: An International Encylopedia* (1998), pp63–65.

6 Konstam (2015), *op cit*, p15.

7 Bekker, Cajus, *Hitler's Naval War* (1974), p33–34.

8 Gardiner, *op cit*, p220.

9 *Ibid*, p225–226.

10 *Ibid*, pp224–244.

11 The structure is outlined in Goerlitz, Walter, *History of the German General Staff, 1657–1945* (1985), pp185–197, with a précis in Konstam (2015), *op cit*, p35.

12 Gardiner, *op cit*, p4.

13 Whitley (1998), *op cit*, pp67–72.

14 Roskill, *op cit*, pp43–46.

15 The directive is published online by Yale Law School, as part of The Avalon Project (http://avalon.law.yale.edu/imt/wardir1.asp)

16 Bekker, *op cit*, pp17–20.

17 Zetterling & Tamelander, *op cit*, p25.

18 *Ibid*, pp26–27. Captain Kennedy of the *Rawalpindi* was the father of Ludovic Kennedy, broadcaster and the author of *Pursuit* (1974).

19 *Ibid*, *op cit*, p30.

20 For a detailed account of the campaign, and its strategic ramifications, see Jackson, Julian, *The Fall of France: The Nazi Invasion of 1940* (2003), particularly pp40–57.

21 Roskill, *op cit*, p291.

22 *Ibid*, pp285–291, 369–372. Also Zetterling & Tamelander, *op cit*, pp42–47.

23 Zetterling & Tamelander, *op cit*, pp44–45.

24 Whitley (1998), *op cit*, pp77–79.

25 Roskill, *op cit*, pp373–375.

26 Zetterling & Tamelander, *op cit*, p63.

27 *Ibid*, pp66–67.

28 *Ibid*, pp67–68. Also Roskill, *op cit*, pp390–391.

29 Zetterling & Tamelander, *op cit*, p72.

30 *Ibid*, pp77–78; Roskill, *op cit*, p375.

31 Roskill, *op cit*, p374; Zetterling & Tamelander, *op cit*, pp64–66.

32 Zetterling & Tamelander, *op cit*, pp78–80.

33 Roskill, *op cit*, pp377–379.

34 *Ibid*, p379.

35 Gröner, *op cit*, p67. For the general strategic situation in early 1941 see Zetterling & Tamelander, *op cit*, pp82–85.

36 Roskill, *op cit*, p486.

37 *Ibid*, p487.

CHAPTER 3: THE HOME FLEET

1 Konstam, Angus, *Jutland 1916: Twelve Hours to Win the War* (2016), p44. Also see Konstam, Angus, *Scapa Flow* (2009), pp7–9.

2 See Brown, Malcolm & Meehan, Patrick, *Scapa Flow* (1968), a series of first-hand accounts of wartime service in and around Scapa Flow, for a detailed picture of the base in wartime. Also see Kennedy (1974), *op cit*, pp37–38, and Konstam (2009), *op cit*, pp43–46.

3 Konstam (2009), *op cit*, pp47–48.

4 *Ibid*, pp49–51.

5 *Ibid*, pp50–51.

6 Kennedy (1974), *op cit*, p38.

7 Sondhaus, *op cit*, pp157–162.

8 Bekker, *op cit*, pp55–73.

9 Roskill, *op cit*, pp249–264.

10 *Ibid*, p345.

11 Heathcote, Tony, *The British Admirals of the Fleet 1734–1995* (2002), p86. Also see Kennedy (1974), *op cit*, pp38–44.

12 Whitley (1998), *op cit*, pp126–136.

13 *Ibid*, pp92–113.

14 *Ibid*, pp113–120.

15 *Ibid*, pp121–127.

16 *Ibid*, pp126–127. Also Roberts, John, *The Battlecruiser Hood* (1982), p9.

17 Whitley (1998), *op cit*, pp137–146.

18 *Ibid*, p146.
19 Winklareth (1998), *op cit*, p48. Also see Campbell, pp28–30.
20 See Friedman, Norman, *Naval Radar* (1981) for a discussion of the relative capabilities of British and German radar during this period.
21 Hobbs, David, *British Aircraft Carriers: Design, Development & Service Histories* (2013), pp68–99. Also p373 for the specifications of the aircraft embarked in these ships. Also see Chesneau, Roger, *Aircraft Carriers of the World, 1914 to the Present* (1992), pp97–105.
22 Hobbs, *op cit*, pp42, 80–82, 90–98.
23 See Friedman, Norman, *British Cruisers: Two World Wars and After* (2010), pp230–251 for a discussion of the role and capabilities of British cruisers during this phase of the war. Friedman has also produced *British Destroyers: From Earliest Days to the Second World War* (2009), a similar volume outlining the capabilities of these smaller warships.

CHAPTER 4: PREPARATIONS

1   Asmussen, *op cit*, p34.
2   Kennedy (1974), *op cit*, pp25–26.
3   *Ibid*, p223. Also quoted in Zetterling & Tamelander (2009), *op cit*, pp54–55.
4   Müllenheim-Rechberg (1990), *op cit*, p69.
5   *Ibid*, p69.
6   Asmussen, *op cit*, p34.
7   *Ibid*, p74.
8   Müllenheim-Rechberg, *op cit*, p70.
9   *Ibid*, p71.
10 Asmussen, *op cit*, p37.
11 Müllenheim-Rechberg, *op cit*, p70.
12 Kennedy (1974), *op cit*, p27.
13 *Ibid*, p27.
14 Müllenheim-Rechberg, *op cit*, p72.
15 *Ibid*, p71.

16 *Ibid*, p71.
17 *Ibid, op cit*, p80.
18 *Ibid*, p81.
19 *Ibid*, p81.
20 *Ibid*, p81.
21 *Ibid*, p85. Also Zetterling & Tamelander, *op cit*, pp92–93.
22 Asmussen, *op cit*, pp37–39.
23 Kennedy (1974), *op cit*, p30.
24 Zetterling & Tamelander, *op cit*, p102.
25 *Ibid*, p103.
26 Asmussen, *op cit*, p43.
27 *Ibid*, p43. Also Kennedy (1974), *op cit*, p32.

CHAPTER 5: THROUGH THE BALTIC

1 Asmussen, *op cit*, p43.
2 Müllenheim-Rechberg, *op cit*, p100.
3 Konstam (2015) *op cit*, p35.
4 Müllenheim-Rechberg, *op cit*, p100.
5 Kennedy (1974), *op cit*, p32.
6 Asmussen, *op cit*, p44.
7 Müllenheim-Rechberg, *op cit*, pp100–101.
8 Asmussen, *op cit*, p44.
9 Müllenheim-Rechberg, *op cit*, p101.
10 *Ibid*, p101.
11 Asmussen, *op cit*, p44.
12 *Ibid*, p44.
13 Müllenheim-Rechberg, *op cit*, p103.
14 Whitley, M. J., *Cruisers of World War Two: An International Encyclopedia* (1996), pp223–224.
15 Müllenheim-Rechberg, *op cit*, p104; Asmussen, *op cit*, p44.
16 Zetterling & Tamelander, *op cit*, p118; Kennedy (1974), *op cit*, pp18–19; and Müllenheim-Rechberg, *op cit*, pp105–106.
17 Müllenheim-Rechberg, *op cit*, p106.
18 Zetterling & Tamelander, *op cit*, p113.
19 *Ibid*, p114.

20 Müllenheim-Rechberg, *op cit*, p107.

21 Asmussen, *op cit*, p45.

22 Müllenheim-Rechberg, *op cit*, p107.

23 Kennedy (1974), *op cit*, p35. Also Müllenheim-Rechberg, *op cit*, p108.

24 Kennedy (1974), *op cit*, pp35–36.

25 Skwiot & Prusinowska, *op cit*, p73.

26 *Ibid*, p74.

27 Zetterling & Tamelander, *op cit*, pp121–122.

28 Skwiot & Prusinowska, *op cit*, p74.

CHAPTER 6: SOJOURN IN NORWAY

1 Müllenheim-Rechberg, *op cit*, p109.

2 *Ibid*, p109.

3 Asmussen, p45.

4 Müllenheim-Rechberg, *op cit*, p109

5 *Ibid*, pp109–110.

6 *Ibid*, pp110–111.

7 Müllenheim-Rechberg, *op cit*, pp111–112. Also Winklareth (1998), *op cit*, pp63–64; Zetterling & Tamelander, *op cit*, pp119–121.

8 Kennedy (1974), *op cit*, p42; Amussen, *op cit*, p45.

9 Skwiot & Prusinowska, *op cit*, p76.

10 Zetterling & Tamelander, *op cit*, p120.

11 *Ibid*, p120.

12 Müllenheim-Rechberg, *op cit*, p111.

13 *Ibid*, p111.

14 *Ibid*, p111.

15 *Ibid*, *op cit*, pp114–116; Zetterling & Tamelander, *op cit*, p123.

16 Zetterling & Tamelander, *op cit*, p123.

17 Müllenheim-Rechberg, *op cit*, p116.

18 Zetterling & Tamelander, *op cit*, p94; Skwiot & Prusinowska, *op cit*, p59.

19 Asmussen, *op cit*, p54.

20 *Ibid*, p54.

21 Müllenheim-Rechberg, *op cit*, p116.

22 *Ibid*, pp116–117.

23 Müllenheim-Rechberg, *op cit*, p116.

CHAPTER 7: MOVE AND COUNTERMOVE

1 Kennedy (1974), *op cit*, p45.

2 *Ibid*, p46; Zetterling & Tamelander, *op cit*, p126.

3 Zetterling & Tamelander, *op cit*, p124; Asmussen, *op cit*, p54.

4 Zetterling & Tamelander, *op cit*, pp119–121

5 Roskill, *op cit*, Map 30, between pp396–397.

6 *Ibid*, pp396–397.

7 Skwiot & Prusinowska, *op cit*, p83.

8 Asmussen, *op cit*, p54.

9 Zetterling & Tamelander, *op cit*, p126.

10 Müllenheim-Rechberg, *op cit*, pp116–117; Asmussen, *op cit*, p55.

11 Müllenheim-Rechberg, *op cit*, p117.

12 Skwiot & Prusinowska, *op cit*, p82; Müllenheim-Rechberg, *op cit*, p116.

13 Müllenheim-Rechberg, p82; Kennedy (1974), *op cit*, pp49, 52; Skwiot & Prusinowska, *op cit*, p82.

14 Kennedy (1974), *op cit*, p51; Zetterling & Tamelander, *op cit*, p140.

15 Kennedy (1974), *op cit*, p56.

16 Zetterling & Tamelander, *op cit*, pp142–145.

17 Kennedy (1974), *op cit*, p42; Zetterling & Tamelander, *op cit*, p143.

18 Kennedy (1974), *op cit*, pp46–47; Zetterling & Tamelander, *op cit*, pp128–129.

19 Kennedy (1974), *op cit*, p47.

20 *Ibid*, p48; Skwiot & Prusinowska, *op cit*, pp84–85; Winklareth (1998), pp66–67.

21 Zetterling & Tamelander, *op cit*, p129.

CHAPTER 8: THE DENMARK STRAIT

1 Zetterling & Tamelander, *op cit*, p144.
2 *Ibid*, p129; Roskill, *op cit*, pp396–397.
3 Kennedy (1974), *op cit*, p54.
4 Zetterling & Tamelander, *op cit*, pp144–145. Also see Friedman (1981) for a discussion of British radar capability.
5 Roskill, *op cit*, pp396–397.
6 Zetterling & Tamelander, *op cit*, p146; Konstam (2015), *op cit*, pp48–49.
7 Müllenheim-Rechberg, *op cit*, p128.
8 *Ibid*, p128.
9 *Ibid*, p128.
10 Roskill, *op cit*, p397.
11 Kennedy (1974), *op cit*, p55; Roskill, *op cit*, p397 (although he says 6 miles).
12 Kennedy (1974), *op cit*, pp55–56.
13 *Ibid*, pp56–57.
14 *Ibid*, *op cit*, p56; Zetterling & Tamelander, *op cit*, p148.
15 Zetterling & Tamelander, *op cit*, p148.
16 Müllenheim-Rechberg, *op cit*, p133.
17 Zetterling & Tamelander, *op cit*, pp153–157 discusses the strategic situation that evening, as does Roskill, *op cit*, pp398–399, from the standpoint of V. Adm. Holland.
18 Müllenheim-Rechberg, *op cit*, p133.
19 *Ibid*, p134.
20 *Ibid*, p134.

CHAPTER 9: DUEL AT DAWN

1 Coles & Briggs, pp148–164 contains a detailed account of the action through Briggs' eyes. A précis is provided in Mearns, David & White, Rob, *Hood and Bismarck: The Deep-sea Discovery of an Epic Battle* (2001), p159. Also Ballantyne, Iain, *Killing the Bismarck: Destroying the Pride of Hitler's Fleet* (2010), pp72–82 for a wealth of personal accounts.
2 Skwiot & Prusinowska, *op cit*, p93.

3 Kennedy (1974), *op cit*, p68.

4 *Ibid*, p70; Asmussen, *op cit*, p60; Winklareth (1998), *op cit*, pp72–73.

5 Kennedy (1974), *op cit*, p69.

6 *Ibid*, p66.

7 Asmussen, *op cit*, p60.

8 Kennedy (1974), *op cit*, p71.

9 Skwiot & Prusinowska, *op cit*, p93. Also Konstam, Angus, *The Bismarck 1941* (2011) for maps showing the approach to contact by both of the protagonists.

10 Kennedy (1974), *op cit*, p74.

11 Asmussen, *op cit*, p60.

12 Müllenheim-Rechberg, *op cit*, p135.

13 *Ibid*, p135.

14 Kennedy (1974), *op cit*, pp75–76.

15 Asmussen, p60.

16 Müllenheim-Rechberg, *op cit*, pp136–137.

17 Winklareth, Robert J., *The Battle of the Denmark Strait: A Critical Analysis of the Bismarck's Singular Triumph* (2012), p84.

18 Müllenheim-Rechberg, *op cit*, p138.

19 Asmussen*, op cit*, pp61–62.

20 Santarini, Marco, *Bismarck and Hood: The Battle of the Denmark Strait – a Technical Analysis for a New Perspective* (2017), pp72–75.
This work provides an exhaustive ballistic analysis of the engagement.

21 *Ibid*, p72. Also Asmussen, *op cit*, pp61–62.

CHAPTER 10: *HOOD* HAS BLOWN UP

1 Winklareth (2012), pp135–137. Also Konstam (2011), *op cit*, p86.

2 Santarini, *op cit*, pp111–116. Also Asmussen, *op cit*, p61.

3 Santarini, *op cit*, pp112–113; Asmussen, *op cit*, pp61–63.

4 Asmussen, *op cit*, p63.

5 Zetterling & Tamelander, *op cit*, p167.

6 *Ibid*, p157; Asmussen, *op cit*, p63.

7 Zetterling & Tamelander, *op cit*, p162.

8 Asmussen, *op cit*, pp63–64.

9 Skwiot & Prusinowska, *op cit*, p99.

10 Asmussen, *op cit*, p63.

11 Skwiot & Prusinowska, *op cit*, p99.

12 Asmussen, *op cit*, p64.

13 Müllenheim-Rechberg, *op cit*, p141.

14 Santarini, *op cit*, pp72–77.

15 *Ibid*, pp116–122.

16 Zetterling & Tamelander, *op cit*, pp171–173 contains several accounts by witnesses on the *Prince of Wales* of the sight of *Hood* blowing up. Also Ballantyne (2010), *op cit*, pp84–88 for similar first-hand reports.

17 Ballantyne (2010), *op cit*, pp93–97.

18 Coles & Briggs, *op cit*, p164.

19 Müllenheim-Rechberg, *op cit*, p142.

20 *Ibid*, p143.

21 Zetterling & Tamelander, *op cit*, p173.

22 *Ibid*, pp176–177.

23 *Ibid*, p180.

24 Santarini, *op cit*, p77.

25 Kennedy (1974), *op cit*, p88; Zetterling & Tamelander, *op cit*, p176.

26 Ballantyne (2010), *op cit*, pp84–87.

27 Skwiot & Prusinowska, *op cit*, p111.

28 Winklareth (2012), *op cit*, p140.

29 Santarini, *op cit*, p77.

30 Asmussen, *op cit*, p69.

31 Kennedy (1974), *op cit*, p90.

CHAPTER 11: BREAKOUT INTO THE ATLANTIC

1 Kennedy (1974), *op cit*, pp90–91; Ballantyne (2010), *op cit*, pp89–92.

2 Zetterling & Tamelander, *op cit*, p180.

3 *Ibid*, p181. Also Ballantyne (2010), *op cit*, pp93–97 for an account of the rescue, and of the plight of the three survivors.

4 Müllenheim-Rechberg, *op cit*, pp147–152. Also Asmussen, *op cit*, p74.

5 Müllenheim-Rechberg, *op cit*, pp150–151.

6 *Ibid*, p152.

7 *Ibid*, p153.

8 *Ibid*, p152. Also pp53–157 for the problems this damage caused Lütjens.

9 Zetterling & Tamelander, *op cit*, p191.

10 Kennedy (1974), p102.

11 Roskill, *op cit*, pp404–408. Also Zetterling & Tamelander, *op cit*, pp193–197 for a full discussion of the British naval dispositions at this juncture.

12 Kennedy (1974), *op cit*, pp103–104.

13 *Ibid*, pp107–108.

14 Müllenheim-Rechberg, *op cit*, p158; Skwiot & Prusinowska, *op cit*, pp123–124.

15 Asmussen, *op cit*, p75.

16 Asmussen *op cit*, p75; Müllenheim-Rechberg, *op cit*, p161.

17 Müllenheim-Rechberg, *op cit*, p163.

18 Ballantyne (2010), *op cit*, p101.

19 *Ibid*, p102.

20 Asmussen *op cit*, p75.

21 Roskill, *op cit*, p408.

22 Zetterling & Tamelander, *op cit*, p199; Ballantyne (2010), *op cit*, p107.

23 Asmussen, *op cit*, p77; Skwiot & Prusinowska, *op cit*, p128.

24 Zetterling & Tamelander, *op cit*, pp201–203; Ballantyne (2010), *op cit*, pp108–111.

25 Müllenheim-Rechberg, *op cit*, p167.

26 Ballantyne (2010), *op cit*, pp111–112; Zetterling & Tamelander, *op cit*, p204.

27 Müllenheim-Rechberg, *op cit*, pp174–175; Zetterling & Tamelander, *op cit*, pp210–211.

28 Müllenheim-Rechberg, *op cit*, pp174–175.

29 *Ibid*, p175.

CHAPTER 12: HUNTING FOR THE *BISMARCK*

1 Zetterling & Tamelander, *op cit*, pp210–211.

2 *Ibid*, pp212–213.

3 Winklareth (1998), *op cit*, p198; Kennedy (1974), *op cit*, pp126–127.

4 Kennedy (1974), *op cit*, p126.

5 *Ibid*, pp127–128; Roskill, *op cit*, p410.

6 Dannreuther, Raymond, *Somerville's Force H* (2005), pp88–89 provides a brief but useful history of Somerville's force.

7 Whitley (1998), *op cit*, p119.

8 Roskill, *op cit*, p410; Kennedy (1974), *op cit*, pp141–144.

9 Ballantyne (2010), *op cit*, pp115–117.

10 Müllenheim-Rechberg, *op cit*, p176.

11 *Ibid*, p176.

12 *Ibid*, p177.

13 *Ibid*, pp182–183.

14 *Ibid*, p183.

15 *Ibid*, p185.

16 *Ibid*, pp188–189.

17 Zetterling & Tamelander, *op cit*, pp220–221.

18 Kennedy (1974), *op cit*, p128

19 Zetterling & Tamelander, *op cit*, pp227–228.

20 *Ibid*, p228.

21 Asmussen, *op cit*, p82.

22 Kennedy (1974), *op cit*, pp151–153.

23 *Ibid*, p154.

24 *Ibid*, p154; Asmussen, *op cit*, p83.

CHAPTER 13: AIR STRIKE

1 Skwiot & Prusinowska, *op cit*, pp147–149.

2 Ballantyne, Iain, *Bismarck: 24 Hours to Doom* (2016), pp21–22; Zetterling & Tamelander, *op cit*, p234.

3 Ballantyne (2010), *op cit*, p132.

4 Zetterling & Tamelander, *op cit*, p235.

5 Asmussen, *op cit*, p83.

6 *Ibid*, p83; Ballantyne (2016), *op cit,* pp16–18.

7 Zetterling & Tamelander, *op cit*, p235.

8 *Ibid*, p235; Kennedy (1974), *op cit*, p160.

9 Zetterling & Tamelander, *op cit*, p236.

10 Ballantyne (2010), *op cit*, p139.

11 *Ibid*, p139.

12 *Ibid*, p139.

13 *Ibid*, p139.

14 *Ibid*, p139.

15 Kennedy (1974), *op cit*, pp165–166.

16 *Ibid*, pp165–166.

17 Asmussen, *op cit*, p85.

18 *Ibid*, p85; Zetterling & Tamelander, *op cit*, p240.

19 Zetterling & Tamelander, *op cit*, p241.

20 Ballantyne (2010), *op cit*, p148.

21 Zetterling & Tamelander, *op cit*, p242.

22 Skwiot & Prusinowska, *op cit*, p154; Asmussen, *op cit*, p228.

23 Zetterling & Tamelander, *op cit*, p243.

24 Ballantyne (2010), *op cit*, p147.

25 Asmussen, *op cit*, p228.

26 Zetterling & Tamelander, *op cit*, p246.

27 *Ibid*, p246; Kennedy (1974), *op cit*, p175.

28 Kennedy (1974), *op cit*, p175.

29 *Ibid*, p172.

30 *Ibid*, p172.

31 Zetterling & Tamelander, *op cit*, p248.

32 *Ibid*, p248.

CHAPTER 14: DESTROYERS IN THE NIGHT

1 Müllenheim-Rechberg, *op cit*, p208.

2 *Ibid*, p209.

3 *Ibid*, p209.

4 *Ibid*, p210.

5 *Ibid*, p212.

6 Kennedy (1974), *op cit*, p27.

7 Müllenheim-Rechberg, *op cit*, p211; Ballantyne (2010), pp158–159; Asmussen, *op cit*, p89.

8 Ballanytne (2016), pp27–29.

9 Kennedy (1974), *op cit*, p183; Zetterling & Tamelander, *op cit*, pp252–253.

10 Ballantyne (2010), *op cit*, p154.

11 Whitley, M. J., *Destroyers of World War Two: An International Encyclopedia* (2002), pp114–121, 220.

12 Zetterling & Tamelander, *op cit*, p251.

13 Asmussen, *op cit*, p89.

14 Müllenheim-Rechberg, *op cit*, p217.

15 Kennedy (1974), *op cit*, p184.

16 *Ibid*, p186.

17 *Ibid*, p186.

18 Ballantyne (2010), *op cit*, p157.

19 *Ibid*, p157.

20 Kennedy (1974), *op cit*, p186.

21 Ballanytne (2016), *op cit*, p46. Also see Zetterling & Tamelander, *op cit*, pp255–256; Müllenheim-Rechberg, *op cit*, p219.

22 Skwiot & Prusinowska, *op cit*, p162.

23 Zetterling & Tamelander, *op cit*, p209.

24 Ballanytne (2016), *op cit*, p41.

25 Kennedy (1974), *op cit*, p189.

26 Ballanytne (2010), *op cit*, pp41–42; Müllenheim-Rechberg, *op cit*, p222.

27 Müllenheim-Rechberg, *op cit*, p223.

28 *Ibid*, p222; Kennedy (1974), *op cit*, pp192–193.

29 Müllenheim-Rechberg, *op cit*, pp229–230.

30 *Ibid*, p231. Also, pp229–234 for an account of the proximity of *Bismarck*'s 'protector' the *U-556* to the stricken battleship, and the inability of her commander to intervene.

NOTES

CHAPTER 15: THE FINAL BATTLE

1 Kennedy (1974), *op cit*, pp198–199.
2 *Ibid*, pp200–201.
3 Zetterling & Tamelander, *op cit*, p264.
4 Ballantyne (2010), *op cit*, p164.
5 Zetterling & Tamelander, *op cit*, p264.
6 Kennedy (1974), *op cit*, p201.
7 Asmussen, *op cit*, p91.
8 Müllenheim-Rechberg, *op cit*, pp248–249.
9 *Ibid*, p247.
10 Kennedy (1974), *op cit*, p204. Also see Ballantyne (2010), *op cit*, pp170–171.
11 Asmussen, *op cit*, p92. For the reaction on the British ships, see Ballantyne (2010), *op cit*, pp170–171.
12 Müllenheim-Rechberg, *op cit*, p248; Asmussen, *op cit*, p93.
13 Asmussen, *op cit*, p92.
14 Müllenheim-Rechberg, *op cit*, p250.
15 Kennedy (1974), *op cit*, p206. Also Konstam (2015), *op cit*, p68.
16 Zetterling & Tamelander, *op cit*, p271.
17 Kennedy (1974), *op cit*, p206.
18 Asmussen, *op cit*, p93.
19 Müllenheim-Rechberg, *op cit*, p250. Also Ballantyne (2016), *op cit*, p61.
20 Müllenheim-Rechberg, *op cit*, p253.
21 Zetterling & Tamelander, p271.
22 *Ibid*, p206.
23 Kennedy (1974), *op cit*, p208.
24 *Ibid*, p207.
25 Ballantyne (2010), *op cit*, p185.
26 Kennedy (1974), *op cit*, pp208–209.
27 Asmussen, *op cit*, p97.
28 Zetterling & Tamelander, *op cit*, p274.
29 Asmussen, *op cit*, pp97–98.
30 Kennedy (1974), *op cit*, p209.

31 For his account of his escape from his ship, and his eventual rescue, see Müllenheim-Rechberg, *op cit*, pp277–282.

32 Ballantyne (2010), *op cit*, pp198–199.

33 Asmussen, *op cit*, p98.

34 Müllenheim-Rechberg, *op cit*, p272.

35 Kennedy (1974), *op cit*, p209.

EPILOGUE

1 Skwiot & Prusinowska, *op cit*, pp186–190.

2 A detailed account of their fate is provided in Ballantyne (2010), *op cit*, pp215–217. Also Chesneau; and Whitley (1996, 1998, 2002).

3 Whitley (1998), *op cit*, p89.

4 Ballard, *op cit*, pp159–169.

5 *Ibid*, p218.

6 Mearns & White, *op cit*, pp194–207.

7 *Ibid*, pp207–211.

Bibliography

Asmussen, John, *Bismarck: Pride of the German Navy* (Cirencester, 2013) Fonthill Media Ltd

Ballantyne, Iain, *Bismarck: 24 Hours to Doom* (London, 2016) Ipso Books

Ballantyne, Iain, *Killing the Bismarck: Destroying the Pride of Hitler's Fleet* (Barnsley, 2010) Pen & Sword

Ballard, Robert D., *The Discovery of the Bismarck* (Toronto, Ontario, 1990) Madison Publishing Inc

Bekker, Cajus, Hitler's Naval War (London, 1974) Macdonald & Co.

Brooks, John, *Dreadnought Gunnery and the Battle of Jutland: The Question of Fire Control* (Abingdon, 2005) Routledge

Broszat, Martin, *Hitler and the Collapse of Weimar Germany* (Oxford, 1987) Berg Publishers

Brown, Malcolm & Meehan, Patricia; *Scapa Flow* (London, 1968) Allen Lane – Penguin Press

Campbell, John, *Naval Weapons of World War Two* (London, 1985) Conway Maritime Press

Chesneau, Roger, *Aircraft Carriers of the World, 1914 to the Present* (London, 1992) Arms & Armour Press

Coles, Alan & Briggs, Ted, *Flagship Hood: The Fate of Britain's Mightiest Warship* (London, 1988) Robert Hale Ltd

Dannreuther, Raymond, *Somerville's Force H* (London, 2005) Aurum Press

Friedman, Norman, *British Cruisers: Two World Wars and After* (Barnsley, 2010) Seaforth Publishing

Friedman, Norman, *British Destroyers: From Earliest Days to the Second World War* (Barnsley, 2009) Seaforth Publishing

Friedman, Norman, *Naval Firepower* (Barnsley, 2013) Seaforth Publishing

Friedman, Norman, *Naval Radar* (London, 1981) Harper Collins

Gardiner, Robert (ed.), *Conway's All the World's Fighting Ships* (London, 1980) Conway Maritime Press

Goerlitz, Walter, *History of the German General Staff, 1657–1945* (London, 1985) Westview Press

Gröner, Erich, *German Warships, 1815–1945, Vol. 1, Major Surface Vessels* (London, 1983) Conway Maritime Press

Heathcote, Tony, *The British Admirals of the Fleet 1734–1995* (Barnsley, 2002) Pen & Sword

Herwig, Holger H., *"Luxury" Fleet: The Imperial German Navy, 1888–1918* (Abingdon, 1987) Ashfield Press Ltd

Hobbs, David, *British Aircraft Carriers: Design, Development & Service Histories* (Barnsley, 2013) Seaforth Publishing

Jackson, Julian, *The Fall of France: The Nazi Invasion of 1940* (Oxford, 2003) Oxford University Press

Kaufmann, Robert G., *Arms Control During the Pre-Nuclear Era* (New York, 1993) Columbia University Press

Kennedy, Ludovic, *Pursuit: The Sinking of the Bismarck* (Glasgow, 1974) William Collins Sons & Co

Kennedy, Paul, *The Rise and Fall of British Naval Mastery* (London, 1983) Macmillan Publishing

Konstam, Angus, *Battleship Bismarck 1936–41, Owners' Workshop Manual* (Yeovil, 2015) Haynes Publishing

Konstam, Angus, *The Bismarck 1941* (Oxford, 2011) Osprey Publishing

Konstam, Angus: *Jutland 1916: Twelve Hours to Win the War* (London, 2016) Aurum Press

Konstam, Angus, *Scapa Flow* (Oxford, 2009) Osprey Publishing

Mahan, Alfred Thayer, *The Influence of Sea Power on History* (1893)

Maiolo, Joseph, *The Royal Navy and Nazi Germany, 1933–39: A Study in Appeasement and the Origins of the Second World War* (London, 1998) Macmillan Press

Mearns, David & White, Rob, *Hood and Bismarck: The Deep-sea Discovery of an Epic Battle* (London, 2001) Channel 4 Books

Ministry of Defence (Navy), *Admiralty Manual of Seamanship* (London, 1979) Vol. 1, HM Stationery Office

Von Müllenheim-Rechberg, Burkard, *Battleship Bismarck: A Survivor's Story* (Annapolis MD, 1990) Naval Institute Press

Roberts, John, *The Battlecruiser Hood* (London, 1982) Conway Maritime Press (Anatomy of the Ship Series)

Roskill, Stephen W., *The War at Sea* (London, 1954) Vol. 1, HM Stationery Office (History of the Second World War Series)

Santarini, Marco, *Bismarck and Hood: The Battle of the Denmark Strait – a Technical Analysis for a New Perspective* (London, 2017) Fonthill Media

Skwiot, Miroslaw Z. & Prusinowska, Elzbieta T., *Hunting the Bismarck* (Marlborough, 2006) Crowood Press

Sondhaus, Lawrence, *The Great War at Sea* (Cambridge, 2014) Cambridge University Press

Vego, Milan, *Maritime Strategy and Sea Denial: Theory and Practice* (Milton, 2018) Routledge

Whitley, M. J., *Battleships of World War Two: An International Encylopedia* (London, 1998) Arms & Armour Press

Whitley, M. J., *Cruisers of World War Two: An International Encyclopedia* (London, 1996) Arms & Armour Press

Whitley, M. J., *Destroyers of World War Two: An International Encyclopedia* (London, 2002) Cassell

Winklareth, Robert J., *The Battle of the Denmark Strait: A Critical Analysis of the Bismarck's Singular Triumph* (Oxford, 2012) Casemate Publishing

Winklareth, Robert J., *The Bismarck Chase: New Light on a Famous Engagement* (London, 1998) Chatham Publishing

Zetterling, Niklas & Tamelander, Michael, *Bismarck: The Final Days of Germany's Greatest Battleship* (Newbury, 2009) Casemate Publishing

Index